ACTORS,
ATHLETES,
AND
ASTRONAUTS

American Politics and Political Economy Series
Edited by Benjamin I. Page

ACTORS, ATHLETES, AND ASTRONAUTS

Political Amateurs in the United States Congress

David T. Canon

The University of Chicago Press
Chicago and London

David T. Canon is assistant professor of political science at Duke University

The University of Chicago Press, Chicago 60637
The University of Chicago Press, Ltd., London
© 1990 by The University of Chicago
All rights reserved. Published 1990
Printed in the United States of America

99 98 97 96 95 94 93 92 91 90   5 4 3 2

Library of Congress Cataloging-in-Publication Data

Canon, David T.
    Actors, athletes, and astronauts : political amateurs in the
United States Congress / David T. Canon.
        p.   cm. — (American politics and political economy series)
    Includes bibliographical references.
    ISBN 0-226-09267-4 (alk. paper). — ISBN 0-226-09268-2 (pbk.
alk. paper)
    1. United States.   Congress.   2. Legislators—United States.
3. Politicians—United States.   4. Amateurism.   I. Title.
II. Series.
JK1140.C36   1990
328.73′073—dc20   89-16765
                                                                CIP

To my wife
Sarah
and
to my parents
Marvis and Neal

Contents

Acknowledgments

I would like to thank the people who have given me the intellectual and emotional support needed to complete this project. My parents, Marvis and Neal, have been instrumental in both areas; they instilled in me an intellectual curiosity from an early age and guided and nurtured me through difficult times. My wife, Sarah, provided needed distractions and unlimited love and support. She always seemed to know when I needed to be pulled away from the computer and when I needed to persevere. Sarah gives me the balance and levity that keep work in perspective.

My intellectual debts are extensive. John Aldrich provided a perfect mixture of encouragement and criticism. His insightful comments forced me to sharpen and tighten my arguments. Dennis Simon helped formulate the ideas for this project. Frank Sorauf gave me continual encouragement and invaluable aid in the organization and structure of the dissertation. His careful reading and editing of the manuscript did much to improve its clarity. Earl Shaw, Thomas Weko, and David Sousa also contributed much along the way. Steven Smith was very generous in sharing his data on amending activity and his advice during my year at the Brookings Institution. Samuel Kernell helped refine my thinking on career structures. David Rohde and Benjamin Page provided very useful comments on the manuscript.

I would like to thank the University of Minnesota Graduate School for providing me with support during the first year of work on this project, and the Brookings Institution, which did the same in my second year.

Introduction

The United States Congress is typically seen as an institution filled with career politicians who have been seasoned by experience in lower levels of political office. This view applies especially to the Senate. Certainly the 1986 Senate class is one of the most experienced ever elected.[1] In the House of Representatives, a growing proportion of new members—almost half since 1978—have served apprenticeships in state legislatures.

But there is another side to the story. Most voters are familiar with celebrities who were elected to Congress without having served in lower office, including Rep. Jack F. Kemp (R-NY), Sen. John H. Glenn (D-OH), and Sen. Bill Bradley (D-NJ), who, after ten years in the Senate, is still trying to shake the prefix "former New York Knicks great" from his name. In 1986, the House added several other notables: Joseph Kennedy (D-MA), NBA player Tom McMillen (D-MD), major-league pitcher Jim Bunning (R-KY), and Fred Grandy (R-IA), known for his role as "Gopher" on the television series "The Love Boat."

Amateurism, defined here as lack of prior political experience,[2] is more widespread in Congress than is suggested by these few celebrity examples. Prominent political journalist George Will recently noted that 24 of the 100 incumbent senators in the Ninety-eighth Congress were serving in their first public office.[3] Political amateurism is even more common in the House, with an average of one-fourth of the members hav-

---

1. Eight House members, one governor, two former governors, a former transportation secretary (and House member), and a state tax commissioner were elected to the Senate in 1986.

2. This definition is in contrast to the previous distinction between machine and "amateur" politicians used by James Q. Wilson in *The Amateur Democrat: Club Politics in Three Cities* (Chicago: University of Chicago Press, 1962).

3. David Brinkley, "This Week with David Brinkley," transcript of show #155, 14 October 1984 (guests: Richard Wirthlin, James Johnson, Sen. Paul Laxalt; interviewers: David Brinkley, Sam Donaldson, George Will), 13.

ing no previous public office experience and more than half in some years having no elective experience.

This book explores why the presence of amateurs is significant. The central questions are (1) Under what conditions are amateurs elected to Congress? and (2) Does it make any difference that they are elected? More specifically, (1) Do political amateurs respond differently to electoral conditions than their experienced counterparts, or do they face a different set of opportunities? and (2) Is there a demonstrable link between candidates' political backgrounds and their behavior within Congress?

Neither question has received extensive scholarly attention. Recent work indirectly addresses the first question by focusing on the importance of previous political experience of candidates in congressional elections.[4] The impression left by this research is that amateurs are the cannon fodder of congressional elections. They enter races that cannot be won because experienced politicians gain nominations when electoral conditions are favorable. A consequence of politicians' collective cautiousness and amateurs' collective ineffectiveness, the literature concludes, is increased incumbency safety. This assertion is only partially correct. Amateurs *do* win races against incumbents and experienced challengers, and a theory of political ambition and careers must recognize this fact.

The extensive use of career and occupational background data has produced some research on the link between political background and behavior in legislatures, but amateurism has never been the central concern.[5] Other work has addressed the question more directly, but the conclusions of these studies are limited by their scope, in terms of both substance and time.[6] I present evidence of behavioral differences both among amateurs and between amateurs and experienced politicians.

---

4. See Barbara Hinckley, "House Reelections and Senate Defeats: The Role of the Challenger," *British Journal of Political Science* 10:4 (October 1980): 441–60; Gary C. Jacobson, "Congressional Elections, 1978: The Case of the Vanishing Challengers," in *Congressional Elections,* ed. Louis Sandy Maisel and Joseph Cooper (Beverly Hills: Sage Publications, 1981), 219–47; and Gary C. Jacobson and Samuel Kernell, *Strategy and Choice in Congressional Elections* (New Haven: Yale University Press, 1983).

5. For example, see Heinz Eulau and John D. Sprague, *Lawyers in Politics* (Indianapolis: Bobbs-Merrill, 1964); James David Barber, *The Lawmakers* (New Haven: Yale University Press, 1965); Kenneth Prewitt, *The Recruitment of Political Leaders: A Study of Citizen-Politicians* (New York: Bobbs-Merrill, 1970); and Donald R. Matthews, *The Social Backgrounds of Political Decision Makers* (New York: Doubleday, 1954).

6. Donald R. Matthews, *U.S. Senators and Their World,* 2d ed. (New York: W. W. Norton and Co., 1973); Michael L. Mezey, "A Multi-Variate Analysis of Committee Assign-

A theory is needed to link amateurs' behavior in the electoral and institutional arenas. Ambition theory, together with an understanding of opportunity structures, can be modified to serve as this missing link. The new theory would provide an understanding of the two questions outlined above; restated in the terms of ambition theory, they are: (1) What conditions promote the "lateral entry"[7] of amateurs into the career structure? and (2) What linkages can be drawn between office-seeking behavior and institutional behavior?

Ambition theory must be modified at several levels to address these questions. At the aggregate level, the assumption of stable career paths must be revised to recognize the dynamics of amateurs' careers. At the individual level, the theory must incorporate the decisions of first-time office-seekers as well as those of career politicians. Finally, ambition theory must strive to explain the behavior of politicians in all phases of their careers, not simply that of those who modify their behavior in anticipation of seeking higher office.

Joseph Schlesinger developed the notion of the opportunity structure to describe the aggregate patterns of political careers. Whenever the supply of potential candidates exceeds the number of available positions, certain preferred routes to higher office will emerge. Schlesinger sees these paths as relatively stable, subject to only slow and predictable change.[8] I show that career structures are not static: amateurs are disproportionately elected in periods of electoral upheaval, and current officeholders rapidly revise their calculations on how to advance their careers. To explain the entry of amateurs into politics, one must first explain the sources of change or continuity in career structures.

Important information is gained by examining the aggregate patterns of careers, but office-seeking behavior must ultimately be understood at the individual level. The link from the aggregate to the individual level comes from a central assumption of ambition theory: experienced politicians respond to the structure of political opportunities and generally attempt to follow the path that will ensure their smooth advancement.

ments in the House of Representatives: 1949–1967" (Ph.D. diss., Syracuse University, 1969); Nicholas A. Masters, "Committee Assignments in the House of Representatives," *American Political Science Review* 55:2 (June 1961): 345–57; Herbert B. Asher, "The Learning of Legislative Norms," *American Political Science Review* 67 (September 1973): 499–513; and James L. Payne, "Show Horses and Work Horses in the United States House of Representatives," *Polity* 12 (Spring 1980): 428–56.

7. "Lateral entry" refers to election to a relatively high office in the career structure (such as the U.S. House or Senate) without prior service in state or local office.

8. Joseph A. Schlesinger, *Ambition and Politics: Political Careers in the United States* (Chicago: Rand McNally, 1966), 20.

(For example, the career structure may reveal that three-fourths of all U.S. representatives elected from a given state had served in the state legislature; therefore, an ambitious politician with an eye on the House will be likely to serve initially in the lower office.) But what of the amateur? Is his or her unwillingness to follow typical routes to Congress irrational?

Ambition theory (in its post-Schlesinger reformulation by David Rohde and others) must be broadened to encompass the behavior of amateurs. Rohde's simplifying assumption that all officeholders are progressively ambitious—at least in that they would accept a higher office if it were offered to them without cost or risk[9]—is not easily applied to amateurs seeking office for the first time or to other nonincumbent candidates. This problem was noted most recently by Abramson, Aldrich, and Rohde in their study of senators who run for the presidency.[10] The increasing incidence of nonofficeholding candidates reduces the utility of a theory that focuses only on incumbents. Including amateurs (such as Jesse Jackson or Pat Robertson) in such a predictive model would be problematic.

The applicability of ambition theory to amateur candidates has similar problems. Considerable evidence indicates that the amateur's risks and payoffs are systematically different from the experienced politician's.[11] Amateurs, at least in the aggregate, are less strategic in their decisions to run for office. Often they do not have as much at stake (e.g., losing the base office), so they may be drawn into an election by benefits less tangible than electoral success.[12]

It is not clear how ambition theory can be revised to include amateurs. The universe of cases one must consider is not simply made up of progressively ambitious politicians, but rather includes all constitutionally eligible candidates. Even if the set could be reduced to some relatively

9. David W. Rohde, "Risk Bearing and Progressive Ambition: The Case of Members of the United States House of Representatives," *American Journal of Political Science* 23:1 (February 1979): 1–26.

10. Paul R. Abramson, John H. Aldrich, and David W. Rohde, "Progressive Ambition among United States Senators: 1972–1988," *Journal of Politics* 49:1 (February 1987): 3–35.

11. Jacobson and Kernell, *Strategy and Choice;* William T. Bianco, "Strategic Decisions on Candidacy in U.S. Congressional Districts," *Legislative Studies Quarterly* 9:2 (May 1984): 351–64; and David T. Canon, "Political Conditions and Experienced Challengers in Congressional Elections: 1972–1984" (paper presented at the annual meeting of the American Political Science Association, New Orleans, 29 August–1 September 1985).

12. Thomas A. Kazee, "The Decision to Run for the U.S. Congress: Challenger Attitudes in the 1970s," *Legislative Studies Quarterly* 5:1 (February 1980): 79–100.

small number of locally prominent individuals—businesspeople, lawyers, celebrities—the assumption of progressive ambition could not be
maintained. It is reasonable to assume that all career politicians would
like a higher political office if they could easily attain it, but this is not the
case with all amateurs. Many a celebrity or successful businessperson or
lawyer would be unwilling to give up higher income and greater security
for the demanding job of a member of Congress. Roger Staubach, Brooks
Robinson, Burt Reynolds, and Charlton Heston have made it clear to
wooing party officials that they would not care to be U.S. senators, thank
you. In other words, there may be actual opportunity costs to winning.

Yet a theory of political careers that ignores as many as a fifth of U.S.
senators and a fourth of House members is not satisfactory. I attempt to
fill this void with a typology of amateurism that draws distinctions among
three types of candidates: ambitious, policy, and hopeless.[13] Ambitious
amateurs resemble their experienced counterparts in that they want to
make a career in politics; policy amateurs are driven by their strong policy
goals; hopeless amateurs are swept into office by national partisan tides,
or in other races they were not expected to win. This typology allows
distinctions to be drawn among amateurs and predictions to be made
about their behavior.

The ultimate significance of the presence of amateur politicians in
Congress lies in potential behavioral differences between amateurs and
experienced politicians. Changes in career paths, explanations for the dynamic nature of opportunity structures, and evidence of differences
between amateurs and experienced politicians in the electoral environment are all important in their own right and are certainly of interest to the
student of Congress. Yet the skeptic's "So what?" must be answered by
demonstrating some institutional or policy significance of the presence of
amateurs. I present differences among amateurs and between amateurs
and experienced politicians in roll call votes, activity on the floor, committee assignments, and legislative careers; in addition, I find that
amateurs may be important agents of policy change during periods of
electoral upheaval.

Chapters 1 and 2 lay out my theory of amateurism and political careers,
setting the stage for the empirical tests in chapters 3–5. Chapter 1 presents the concepts of amateurism and political career structures and
defines the factors that influence the election of amateurs to high office.

---

13. The term hopeless is not intended in a pejorative sense (often hopeless amateurs have
well-developed political skills). Rather, the term refers to the surprising nature of the amateur's campaign which an objective analysis may have deemed hopeless.

Chapter 2 discusses alternative theoretical perspectives and then presents my typology of amateurism. Chapter 3 examines changes in levels of political amateurism in the House from 1930 to 1986 and in the Senate from 1913 to 1986 and offers explanations for those changes. Chapter 4, using data from the years 1972–88, determines the conditions under which it is most likely that amateurs or experienced politicians will run for Congress.[14] (An understanding of the nature of amateur candidacies can be gained by examining decisions to run in primaries as well as general elections.) Chapter 5 presents evidence of behavioral differences among the three types of amateurs and between amateurs and experienced politicians in the House and Senate on the range of topics mentioned above. Finally, in chapter 6 I summarize the central argument and speculate on the broader consequences of amateurism in Congress.

Special attention is given throughout to important differences in the nature of amateurism in the House and in the Senate—for example, amateurs in the Senate tend to be highly visible celebrities; in the House, they are more likely to be local businessmen or attorneys who are seeking public office for the first time.

14. Originally the data for chapters 4 and 5 covered the years 1972 through 1984. In the process of revising the manuscript, I included the 1986–88 period in chapter 4, but time constraints did not permit a parallel expansion for chapter 5. The process of including more recent data is never-ending, so I had to draw the line somewhere.

One

Theory: When Amateurs Appear

Political amateurs make good copy for journalists covering Congress. The "human interest" angle is pursued in stories on the latest Kennedy, actor, or basketball player elected to the House.[1] Other stories cover more serious implications of amateurs in politics. Christopher Buchanan noted the 1980 election of six Republican representatives who were all under the age of thirty and all without experience in public office.[2] These "Young Turks" brought with them a confrontational attitude that differed sharply from the House minority party's practices in the past. George Will described a similar trend in the Senate.[3] Kevin Phillips reported on the wave of celebrities who have entered politics in the last decade. Athletes, football coaches, actors, astronauts, and prisoners of war have been nominated and elected to the House, Senate, and governorships. Phillips notes that the trend is most prominent in the Republican party and in the Sun Belt, where "there's little political tradition more ancient than television and shopping centers."[4]

Political scientists have not systematically studied the impact of amateurs in the political system. Often the topic appears as the complement of a focus on political careers or strategic politicians.[5] In the former, amateurs in high public office are seen as the exception to the normal

1. R. W. Apple, "Clues to Watch for in a Close Election as the Results Unfold on Television," *New York Times,* 4 November 1986, 11.

2. Christopher Buchanan, "Youth Is on the Right in House Freshman Class," *Congressional Quarterly Weekly Report* 39 (3 January 1981): 3.

3. David Brinkley, "This Week with David Brinkley," transcript of show #155, 14 October 1984 (guests: Richard Wirthlin, James Johnson, Sen. Paul Laxalt; interviewers: David Brinkley, Sam Donaldson, George Will), 13.

4. Kevin Phillips, "At Election Time, Celebrities Can Make Political Party's Day," *Minneapolis Star and Tribune,* 18 June 1985, 11A.

5. See Joseph A. Schlesinger, *Ambition and Politics: Political Careers in the United States* (Chicago: Rand McNally, 1966), for the perspective on political careers, and Gary C. Jacobson and Samuel Kernell, *Strategy and Choice in Congressional Elections* (New Haven: Yale University Press, 1983), on the individual-level approach.

progression of political careers, whereas strategic politicians are defined as those who have held prior elective office. Amateurs are generally viewed as weak candidates who have naive views about the political world.[6] While this observation may be true for many or even most amateur candidates, there is, as indicated in the introduction, a significant subset of amateurs who run strong campaigns and win. An average of one-fourth of U.S. representatives have no previous public experience and more than a fifth of all popularly elected senators have not held elective office (though fewer than 10% of senators are complete amateurs).

How do these amateurs win seats in Congress? The first place to look for an explanation is in the nature of the political system and the types of constraints and incentives it provides for individuals seeking to establish a political career. If nominations are controlled by strong parties, or if rigid career ladders are in place, amateurs stand little chance of winning high office. On the other hand, amateurs may have easy access to public office either through design (as in Yugoslavia, where the leadership attempted to implement a "more participatory and truly Marxist system" by requiring that a majority of the legislators be amateurs)[7] or through norms, as with the practice of rotation in the United States in the nineteenth century.[8] In this chapter I will describe the determinants of the career structure—that peculiar mix of factors that influences the election of amateurs to high office in the United States: the "rules of the game," the role played by political parties, the scope of political participation, and the relative desirability of political offices within the career structure.

Amateurism: A Definition and Its Political Implications

The word "amateurism" has pejorative connotations. *The American Heritage Dictionary* defines an amateur as "a person who engages in any art, science, study, or athletic activity as a pastime rather than as a profession . . . one lacking professional skill." While my definition is based simply on the presence or absence of previous political experience,[9] some implications of the dictionary definition should be noted. The first part is not relevant here (although politics was not the amateur's primary career, it can no longer be considered a pastime once he or she is elected

6. David A. Leuthold, *Electioneering in a Democracy* (New York: John Wiley and Sons, 1968).

7. Lenard J. Cohen, "Politics as an Avocation: Legislative Professionalization and Participation in Yugoslavia," *Legislative Studies Quarterly* 5:2 (May 1980): 175.

8. Samuel Kernell, "Toward Understanding Nineteenth Century Congressional Careers: Ambition, Competition, and Rotation," *American Journal of Political Science* 21:4 (November 1977): 669–93.

9. See Appendix A for a complete listing of offices coded.

to Congress). The second part, however, is significant: amateurs' lack of proven political skills affects their chances of winning office and may influence their effectiveness in Congress when they do win.

Three aspects of amateurs' backgrounds hurt their chances of gaining office: the absence of prior campaign experience,[10] low name recognition (celebrities are the exception), and a general preference among voters for candidates who have prior experience.[11] These obstacles are not insurmountable. The successful campaigns of senators Rudy Boschwitz (R-MN) and Frank Lautenberg (D-NJ) and former representative Ed Zschau (R-CA), among many others, indicate that large expenditures on consultants, staff, and advertising permit amateurs to overcome initial deficits. The impact of the last point—voters' preference for experience—can also be overstated. The career structure in the United States is relatively open. Compared to nations with stronger party systems, the United States requires little in the way of party or office apprenticeship, even for the highest offices. Furthermore, not all voters automatically prefer experience. The suspicions many Americans hold about career politicians, as well as the long-standing tradition of "running against Washington," can be exploited by amateurs who can credibly claim that they are not "one of them."

Although an amateur's deficiencies in electoral politics can be overcome with money and effective campaign strategy, nonpolitical backgrounds may be more of a liability in Congress. Robert Dahl says, "To suppose that one can run a complex political system without first learning the trade is, as Plato pointed out, as silly as to suppose that one can be a doctor or a carpenter without prior training."[12] Another political observer commented, "The sooner we spurn celebrity and revert to expertise the better."[13] Others do not share this concern. Richard Fenno speaks favorably of Jim Johnson (R-CO), a "citizen-legislator" of the early 1970s who became interested in politics because of the Vietnam War. Once in Congress, he brought substantial skill and energy to bear on issues that concerned him.[14]

Amateurism is not always a liability, but questions about the desir-

10. Louis Sandy Maisel, *From Obscurity to Oblivion: Running in the Congressional Primary* rev. ed. (Knoxville: University of Tennessee Press, 1986).

11. Leuthold, *Electioneering in a Democracy*, 23–31.

12. Quoted in the foreword to Joseph A. Schlesinger, *How They Became Governor: A Study of Comparative State Politics, 1870–1950* (East Lansing: Governmental Research Bureau, Michigan State University, 1957), 3.

13. Phillips, "At Election Time," 11A.

14. Richard F. Fenno, Jr., "What's He Like? What's She Like? What Are They Like?" in *The United States Congress: Thomas P. O'Neill, Jr., Symposium on the U.S. Congress,* ed. Dennis Hale (New Brunswick: Transaction books, 1983), 118–25.

ability of amateurs in Congress are not easily answered. Evaluating the amateurs' effectiveness in Congress is not the central aim of this research; rather, the goal is to outline the distinctiveness and significance of their careers.

The Career Structure

The career structure defines the distinctiveness of amateurs in high office. If all aspirants had an equal chance of attaining a seat in Congress regardless of their previous experience, amateurs would be more common. But the structure of careers, which gives certain office-seekers a competitive edge over others by virtue of their place in the structure, tends to hinder amateurs in the manner described above. How exactly does this work?

A career structure is the loose hierarchy of offices that begins with the least desirable and most numerous local offices and builds to the more attractive, less numerous federal offices. Figure 1.1 depicts the career structure in the United States. Its levels roughly follow the three levels of government—local, state, and federal—with the exception of governorships, which rank with Senate seats in the hierarchy.[15] As one progresses up the career structure, the proportion of amateurs decreases.

It is more difficult for a newcomer to be elected to the U.S. Senate than to a city council. This is especially true in stable political systems with strong parties, where access to higher office can mostly be limited to those with prior experience. Hugh Bone wrote:

> It becomes essential in most communities for the citizen to be
> an active party member, a ward or district leader, or a
> committee member. From here the individual may work up
> through the ranks to obtain a nomination for a lesser local
> office, the state legislature, and so on, possibly to Congress.[16]

The career structure described here, from the 1940s, would leave little room for amateurs in Congress. In reality, career paths in the United States have never been that rigidly structured, even when parties exerted

---

15. There is some variation in the ranking of offices within levels based on the relative desirability of an office. (The variations are indicated by the irregular breaks in levels.) For example, mayoralties of large cities and some constitutional offices in large states will have higher places in the career structure than comparable offices with less power or prestige.

16. Hugh A. Bone, *American Politics and the Party System* (New York: McGraw-Hill, 1949), 740. In this same passage, Bone notes that low-level politicians generally cannot make politics their only career.

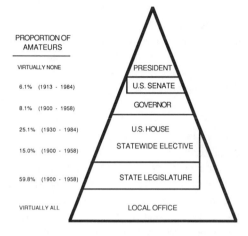

Fig. 1.1 The Political Career Structure in the United States.
SOURCE: Data for the House and Senate gathered by author. Data for state offices are from Schlesinger, *Ambition and Politics*, 91–92. Schlesinger's data understate the total proportion of amateurs because they are only for those in state office who later served in the Senate or a governorship.

more control over nominations. Harold Lasswell makes a more realistic observation: "In American politics the escalator to the top is not a regimented, orderly lift, but a tangle of ladders, ropes, and runways that attract people from other activities at various stages of the process, and lead others to a dead end or a drop."[17] This "tangle" of political careers implies a "permeable" (open to amateurs) rather than rigid structure. To understand *why* some career structures are "permeable tangles" and others are more rigid, one must examine the relationship between the characteristics of the political system and those of the career structure.

Determinants of the Career Structure: Why Amateurs Are Elected
Rules of the Game

The "rules of the game" set boundaries and guide the ambitions of politicians. Two types of rules are central: those that define office and term requirements and those that define electoral conditions. Constitutional provisions that establish the number of elective offices define the number of opportunities to run for office at various levels of government.

17. Harold D. Lasswell, *Psychopathology and Politics* (Chicago: University of Chicago Press, 1930), 303.

These rules shape political careers by ensuring that the initial outlets for political ambition are usually at the local level, where opportunities are the most numerous. Term restrictions also direct ambition. An office with a one- or two-term limit does not arouse the same ambition as an office in which one could make a career. (Jimmy Carter may not have had his eyes on the White House when he ran for governor of Georgia, but the rules of the game determined that the office would be either a stepping-stone or a political dead end.) Congressional office is a more likely outlet for those wishing to establish a long-term career.

While office and term restrictions must be taken as givens, one factor that helps define the nature of political opportunities is subject to manipulation: the drawing of district lines. Gerrymandering,[18] the practice of tinkering with district lines for partisan advantage, can create substantial distortions in the geographic distribution of votes. Recently the most blatant instances have been rejected by the courts, but in many states this decennial practice can affect the strategic calculations of candidates for office. Amateurs may have fewer opportunities to run if experienced . challengers exploit the uncertainty created by new district lines and voters who are not familiar with the incumbents.

The second set of constitutional rules of the game defines electoral conditions. Whether elections are decided by a majority or by a plurality, in single-member or proportional districts, has an impact on the nature of the party system, and thus on the nature of political careers.[19] Runoff primaries in the South have often discriminated against blacks, while third parties have never taken hold in the United States largely because of single-member districts and plurality elections. Third parties are more concerned with ideological goals than with winning elections,[20] and, by the nature of their electoral status, third-party candidates are more likely to be amateurs. This relationship between third parties and amateurism may be uniquely American, or, more accurately, unique to the particular mix of rules found in the United States. Successful third parties in nations with proportional representation are more likely to resemble the two ma-

18. The term "gerrymander" arose from the Massachusetts governorship of Elbridge *Gerry,* who was responsible for a sala*mander*-shaped congressional district in 1811. See Frank J. Sorauf, *Party Politics in America* (Boston: Little, Brown, 1984), 248. Today's machinations make Gerry's effort look like child's play. Phil Burton's attempt to aid his brother John in California in 1982 and Indiana's plan to pack three Democratic incumbents in one district in 1982 are two of the more notorious examples.

19. See E. E. Schattschneider, *Party Government* (New York: Holt, Reinhardt, and Winston, 1942) and Maurice Duverger, *Political Parties* (New York: Wiley and Sons, 1954).

20. Sorauf, *Party Politics in America,* 46–52.

jor U.S. parties in their mix of electoral and policy goals and the level of prior office experience of their candidates.[21]

The rules governing the actual selection process can also have an effect on the career structure. The transition from the party ballot to the Australian ballot and the implementation of the direct primary both had significant effects on the party's control over general elections and nominations.[22] The Seventeenth Amendment, which provided for the direct election of U.S. senators, also moved election control from the party elite to the public. Both of these changes may have created more opportunities for amateurs in the early twentieth century.

There is some work that has examined the link between the rules of the electoral process and political careers. Richard Tobin and associates find that closed primaries are more likely than open primaries to produce politically experienced candidates in state legislative races.[23] The current presidential nomination process also influences the types of candidates that emerge. Abramson, Aldrich, and Rohde cite the recent candidacies of Jimmy Carter, Ronald Reagan, Walter Mondale, and Gary Hart as evidence of the growing advantage of nonincumbency.[24]

The importance of constitutional rules cannot be overstated. The direct primary and the secret ballot had a great hand in creating candidate-centered rather than party-centered political campaigns. While this has opened possibilities for amateur candidates, single-member plurality-rule districts have potentially limited these types of campaigns. In specific cases, redistricting has an impact on the type of candidate who runs and is elected. Finally, the nature of the electoral process can alter career paths and affect the place of amateurs in the career structure.[25]

21. Herbert Kitschelt and Staf Hellemans, *Beyond the European Left: Ideology and Political Action in the Belgian Ecology Party* (Durham, N.C.: Duke University Press, 1990).

22. Sorauf, *Party Politics in America*, 235–41; Joseph A. Schlesinger, "The New American Political Party," *American Political Science Review* 79:4 (December 1985): 1155–56.

23. Edward Keynes, Richard J. Tobin, and Robert Danziger, "Institutional Effects on Elite Recruitment: The Case of State Nominating Systems," *American Politics Quarterly* 7:3 (July 1979): 283–302; Richard J. Tobin, "The Influence of Nominating Systems on the Political Experiences of State Legislators," *Western Political Quarterly* 28:3 (September 1975): 553–66; and Richard J. Tobin and Edward Keynes, "Institutional Differences in the Recruitment Process: A Four State Study," *American Journal of Political Science* 19:4 (November 1975): 667–82.

24. Paul R. Abramson, John H. Aldrich, and David W. Rohde, "Progressive Ambition among U.S. Senators: 1972–1988," *Journal of Politics* 49:1 (February 1987): 32–34.

25. Many of the "rules of the game" have been relatively constant in the period of this study. The "rules" that are relevant here are redistricting, the open or closed nature of the primary election, the rules governing voting, and the pre-primary endorsement practices. All of these have significant variation in the cross-section and some change over time (both among and within states).

Political Party

Political parties help shape the career structure in three ways: (1) by structuring competition through the two-party system, (2) by nominating political candidates, minimally through supplying them with a party label and more substantially through participating in their recruitment and selection, and (3) by stimulating political participation among voters.

The two-party system has a profound impact on the career structure. In its simplest terms, "two-party system" means that third parties do not compete realistically for public office; i.e., few candidates can consider running without the Democratic or Republican label. The party's competitive standing in a given state or congressional district will further define potential candidates' ambitions and careers. Republicans considering a career in politics will face a different set of opportunities on the South Side of Chicago than in the suburbs of Dallas. Candidates in a weak minority party will not have the opportunity to follow the typical progression of the political career. Therefore, in states in which one party is dominant it is more likely that career structures will be divergent. Note the example of Mississippi, where very few Republicans—7 of 122 in 1987—are ever elected to the state legislature. In such states, it is much more likely that a Republican candidate for the U.S. House will be an amateur than a Democratic candidate, who probably will have a base office in the state legislature or a local elective office. If parties are competitive there is a greater chance that their career structures will be similar, because they will share control of base offices.[26]

The competitive position of the parties at the national level will also affect the types of candidates who are elected in a given year. This is recognized in the literature as the impact of "national tides" in congressional elections. Thus, 1932, 1964, and 1974 were years in which many Democratic candidates were swept into office; in 1980, some Republicans found themselves in Washington who normally would not have had much of a chance. A hypothesis arising from this observation is that when the normal competitive balance between the parties is disrupted, career paths will temporarily change as a disproportionate number of amateurs are elected. This may be observable for several elections in the case of a major realignment, as in the 1930s, or may be a one-time "blip" that disappears in the following election.

Parties also influence the career structure through nominations for political office. It is obviously in the party's interest to field the strongest possible candidate for the general election. Ideally, this is done by

26. Schlesinger, *Ambition and Politics*, chap. 7.

grooming candidates who work up through party ranks. Parties also would like to control politicians' ambitions and deter primary competition for the strongest candidate to prevent primaries from turning into free-for-alls. Pre-primary endorsement, as exercised in Minnesota in its purest form and in other states in some manner, can provide an effective means of choking off outside candidacies. Kunkel finds that in 1986, 99% of the Minnesota Democratic Farmer-Labor Party's endorsees (373 of 377) won in open-seat and incumbent races.[27] The closed primary is another minimal but widely used step in exerting some party control. Parties have recently attempted to play a larger role in candidate recruitment through aggressive contacts and candidate training schools.[28] An expanding resource base enhances the party's role in recruitment.

The party's involvement in recruitment has a variable effect on candidacies of political amateurs. In some instances the amateur is a well-known celebrity or a well-connected and well-financed businessperson who is actively recruited. More frequently, amateur candidacies are among those that the party is trying to deter.[29] While there is great variation, the impact of party recruitment on amateur candidacies does not occur randomly. Schlesinger indicates that the Republican party provides more opportunities for nonofficeholders than the Democratic party; he notes that "only Republican state parties make a practice of selecting nominees for both the governorship and the Senate outside the ranks of officeholders."[30]

While parties clearly have some impact on the types of candidates that emerge in congressional elections, this role can be overstated. Studies of recruitment consistently reveal that the party does *not* play a central role in the eventual decision to run for office.[31] Candidates usually seek the

27. Joseph A. Kunkel, "Party Endorsement and Incumbency in Minnesota Legislative Nominations," *Legislative Studies Quarterly* 8:2 (May 1988): 211–23.

28. Marjorie Randon Hershey, *Running for Office: The Political Education of Campaigners* (Chatham, N.J.: Chatham House Publishers, 1984), 139–45; Paul S. Herrnson, *Party Campaigning in the 1980s* (Cambridge, Mass.: Harvard University Press, 1988).

29. Though there is no systematic evidence for this claim, Linda L. Fowler provides some limited evidence in "The Cycle of Defeat: Recruitment of Congressional Challengers" (Ph.D. diss., University of Rochester, 1977). In chap. 4, I present indirect evidence based on competition for nominations in primary elections.

30. Schlesinger, *Ambition and Politics*, 153. Part of the Republican penchant for amateur candidates can also be explained by their traditional ties with the business community. Republicans may simply be more comfortable with candidates who do not have political backgrounds.

31. John W. Kingdon, *Candidates for Office* (New York: Random House, 1968); Leuthold, *Electioneering in a Democracy*; Kenneth Prewitt, *The Recruitment of Political Leaders: A Study of Citizen-Politicians* (New York: Bobbs-Merrill, 1970). See Herrnson, *Party Campaigning in the 1980s*, for an alternative view.

blessing of the party organization, but nominations are not (except in a few cases) rewards handed out to the party faithful. In New York congressional races, for example, the party is determinative in the decision to run only when "sacrificial lambs" are needed for the ticket.[32]

Congressional campaigns are now viewed as independent affairs run by political entrepreneurs in the political market.[33] Therefore, as in many other areas of American politics, parties' impact on the career structure is partly explained by what they do *not* do. The absence of elite control facilitates the permeability of the political career structure: amateurs are free agents who are more concerned about other ambitious politicians than about the approval of the local party.

Participation

The final way in which parties can affect the career structure—by stimulating increased political participation among voters—is less direct than the previous two. Parties provide the link between the public and the most immediate form of participation in a democracy: choosing elected leaders. Parties have always played a role in broadening the base of political participation in the United States through voter-registration and get-out-the-vote drives.

Citizens may participate in the political system in four ways: by holding political office, by direct involvement in the electoral process (either through running for office or through campaign activity), by participation in the selection of leaders, or by nonelectoral activity, such as lobbying or interest-group participation. All of these will be influenced by the constitutional and systemic variables outlined above. The main hypothesis introduced in this section is that the broader the base of participation, the more likely it is that career structures will be open to amateurs.

The subset of the population that can realistically hold some expectation of gaining public office will be reflected in the career structure. For many years, white Protestant men with previous political experience were the most advantaged—if not the only—candidates for office. As the subset broadens, there will be increased opportunities for people with various backgrounds to run for office, including those with no previous political experience.

One factor that tends to increase the size of the pool of potential candidates is political modernization. As systems become more developed,

32. Fowler, "Cycle of Defeat," 135–137.

33. Gary C. Jacobson, *The Politics of Congressional Elections*, 2d ed. (Boston: Little, Brown, 1987), 7–8 and chap. 3.

participation increases, which should in turn be reflected not only in increased suffrage and turnout within the general population, but also in the characteristics of elected officials.[34] There is a counter-argument. While modernization broadens the base of participation, political offices become institutionalized,[35] political careers become more developed and stable,[36] and expectations for the political credentials of candidates for high office may be heightened. These factors tend to limit the access of amateurs to high office. Bogue and colleagues note this effect for the House in the twentieth century:

> These trends suggest that the House has become a professional body with a highly stable membership and that an elite of professional lawmakers gradually replaced a cadre of amateurs whose primary career and occupational concerns were in other areas.[37]

Thus there are theoretical reasons for believing that career structures will be less open or more open to amateur candidacies as political systems develop and the base of participation broadens. I argue that there is a threshold of minimum participation that is a necessary condition for amateurs to have a chance in the career structure, but that after this threshold is passed, increased development of the political system may work to close high office to political amateurs.

It is beyond the scope of this research to determine whether the extent of participation has a significant impact on the emergence of the career structure, but some speculation is in order. A link between the nature of participation in elections and the type of candidate who is elected seems plausible. If nominations and selection are controlled by a party elite, candidates are likely to be careerists. If the base of participation is larger, political amateurs are likely to have a greater chance of being elected. Participation has increased with the proliferation of the direct primary

34. Allan G. Bogue, Jerome M. Clubb, Carroll R. McKibbin, and Santa A. Traugott, "Members of the House of Representatives and the Process of Modernization: 1789–1960," *Journal of American History* 63 (September 1976): 280.

35. Samuel P. Huntington, *Political Order in Changing Societies* (New Haven: Yale University Press, 1968); Nelson W. Polsby, "The Institutionalization of the U.S. House of Representatives," *American Political Science Review* 62:1 (March 1968): 144–69.

36. Samuel Kernell, "Congress and the Emergence of a Political Career Structure" (paper presented at the Project '87 Conference on Congress, Washington, D.C., 1–4 February 1981); Samuel Kernell, "Ambition and Politics: An Exploratory Study of the Political Careers of Nineteenth Century Congressmen" (paper presented at the annual meeting of the American Political Science Association, Chicago, Illinois, 1976).

37. Bogue, Clubb, McKibbin, and Traugott, "Process of Modernization," 300.

throughout the twentieth century, the enfranchisement of women and eighteen- to twenty-year-olds, and the gradual enfranchisement of blacks in the 1960s with the abolition of the poll tax, the 1964 Civil Rights Act, and the 1965 Voting Rights Act. Variations in state laws concerning registration and voting in primaries and general elections have a significant impact on participation.[38] In chapter 4, I will show whether different rates and types of participation in the electoral arena have an impact on the types of candidates who are elected.

Desirability of Office

Characteristics of an office such as its powers, its salary, the size of its constituency, and its value as a stepping-stone to higher office all affect its place in the opportunity structure. The desirability of holding an office encompasses all these characteristics, but also is based on less tangible factors, such as the position of the office in the federal system and a difficult-to-document but commonly recognized fact: that impressions of the inherent attractiveness of various offices can change.

One by-product of the nationalization of U.S. politics in the past century is that the hierarchy of political careers has firmly cemented federal offices in the top tier of the career structure. This "rationalization of authority,"[39] by which the central government more closely defines and enforces its power, is part of the process of political modernization. In the early nineteenth century this process had not yet begun; Washington, D.C., was a southern backwater compared with its centrality today. In that period it was common for congressmen to "give up the duress of Washington to return to some local office or state assembly nearer home."[40] It is not surprising that the relative desirability of political life in Washington was reflected in the career structure. With national office having little advantage over the convenience of local and state office, the pattern of officeholding resembled a game of musical chairs in which a group of politicians rotated terms in the U.S. Congress and moved more freely—and in both directions—between levels of the career structure.[41] Kernell comments:

38. Raymond E. Wolfinger and Steven J. Rosenstone, *Who Votes?* (New Haven: Yale University Press, 1980).

39. Huntington, *Political Order in Changing Societies*.

40. Kernell, "Emergence of a Political Career Structure," 12.

41. Polsby notes the "kaleidoscopic career" of Henry Clay, who made *ten* different career moves in and out of the House, Senate, and Kentucky state legislature, plus stints as a commissioner to negotiate the Treaty of Ghent and as Secretary of State, and who left politics completely for periods of two and five years. Polsby notes that Clay's career was

In an undeveloped career structure the game of musical chairs can be frenetic. And because many part-time politicians are temporarily leaving public life, numerous vacancies open up which further encourages movement among those who remain in politics. When the music starts many offices become vacant with many politicians—current officeholders, returnees, and novices alike—taking chances.[42]

With the nationalization of the political system came a more regularized succession of officeholding that was clearly in one direction: from local to state to federal. Previous patterns of office succession were replaced by competition for national office by career politicians. The growing importance of Congress's work during the late nineteenth century made the job of congressman increasingly attractive.

The changing relative attractiveness of political offices is difficult to document directly, though the movement of politicians between offices gives strong circumstantial evidence of the direction of change. For example, in the 1960s, when governors faced especially difficult political times, career paths leading to and from governorships changed. When governorships are less attractive, fewer representatives will risk their usually safe Washington seats for a chance to return to their home states. In the years 1900–1959, 9.5% of all governors came from the U.S. House;[43] for 1960–69, when governors were increasingly vulnerable, this figure falls to 7.3%. During the 1970s, gubernatorial vulnerability decreased, two former governors were elected president, and state budgets were generally in better shape than the federal government's. In this period the percentage of U.S. representatives in the statehouses jumped to 11.4% (data for the 1960s and 1970s compiled by the author).

Similar patterns are evident for paths leading from governorships. Shortly after the 1960 presidential election, Richard Scammon observed, "The old formula of 'Get elected to be governor and then you might make it to the White House' is being replaced by 'get elected to be governor and you are on the path to oblivion.' "[44] By 1976, governors once again occupied a rung on the presidential career ladder. In the 1960s they were more likely to abandon state politics, taking roughly

---

remarkable even for that period, yet it demonstrates the relative ease of lateral movement in the career structure of the nineteenth century. See Polsby, "Institutionalization of the U.S. House," 148.

42. Kernell, "Emergence of a Political Career Structure," 14.

43. Schlesinger, *Ambition and Politics,* 91.

44. Quoted in Lattie Finch Coor, "The Increasing Vulnerability of the American Governor" (Ph.D. diss., Washington University, St. Louis, 1964), 1.

20% of all opportunities to run for the Senate. For 1970–76 this figure falls to about 4%.[45]

The career movement of U.S. House members provides more evidence for the claim that ambitious politicians are sensitive to the changing desirability of various offices. Paul Brace shows that after controlling for most other factors, the nature of service in the U.S. House in the 1970s (i.e., the impression that the job was less rewarding and more demanding than it had been in previous periods) was a strong explanatory variable in a representative's decision to run for the Senate.[46]

The impact of ambitious politicians' strategic calculations and career movements on the potential careers of political amateurs may be far-reaching. This can be stated in terms of a hypothesis: opportunities for amateurs open up as career politicians move away from less desirable offices. Thus one would expect more amateurs to run for governorships in the 1960s and for the House in the 1970s. In the nineteenth century, when movement between levels of the career structure was less regularized, one would expect more opportunities for amateurs as well. I will not test the latter point or opportunities to run for governorships, but the concern with the relative attractiveness of various offices is important in developing a theory of career structures and structural change.

Conclusion

My career-based definition of political amateurism as the lack of previous political experience must be understood within the context of the political career structure, the political system, and the historical period. In an ordered yet "permeable" structure, as in the United States, amateurs are able to bypass normal career paths. In other nations, such as Great Britain, opportunities for amateurs to reach high office are more limited. As shown in Figure 1.2, the career structure in a representative democracy can vary from nonexistent (b) to hierarchical and permeable or rigid (c,d). Which of these shapes the career structure takes will determine whether amateurs have access to high levels of the structure. What explains these differences? That is, what are the conditions in participatory democracies that produce open but hierarchical career structures, as in variant c? In the United States, the constitutional rules, role of parties, and desirability of office define a scope of participation that encompasses the potential involvement of amateurs.

45. Frank Codispoti, "American Governors and Progressive Ambition: An Analysis of Opportunities to Run for the Senate" (Ph.D. diss., Michigan State University, 1981), 117.

46. Paul R. Brace, "Progressive Ambition in the House: A Probabilistic Approach," *Journal of Politics* 46:2 (May 1984): 556–71.

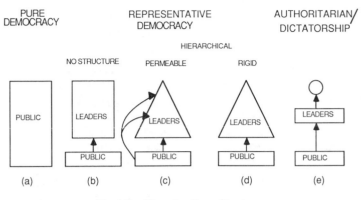

Fig. 1.2   Alternative Career Structures

Another theme in this chapter is the variability of opportunities to run for high office. The current literature does not systematically address the question of changes in career structures.[47] The common thinking is that, because career structures are simply the aggregation of thousands of individual decisions, structures are not likely to change unless individual-level factors change. District-level considerations are central in determining what type of candidate will emerge from a given race. Experienced challengers usually get the upper hand when conditions are favorable, thus creating stability in career paths.

Yet career structures *do* change. Changes in the rules of the game, swings in partisan balance or control over nominations, significant changes in participation, and shifts in the relative desirability of offices all help explain changing career structures and provide a basis for predict-

47. The exception is some research on the presidential career structure; see Robert L. Peabody, Norman J. Ornstein, and David W. Rohde, "The United States Senate as a Presidential Incubator: Many Are Called But Few Are Chosen," *Political Science Quarterly* 91:2 (Summer 1976): 237–58, and Abramson, Aldrich, and Rohde, "Progressive Ambition among U.S. Senators." These scholars note changes in the structure, but there is little theoretical treatment of the changes and no discussion of change at lower levels in the career structure. In his seminal work, Schlesinger notes cross-sectional variation in career structures among states, but does not address variation over time (*Ambition and Politics,* esp. chap. 8). In more recent work, Schlesinger notes that career structures can change due to changes in rules or the competitive position of parties ("The New American Political Party," 1154). While the basis for a comprehensive treatment of changes in career structure lies within this definition, Schlesinger chooses to focus on the strength of partisan identification as his indicator of changes in party systems ("The New American Political Party," 1159). This emphasis is well placed, but it leads him to overlook the importance of the *direction* of partisan identification and the significance for political careers of changes in the electoral strengths of the parties. In chap. 3, I will examine changes in career structures during periods of electoral upheaval.

ing what types of candidates will be elected. Vilfredo Pareto discusses the dynamic nature of leadership and points out the importance of shocks or disturbances to the normal pattern of careers:

> The governing elite is always in a state of slow and continuous transformation. It flows on like a river, never being today, what it was yesterday. From time to time sudden and violent disturbances occur. There is a flood—the river overflows its banks. Afterwards, the new governing elite again resumes its slow transformation. The flood has subsided, the river is again flowing normally in its wonted bed.[48]

The determinants of career structures outlined here provide a theoretical basis for understanding the impact of Pareto's "floods" on the career structure, and also can explain the incidence of amateurism in the cross-section. Five testable hypotheses emerge: (1) The "rules of the game" (such as the open or closed nature of primaries, the use of party endorsements, and the impact of redistricting) influence that incidence of amateurism in Congress; (2) The minority party in a one-party region is more likely to produce amateurs; (3) When normal patterns of partisan competition are disrupted, amateurs are more likely to win a House or Senate seat; (4) A broader base of political participation leads to more opportunities for amateurs; and (5) As career politicians leave less desirable offices, opportunities for amateurs increase. Each of these hypotheses is examined in chapters 3 and 4. In chapter 2, I present the theoretical basis for my analysis of behavioral differences between amateurs and experienced candidates in congressional politics.

48. Quoted in Bogue, Clubb, McKibbin, and Traugott, "Process of Modernization," 301.

Two

Theory: What Amateurs Do

How are amateurs elected to Congress? Is the context of their campaigns different from that of their experienced counterparts? Does it matter that amateurs are elected? The literature provides some guidance in answering these questions, though current research is often limited by a simplistic view of the amateur as a single type, or by the assumption that all politicians hold similar goals. Rather than viewing *all* inexperienced candidates as nonstrategic and ineffective, one should recognize that amateurs run the full range of quality—from the most hopeless neophytes in House elections to the Bill Bradleys and John Glenns in the Senate.

The aim of this chapter is to provide a basis for understanding the place of the amateur in electoral and congressional politics. First, I discuss the two dominant theoretical traditions that have attempted to explain amateurs' behavior. After indicating the limitations of these approaches, I present a theory outlining the complex goals amateurs hold and describing the distinct political environment they face.

The Existing Theoretical Arguments
Amateur and Experienced Politicians in Elections

The questions of who is elected to Congress and why have been approached from two theoretical perspectives. The "inherent differences" approach, which includes sociological and psychological theory, argues that there are differences in background, attitude, and personality that influence candidates' behavior; "rational choice" theory assumes that *all* politicians are rational utility maximizers.

The inherent-differences approach asks the question, "Which social and individual-level factors influence the selection of political leaders?" From this view, the election of amateurs to high office is more likely to depend on occupation, social status, and social mobility than strictly on political experience.[1] This attitudinal approach focuses on psychological dispositions and personality traits as the basis for political motivation and behavior.[2] Two of the most important contributions in this tradition are integrative. Prewitt's study of San Francisco Bay Area city councilmen combines institutional and individual-level approaches to examine the impact of the characteristics of leaders on the political order.[3] Fishel used both socioeconomic and attitudinal approaches in his study of challengers in the 1964 congressional elections.[4] Common to all this work is the assumption that some people are more predisposed to politics than others due to their place in society, their lust for power, or their "political personality."

Rational-choice and ambition theorists assume that all people process information and assess the costs and benefits of their actions in the same way. While motivational and background differences may be important, the decision to run for office is seen as primarily a matter of context and opportunity. Thus if an amateur were suddenly placed in a state legislature and given the option of running for the U.S. House, he or she would make strategic calculations in the same manner as a career politician who started lower on the political ladder. Amateurs who may be willing to take a greater risk in running would not do so if they had to give up their state legislative seats to run. In contrast, the personality approach predicts that differences will persist even when the context changes because the psychological development of the political personality is what matters.[5]

1. Donald R. Matthews, *The Social Backgrounds of Political Decision Makers* (New York: Doubleday, 1954); Joseph A. Schlesinger, "Lawyers and American Politics: A Clarified View," *Midwest Journal of Political Science* 1:1 (February 1957): 26–39; Eulau and Sprague, *Lawyers in Politics* (Indianapolis: Bobbs-Merrill, 1964).

2. James David Barber, *The Lawmakers* (New Haven: Yale University Press, 1965); Rufus P. Browning, "The Inter-Action of Personality and Political System in Decisions to Run for Office: Some Data and a Simulation Technique," *Journal of Social Issues* 24:3 (July 1968): 93–110; Harold D. Lasswell, "The Selective Effect of Personality on Political Participation," in *Studies in the Scope and Method of the Authoritarian Personality,* ed. Richard Christie and Marie Jahoda (Glencoe, Ill.: Free Press, 1954), 197–225.

3. Kenneth Prewitt, *The Recruitment of Political Leaders: A Study of Citizen-Politicians* (New York: Bobbs-Merrill, 1970).

4. Jeff Fishel, *Party and Opposition: Congressional Challengers in American Politics* (New York: David McKay, 1973).

5. The exception to this assertion is Rohde's concept of "risk takers," which recognizes the effect of psychological differences on choices that are made in identical contexts. However, the distinction is generally valid. Gordon Black notes the differences between purposive theory and psychological perspectives: "This description of the development of ambition differs markedly from the view that sees the politician as a driven man who decides

Schlesinger's seminal discussion of the "structure of opportunities" outlines the context of choice at the aggregate level;[6] in the last decade, research has moved to an individual-level analysis of office-seeking. This new direction of research coincided with a change in the nature of congressional elections. As early as 1963, a leading scholar of political parties noted the advent of candidate-centered campaigns and the declining role of political parties.[7] By 1983, the notion had almost achieved "common wisdom" status, as Jacobson was able to assert: "The most striking feature of contemporary congressional elections is the ascendant importance of individual candidates and campaigns."[8] Once political campaigns are viewed in these terms, it makes sense, analytically speaking, to make assumptions about the rational calculations of the individual political entrepreneur. If, indeed, the candidate bears the "risks, rewards, and pains" of campaigns, the specification, operationalization, and measurement of these factors should be made from an individual-level perspective.

Gordon Black and David Rohde pioneered individual-level studies of ambition.[9] Black's simple formulation of an ambitious politician's strategic calculus was the first formal statement of the decision to run for higher office. His specification reads, $Uo = (PB) - R$, where Uo = utility of the target office O, P = probability of winning election to office O, B = value of office O, and R = risk (e.g., cost of campaigning, intrinsic value of the base office, opportunity cost of losing the base office).

There are two important implications of this equation. First, it states that ambitious politicians will always aspire to higher office if expected net benefits are positive (i.e., $PB > R$). This approach has proven useful

---

his course early and plans his whole life accordingly. Perhaps there are such men, but we suspect they are a distinct minority. The tides of politics are too great to permit men to chart an undeviating route through the uncertain and troubled waters of political life" ("A Theory of Political Ambition: Career Choices and the Role of Structural Incentives," *American Political Science Review* 66 [March 1972], 159).

6. Joseph A. Schlesinger, *Ambition and Politics: Political Careers in the United States* (Chicago: Rand McNally, 1966), esp. chaps. 2 and 3.

7. Frank J. Sorauf, *Party and Representation* (New York: Atherton Press, 1963), chap. 5.

8. Gary C. Jacobson, *The Politics of Congressional Elections,* 1st ed. (Boston: Little, Brown, 1983), 8.

9. Gordon Black, "A Theory of Political Ambition: Career Choices and the Role of Structural Incentives," *American Political Science Review* 66 (March 1972): 144–59; David W. Rohde, "Risk Bearing and Progressive Ambition: The Case of Members of the United States House of Representatives," *American Journal of Political Science* 23:1 (February 1979): 1–26.

for the Senate and governorships[10] and for the presidency[11] but is not easily applied to congressional elections, for two reasons: (1) the potential pool of candidates for the House is far too large to analyze, even for a single election,[12] and (2) this formulation is much more difficult to apply to potential candidates who do not currently hold political office because the R term is not easily evaluated. It is possible to compare the value of the current office and the opportunity costs incurred by two state legislators who give up their seats to run for the House, but it is far more difficult to compare the same variables for a prominent attorney and a businessperson. This does not pose as significant a problem for Senate or presidential campaigns because a relatively small proportion of those candidates are amateurs; however, it is a concern for House races, where more than 70% of congressional challengers and approximately one-fourth of all representatives have not previously held public office.

Of greater interest to my work is a second implication of Black's equation that reveals systematic differences between the calculations of candidates who are current officeholders and those of amateurs: The greater the risks of running, the higher the probability of winning must be before the candidate will decide to run. Office holders have certain advantages in seeking higher office (e.g., shared constituencies, previous campaign experience), but they also have more to lose if they are not elected, a defeat may not merely interrupt a career, but end it. Therefore, only amateurs are expected to run when the chances for success are remote.

Jacobson and Kernell were the first to develop this implication of ambition theory. They offer convincing arguments that experienced politicians are more strategic in their office-seeking behavior than amateur candidates and thus are more sensitive to national and district conditions that affect their chances for success.[13] But the distinction between experienced and amateur candidates can be overdrawn. When is the distinction

10. Rohde, "Risk Bearing and Progressive Ambition"; Paul R. Brace, "Progressive Ambition in the House: A Probabilistic Approach," *Journal of Politics* 46:2 (May 1984): 556–71.

11. Paul R. Abramson, John H. Aldrich, and David W. Rohde, "Progressive Ambition among U.S. Senators: 1972–1988," *Journal of Politics* 49:1 (February 1987): 3–35.

12. A group of scholars, led by Louis Sandy Maisel, is attempting to tackle these two problems by identifying a pool of *all* potential congressional candidates, and determining the factors that influence their decisions to run for office, in a small sample of districts. Abramson, Aldrich, and Rohde claim that "there is no practical way" that all potential candidates can be identified, even for the presidency ("Progressive Ambition among U.S. Senators," 6).

13. Gary C. Jacobson and Samuel Kernell, *Strategy and Choice in Congressional Elections* (New Haven: Yale University Press, 1983), 30–34.

valid and when is it not? What about amateurs who are successful? Do they resemble their experienced counterparts? My theory of amateurism offers some answers.

Amateur and Experienced Politicians in Congress

Behavioral differences between amateurs and experienced politicians are predicted by two approaches that I call recruitment theory and socialization theory.[14] Note that these labels for the theories are mine; as will be clear from the discussion below, the overlap is only partial with the large bodies of "recruitment" and "socialization" literature. Schlesinger presented a third approach, ambition theory, as a critique of social and psychological theories. When applied to electoral politics, ambition theory is clearly in the rational-choice camp, but its applications to institutional behavior more closely resemble a theory of motivation and thus fall within the purview of recruitment theories.

Recruitment theory is the same as the "inherent differences" approach outlined above. In its application here, the theory holds that people who choose politics as a vocation and embark on political careers early in their professional lives are apt to bring with them a different picture of politics and a different mode of behavior than amateurs who enter politics after establishing themselves in nonpolitical careers. (For example, Tip O'Neill, who entered politics at age twenty-four and served continuously in a legislature for almost fifty years, probably had a different view of politics *coming in* to the U.S. House than Rudy Boschwitz had when he entered the Senate at age forty-eight after amassing a fortune selling plywood in Minnesota.)

Lasswell has provided the strongest theoretical arguments in this tradition. In his early work, Lasswell saw power as the central value pursued by "political man."[15] Those who enter politics at a base office and

14. Schlesinger does not address the behavioral implications of ambition theory in his seminal work. However, many scholars have demonstrated a strong relationship between ambition and behavior. Murray Frost examines the impact of progressive ambition on U.S. House members and confirms some of his hypotheses ("Senatorial Ambitions and Legislative Behavior" [Ph.D. diss., Michigan State University, 1972]). See also Prewitt, *Recruitment of Political Leaders;* Fishel, *Party and Opposition;* John R. Hibbing, "Ambition in the House: Behavioral Consequences of Higher Office Goals among U.S. Representatives," *American Journal of Political Science* 30:3 (August 1986): 651–65; and Peverill Squire, "Member Career Opportunities and the Internal Organization of Legislatures," *Journal of Politics* 50:3 (August 1988): 726–44.

15. Harold D. Lasswell, *Psychopathology and Politics* (Chicago: University of Chicago Press, 1930)

choose to make their career in politics are more likely than amateurs to have power-centered personalities because they have made a commitment to the risk-fraught climb up the tier of offices. In subsequent work, Lasswell recognizes that power-centered personalities are not likely to be effective in politics.[16] He focuses instead on the dominance of cooperation and compromise in the democratic process. Prewitt commented on the significance of this revision of Lasswell's work:

> Success in such a political environment is withheld from rigid personality types, from those who are unable to adapt, adjust, and realistically appraise the situation. The selection process weeds out the intensely power-oriented person; his personality precludes flexible give-and-take politicking. "Young people with rigid personalities may discover that the ladder of advance in politics is less congenial than the more regular steps provided by standard professions and vocations."[17]

This process of natural selection of a dominant political type increases the likelihood that career politicians will have similar characteristics when they initially reach the U.S. Congress. On the other hand, amateurs— who have chosen other careers—are more likely to possess "nonpolitical" personalities because they have not been homogenized by the requirements of advancement in a political career. This line of argument leads to the prediction that "mavericks" in the body are more likely to be amateurs (for example, the "Young Turks" mentioned earlier).[18]

What does this theoretical perspective say about the persistence of differences between amateurs and those who have chosen politics as their vocation? Do amateurs and experienced politicians continue to diverge in their behavior, or do amateurs adapt to the norms of cooperation and compromise, just as their experienced counterparts did early in their political careers? Three patterns of behavior are possible: (1) amateurs adapt to political life and eventually resemble their experienced counterparts, (2) amateurs do not adapt, and therefore, as Lasswell predicts, their political careers are relatively short, and (3) amateurs do not adapt, but are nonetheless able to make successful careers in politics. Recruitment theory most clearly predicts the second scenario: differences between amateurs and experienced politicians are likely to persist because they are rooted in

16. Lasswell, "Effect of Personality on Political Participation."

17. Lasswell, quoted in Prewitt, *Recruitment of Political Leaders*, 116.

18. Clearly this is not always the case. The most prominent exception in the twentieth century is probably Huey Long, who came to the Senate as the most powerful politician in Louisiana history, yet was one of the most famous (or notorious) mavericks of the past century.

background characteristics that do not change or in psychological traits or dispositions that evolve very slowly. The first scenario—that amateurs adapt—is the central argument of socialization theory. After noting the many different types of candidates who are elected, Randall Ripley concludes, "In short, members come to Congress (or lose races for Congress) for many different reasons and with many different self-images. Once in Congress, socializing pressures may impose more uniformity on what was at the outset a reasonably diverse lot of people."[19] John Hiler (R-IN) is a prime example of a representative who lost his ideological zeal. Elected in 1980 at age twenty-seven, Hiler was typical of the "new breed" GOP House member. In his first term he was so committed to the goal of cutting pork-barrel spending that he turned down a plea from South Bend mayor Roger Parent to help secure a loan for an ethanol plant in the district. Also committed to free-market principles, he did not help the United Auto Workers in their effort to keep Bendix Corporation, the district's largest employer, from moving south. Within one year he was "Housebroken," and for good reason: in 1986 he survived by forty-seven votes in the nation's closest House race.[20]

Socialization theory also has an alternative explanation of the source of behavioral differences: the unevenness of political socialization, rather than inherent differences among types of candidates, is what causes behavioral differences between the two groups. Differences begin with the electoral process—the "training ground" that exposes politicians to the requirements of political life. David Easton says, "The process of competing for positions of authority in itself trains the leadership in many of the competencies required by the system."[21]

Differences carry over into the institution. Politicians who move to the U.S. Congress after serving in a state legislature or other elective office will already have been exposed to the give-and-take of politics. They are more likely to be pragmatic in their political concerns, willing to compromise, and cognizant of the moderate position taking that is often necessary to cultivate broad electoral coalitions. Amateurs who lack such previous experience would not be acclimated to the political world.[22] That

---

19. Randall B. Ripley, *Congress: Process and Policy* (New York: W. W. Norton and Company, 1983), 86.

20. Fred Barnes, "The Unbearable Lightness of Being a Congressman," *New Republic*, 15 February 1988, 18–22.

21. David Easton, *A Systems Analysis of Political Life* (New York: John Wiley and Sons, 1965), 451.

22. Walter J. Oleszek, "Congressional Career Patterns: 1910–1960" (Ph.D. diss., State University of New York at Albany, 1968), 198.

political apprenticeship is necessary for competent service in high public office is debatable, yet some have argued the point. Walter Oleszek notes the significance of prior training for U.S. congressmen and for the operation of the institution:

> Few political neophytes reach the national legislative arena. This in itself is an important fact for it reflects upon the capability of Congress to resolve difficult problems. Just as most occupations require some period of apprenticeship, it seems that the party leadership corps and the electorate generally expect congressional candidates to acquire political, administrative, and substantive skills.[23]

Steven Roberts reports that House Speaker Tip O'Neill holds amateur House members responsible for some of the problems the Democratic House leadership had in maintaining their coalition in the first year of the Reagan administration. Roberts says:

> Speaker O'Neill and other veterans refer caustically to some of these younger lawmakers as "bedwetters." Since they did not have to wait their turn to climb the party ladder, few had legislative experience before arriving in Washington, and thus had seldom been subjected to the kind of white-hot pressure applied by the Reagan administration. As a result, they melted quickly.[24]

The predicted behavioral differences generated by these two perspectives differ greatly. As argued above, recruitment theory predicts that differences in behavior will persist for the duration of the political careers of amateurs and experienced politicians alike once they are elected to the same body. Socialization theory predicts that once amateurs learn the political "ropes" and become "socialized," they will resemble their experienced counterparts (i.e., the "bedwetters" would not have given in to Reagan's pressure if they had been experienced). The learning process would take a term or two, after which previous political background would be irrelevant.

A Theory of Amateurism

In explaining behavior in the institution, both recruitment theory and socialization theory are overly simplistic and determinative. In reality,

---

23. Ibid., 197–98.
24. Steven V. Roberts, "Congressmen and Their Districts: Free Agents in Fear of the Future," in *The United States Congress: Thomas P. O'Neill, Jr., Symposium on the U.S. Congress,* ed. Dennis Hale (New Brunswick: Transaction Books, 1983), 82.

some amateurs will have different views of politics and behavior that probably will persist for their tenure in Congress. Some may resemble their experienced counterparts upon entry into office; others may reach that point when they "learn the ropes." In electoral politics, greater recognition is needed for the complex nature of amateurs' goals and aspirations. Some amateurs will resemble experienced politicians in their strategic behavior by carefully weighing the costs and benefits of running. Others will pursue policy goals without much consideration for their electoral fortunes or in order to promote nonpolitical careers. A theory is needed to help disentangle the complexity of empirical reality and provide a basis for explaining differences and similarities between amateurs and experienced politicians.

A Typology of Amateurism

Amateurs generally start at a disadvantage in the process of winning a House or Senate seat and must pursue aggressive campaign strategies to overcome their deficits in name recognition and experience. While career politicians can emphasize their accomplishments in politics and rely on a proven base of supporters, amateurs often must attack, and consequently are often risk-takers who are willing to challenge incumbents or other experienced politicians in primaries and general elections. Others pursue aggressive policy-based campaigns. This view is a significant departure from previous work that has viewed amateurs as hopelessly naive or motivated by nonpolitical considerations.[25] While the behavior of many amateurs is consistent with this common view, many others pursue aggressive, rational strategies that land some of them in Congress.

Amateurs who are elected to Congress are of three types: ambitious, policy, and hopeless. (Categories are not exclusive; I also examine two mixed types.) Differences in how they behave in Congress are examined in chapter 5. Chapter 4 examines the strategic behavior of ambitious amateurs in congressional elections.[26]

25. David A. Leuthold, *Electioneering in a Democracy* (New York: John Wiley and Sons, 1968); John W. Kingdon, *Candidates for Office* (New York: Random House, 1968); Linda L. Fowler, "The Cycle of Defeat: Recruitment of Congressional Challengers" (Ph.D. diss., University of Rochester, 1977); Thomas A. Kazee, "The Decision to Run for the U.S. Congress: Challenger Attitudes in the 1970s" *Legislative Studies Quarterly* 5:1 (February 1980): 79–100; Jacobson and Kernell, *Strategy and Choice*.

26. The behavior of policy amateurs in elections will not be examined because determining the policy goals of all congressional candidates is beyond the scope of this project. Little information is readily available on the importance of policy goals to defeated congressional candidates. Because more than four thousand races will be examined (all House and Senate races from 1972 to 1988), using questionnaires or relying on local papers is not feasible.

THE AMBITIOUS AMATEUR

Some amateurs are more political than the typical ladder climber. Many prominent young attorneys and businessmen or local activists are extremely ambitious and do not want to waste time in lower office. For example, Andrew Maguire (D-NJ), a former Peace Corps volunteer, won a 1974 election with no previous political experience. Maguire notes that he "cut in from the side. . . . A high risk strategy made sense to me. I wanted to do reasonably well in a short period of time."[27] Maguire is hardly the image of the sacrificial-lamb amateur that is conjured up in the literature.

Ambitious amateurs are identified on the basis of their celebrity status and ambition as revealed through strategic behavior (whether or not they defeat an experienced politician in the primary, and whether or not they received 40% of the vote in a previous attempt for the House). This identification process is discussed in more detail in chapter 4 (pp. 87–92).

How does this type of amateur differ from that of the simple definition based on lack of previous political experience? I expect that ambitious amateurs' strategic behavior in the decision to run for office will resemble their experienced counterparts' behavior, because both types are primarily concerned with electoral goals. Ambitious amateurs will be more likely to run in open-seat races or when other district and national conditions are in their favor. Whether one predicts differences between ambitious amateurs and all other amateurs in the institution depends on the theoretical perspective one adopts. Recruitment theory would hold that ambitious amateurs are more likely to resemble their experienced counterparts. Ambitious amateurs have personalities and ambitions that are similar to those of experienced politicians who work their way up the career ladder; therefore, their views of politics and political careers are not likely to differ. Socialization theory, on the other hand, would maintain that it is not revealed ambitions or "political types" that matter, but rather the range of political experiences to which the candidate has been exposed; therefore, an ambitious amateur is just as likely as the other types of amateurs to behave differently at first in the institution. The expectation of my theory is that ambitious amateurs are likely to hold the same set

---

More detailed information is available for candidates who are elected, so the importance of policy goals will be determined for this subset of amateurs. Hopeless amateurs are defined by their performance in the election, so they are excluded from the analysis in chap. 4 as well.

27. Roberts, "Congressmen and Their Districts," 73.

of goals as experienced politicians; thus their behavior will not differ systematically.

THE POLICY AMATEUR

Two types of policy goals may motivate behavior: policy advocacy and policy seeking.[28] Policy advocates are interested in bringing a specific issue before the public, while policy seekers are concerned with actually shaping policy. Although policy amateurs do not have a monopoly on policy-based political careers, their relative lack of concern for electoral goals is distinctive.

Policy advocates are less strategic in their behavior than experienced politicians because they are less concerned with electoral goals. Often these amateurs run issue-based campaigns with little hope of being elected, as did John Orman, the 1984 Democratic nominee in Connecticut's Fourth District. He says:

> As a citizen who had strong anti-nuclear views and strong anti-Reagan views, I was able to get the nomination essentially because no professional politician wanted it. . . . I had never even thought of running for political office before since I enjoyed operating as a citizen activist on the edges of the political system, but since no opposition was developing in the "safe" district, I felt that it was a great opportunity to discuss national issues and to represent a progressive constituency.[29]

It is not likely that similar campaign goals would ever be expressed by an experienced challenger whose political career was on the line.[30]

Policy seekers have a mix of office-seeking and policy goals (obviously, to have the greatest possible impact in shaping policy, one must be elected). In the last 1960s and early 1970s, many amateurs entered politics in order to change U.S. policy on the Vietnam War or the environment. More recently, abortion and school busing issues have stimulated amateur campaigns. These amateurs may resemble the citizen-politicians of the nineteenth century who entered politics for a brief time and then returned to

28. John H. Aldrich, *Before the Convention: Strategies and Choices in Presidential Nomination Campaigns* (Chicago: University of Chicago Press, 1980), 43.

29. John Orman, "Media Coverage of the Congressional Underdog," *PS* 18:4 (Fall 1985): 755.

30. This is not to say that there is a complete lack of policy content in such campaigns—only that policy advocacy will not be the central goal in running for office, or, perhaps more accurately, will not be the central way in which the campaign is run. Instead of focusing on issues, these experienced challengers will run on more vote-profitable grounds.

their permanent occupations. Jim Johnson (D-CO), an anti-war candidate in the early 1970s, is a good example. Fenno says, "We should think of Jim Johnson as a citizen legislator." He continues:

> He is a man who got agitated about a public problem, went to Washington to see what he could do about it, did what he felt he could do about it, and then returned home to resume his career. From beginning to end, issues of war and peace were the ones that Johnson cared most about. When he decided he could do nothing about these matters, he decided to leave.[31]

More recently, Gordon Humphrey (R-NH) announced that he would not seek third-term reelection to the Senate, fulfilling his 1978 and 1984 campaign pledges that he would be a citizen-legislator and serve only two terms. Humphrey cannot be labeled easily, but his extreme ideological positions are motivated by strong policy concerns.[32]

Amateurs who use issue positions as the basis for their campaigns are coded as policy amateurs.[33] Though many classifications of issue campaigns are possible, four types seem dominant: negative or attack, valence, positive, and ideological. To narrow the focus, I followed Barbara Hinckley's definition of issues as "questions of public policy held by some people to be controversial and worth debate and discussion."[34] With this definition as a guide, negative and valence campaigns are not coded as policy campaigns; while negative campaigns may have some issue content (such as attacks on a member's voting record), the two tend

31. Fenno, "What's He Like? What's She Like? What Are They Like?" in *The United States Congress: Thomas P. O'Neill, Jr., Symposium on the Senate,* ed. Dennis Hale (New Brunswick: Transaction Books, 1983), 118.

32. Rhodes Cook, "New Hampshire Conservative Humphrey to Quit in 1990," *Congressional Quarterly Weekly Report* 47 (11 March 1989): 544.

33. Information about the general-election campaign was gathered from issues of *Congressional Quarterly Weekly Report, Politics in America, The Almanac of American Politics,* the *Washington Post,* the *New York Times,* and some local newspapers between 1972 and 1984. Specific coding rules are discussed in the text.

It is possible, as Anthony Downs (*An Economic Theory of Democracy* [New York: Harper and Row, 1957]) argues, that candidates do not get elected in order to take policy positions, but take policy positions in order to get elected. My assumption is that candidates who make policy positions central in their campaigns are *not* doing so simply to get elected but rather because the positions are true reflections of their ideologies and their desires to affect public policy. This is plausible because the optimal strategy is to pursue the median position or obfuscate issues (see Benjamin I. Page, "The Theory of Political Ambiguity," *American Political Science Review* 70:3 [September 1976]: 742–52).

34. Barbara Hinckley, *Congressional Elections* (Washington, D.C.: Congressional Quarterly Press, 1981), 96.

to be mutually exclusive.[35] This is not to say that attack themes are not crucial in many campaigns, only that this type of campaign is not a guide to future behavior. Valence issues also do not reveal anything about the true policy views of the candidate; all politicians are "for" no drugs, clean government, and low inflation.

Candidates occasionally address a valence issue in terms of specific policy proposals. Those who take this additional step are coded as policy amateurs because they have articulated a positive policy position. Other positive issue appealers may take on more controversial issues; these are the policy seekers discussed above who addressed issues like Vietnam, the environment, and consumer concerns. Finally, amateurs who are elected on the basis of general ideological appeals are considered policy amateurs. The "Young Turks" elected in 1980 fall into this category (fifteen of the nineteen Republican amateurs elected in 1980 were policy amateurs). These amateurs tend to be young, ambitious, and committed to conservative principles that are centered around belief in the free market and limited government.

It is generally very clear from the public record whether issues played a central role in a given campaign.[36] The campaigns of two amateurs elected from Oregon in 1980 are instructive. In one, Denny Smith (R), a wealthy newspaper owner, defeated Al Ullman, the Ways and Means Committee chairman, by spending $700,000 in an extremely negative campaign. Though an ideological conservative, *Congressional Quarterly* reported, Smith "concentrated more on attacking Ullman than discussing his own positions."[37] Therefore, Smith is not considered a policy amateur. In the other, Ron Wyden (D), an ambitious thirty-one-

35. Fred Barnes chronicles some of the more outrageous campaign "issues" ("Our Cheesy Democracy: Stupid Politician Tricks," *New Republic,* 3 November 1986, 18–21). Included are the "urine sample wars," wherein opponents charge each other with drug abuse. Bill Clinton, governor of Arkansas, was pressured into taking a drug test, but that did not satisfy his opponent, who demanded that Clinton's wife comply as well. (She did, and passed.) Tom Daschle, who eventually defeated James Abnor (R-SD), was criticized for taking a contribution from Jane Fonda, who had urged people not to eat red meat, which is important to the South Dakota economy. Fonda later was shown in a commercial eating a Big Mac to assure people that she was not trying to undermine the farm economy. The most pressing issue in Fred "Gopher" Grandy's (R-IA) successful campaign was his poking fun at Iowa on "The Tonight Show." Grandy had likened the Miss Sioux City Rivercade to "a big testimonial to ringworm."

36. Some cases are not as obvious. In these instances I consulted several sources, looking for clues about the nature of the campaign. I then evaluated the public record in two independent readings, coding the amateur both times. In all but three of the cases the codings were in agreement.

37. *Congressional Quarterly Weekly Report* 39 (3 January 1981): 25.

year-old lawyer, defeated Rep. Robert Duncan in the Democratic primary. Wyden defeated Duncan by attacking him for being "out of touch with the district," but he also ran an issues campaign. *Congressional Quarterly* labeled Wyden an "outspoken urban advocate" who had a "high-profile" image on issues concerning senior citizens, speculating that, as the executive director of the Gray Panthers, he could become "a national spokesman for the elderly."[38] Wyden is clearly a policy amateur.

Policy amateurs are likely to behave very differently in both electoral and institutional politics. They will be less concerned with the office-seeking goal and more concerned with policy goals. Politics is not a career for many of these people; they enter politics after establishing another career. Typically they have a strong worldview and concrete goals. After achieving those goals, or being frustrated in the process, some will retire from politics.

Are differences between policy amateurs and experienced politicians likely to persist? If socialization theory is ever relevant, it is likely to hold here. Washington is full of tales of the bright-eyed ideologue who plans to push for a specific policy agenda, only to be seduced by constituency pressures and the reelection goal.[39] Furthermore, this breed of amateur may quickly realize that Congress is not suited to the pursuit of specific policy goals. Although individual members can often influence specific bills or raise specific policy concerns, immediate changes of national significance are difficult to bring about, especially for freshman members.

THE HOPELESS AMATEUR

A majority of amateurs in the electoral arena will be of the hopeless type (see Introduction, note 13). Experienced and qualified politicians are reluctant to challenge incumbents, given their tremendous advantage. Many amateurs run because of a feeling of duty to their party, or just for the thrill of the battle.[40] Not many of these amateurs are elected because, by the nature of their candidacies, they are poorly funded and are running

38. Ibid.

39. The example of John Hiler was noted above. Vin Weber (R-MN) also moderated his conservative positions in the face of a tough reelection fight in 1986. Weber tried to put some distance between himself and Reagan by opposing Reagan's farm policy, by voting for rigid controls sponsored by Iowa's liberal Democratic senator, Tom Harkin, and by serving as ombudsman for the district's farmers. "That's a far cry from riding shotgun for Rep. Newt Gingrich in the Conservative Opportunity Society," Evans and Novak commented (Rowland Evans and Robert Novak, "Reverse Realignment," *Washington Post,* 7 April 1986, A15).

40. Kingdon, *Candidates for Office;* Kazee, "The Decision to Run."

against tremendous odds. A fair number of hopeless amateurs have been swept into office in years such as 1932, 1964, and 1980. Hopeless amateurs are also elected in normal electoral periods. Every year there are a few amateurs who pull stunning upsets over incumbents who had become inattentive or out of step with the district. These amateurs are responsible for the "random terror" component of elections that all incumbents fear. They play an important role in the democratic process by adding an additional measure of accountability.

Hopeless amateurs are identified as the outliers in a regression of thirteen district- and national-level variables on the winner's share of the vote.[41] In open-seat races the outliers were defined as those winners whose predicted vote was less than 45%; in incumbent races, surprise victories are those in which the incumbent was predicted to receive 60% of the vote, but lost. Thirty-two candidates are defined by this process; twenty-five are amateurs and seven had some political experience (only one had elective political experience). Only eight amateurs would be expected by chance (the difference is significant at the .001 level). This finding is consistent with the theoretical expectation that experienced candidates are not likely to run when the chances for success are low.

MIXED TYPES

In the coding process it became clear that the types are not mutually exclusive; therefore, two mixed-types are also included: ambitious/policy amateurs and hopeless/policy amateurs. These are candidates who are defined as either ambitious or hopeless by the objective tests outlined above, but who also have a strong issue component in their campaigns. These cases make the task of predicting behavioral patterns more difficult and will be treated separately in the analysis.[42]

41. In incumbent races the dependent variable is the vote percentage received by the incumbent; in open-seat races it is the winner's vote total. The independent variables are a dummy for first-term members, a scandal dummy, real income change for the party in and out of power, the change in the unemployment rate for the party in and out of power, a dummy for whether the incumbent was hurt by redistricting, the normal vote of the district, the previous challenger's vote, two Watergate dummies, and a three-level variable to measure the strength of the challenge to an incumbent in his or her primary. All the variables were in the expected direction and all except real income were significant at the .00001 level; the R^2 was .44. Some of the more noteworthy coefficients were: a scandal cost the incumbent 3.2% of the vote, unfavorable redistricting 4.3%, a strong primary challenge 2.3%, Watergate 8.8% (for Republicans, it helped Democrats by 3.8%).

42. Two additional groups are treated separately in the analysis because of their distinctive backgrounds: from 1972 to 1984, seven widows of former congressmen were elected (six of whom were amateurs), as well as fifteen "super-freshmen," members of Congress who returned to the House after a previous defeat.

The other possible overlap—ambitious and hopeless—occurred with eight of the thirty-two members identified as hopeless amateurs.[43] In these cases, candidates are coded as hopeless amateurs. Mick Staton is a nearly perfect example of the hopeless amateur, illustrating why the hopeless type is probably the more central of the two. *Congressional Quarterly Weekly Report* describes his victory in 1980, the first by a Republican in West Virginia's Third District since 1926, as a combination of "persistence and good luck."[44] Ehrenhalt reports that "the election of Staton had been regarded as a bit of a fluke. Only the combination of the conservative tide—with Ronald Reagan at the head—and local Democratic infighting had swung the seat to the GOP."[45] Staton was a virtual unknown without ties to the party or to the Charleston business community when he decided to challenge thirty-year House veteran John Stack in 1978. After Staton mortgaged his house to fund the race and gained 41% of the vote, the party took notice. When Stack died early in 1980, Staton narrowly lost in the special election. He came back to beat the special-election winner, John Hutchinson, in the fall.

Staton is not a pure hopeless amateur because of his three attempts at the seat (recall, this is one of the criteria for defining ambitious amateurs). Yet several factors make this a clear-cut case. First, the "fluke" conditions of Reagan's coattails and the normally Democratic nature of the district firmly place Staton in the statistically defined category of hopeless amateurs (his predicted vote was 41.7%). Second, at forty years of age, Staton is older than the typical ambitious amateur. Finally, he is by his own description a "citizen legislator rather than a career politician." He indicated that he did not plan to serve in Congress more than four or five terms.[46] Staton received his wish, a bit prematurely. In 1982 he was swamped by Bob Wise, a Democratic state senator, 58% to 42%.

Behavior in Elections

A more detailed examination of the behavioral implications of the theory and how it will be tested is in order. My treatment of the decision to run for a House or Senate seat represents a theoretical advance in two

43. In two of the eight cases, the hopeless amateur defeated an experienced candidate in the primary election; in the other six cases, that amateur was making his or her second attempt for the House seat.

44. *Congressional Quarterly Weekly Report* 39 (3 January 1981): 32.

45. Alan Ehrenhalt, *Politics in America, 1984* (Washington, D.C.: Congressional Quarterly Press, 1983), 1626.

46. *Congressional Quarterly Weekly Report* 39 (3 January 1981): 32.

ways. First, it combines the assumptions of purposive behavior, viewing recruitment as an individual's "calculus of candidacy," with an awareness of the structural and institutional contexts of the decision to run (as described in the previous chapter). This approach allows more accurate predictions of the types of candidates who will run in varying contexts. Second, it recognizes that many amateurs have systematically different preferences and are guided by a different array of costs and benefits than are experienced politicians, and that amateurs in general are motivated by a variety of goals. Before developing these points, I will place my typology within the context of purposive theory.

In its simplest form, the purposive approach reduces the decision to run to statements like, "A candidate will run if the benefits of doing so exceed the costs and the net benefits exceed the utility of the candidate's best alternative."[47] This statement is obviously true, but it is not very helpful until one starts to analyze the varying costs and benefits involved and the likelihood of success. This has been the basic approach of research in this area in the last decade. Factors such as the size and competitiveness of the district,[48] the characteristics of the higher office,[49] various district- and national-level conditions,[50] and whether candidates must give up their current seats to run for higher office[51] have all been related to candidates' strategic calculus. Unfortunately, this work examines the decisions of current officeholders to run for higher office and ignores the amateur's initial decision to run. How could purposive theory be applied to this decision?

A purposive model of the initial decision to run would be based on several assumptions. First, one would assume that amateurs maximize expected utility just as experienced politicians do. They consider all alternatives, assess the likelihood of various outcomes and their consequences, and then choose the alternative that is most likely to achieve their goals. Beyond this basic assumption, one should recognize that the choice situation is fundamentally different for the amateur.

While I accept the assumption that amateur and experienced politicians

47. See, for example, Black, "A Theory of Political Ambition."

48. Ibid., 147–48.

49. Rohde, "Risk Bearing and Progressive Ambition," 5–8.

50. Ibid.; Brace, "Progressive Ambition in the House"; Jon R. Bond, Cary Covington, and Richard Fleisher, "Explaining Challenger Quality in Congressional Elections," *Journal of Politics* 47:2 (May 1985): 510–29.

51. Paul L. Hain, Philip G. Roeder, and Manuel Avalos, "Risk and Progressive Candidacies: An Extension of Rohde's Model," *American Journal of Political Science* 25:1 (February 1981): 188–91.

are rational, purposive actors, it strikes me as similar to the tautology expressed above concerning net benefits outweighing net costs in the decision to run. That assertion leaves open the question of *identifying* the relevant costs and benefits. Clearly, the decision to run for office is freely made, based on available information; therefore, by definition, net expected utility must be positive for all candidates. My argument is that there are systematic differences in many amateurs' utility functions and in their costs and benefits of running when compared to those of their experienced counterparts. Furthermore, these differences are due to their status as amateurs rather than to the specific context of a given race. It is a mistake to allow the assumption of rationality to mask significant differences in the components of strategic decisions, as the current literature has done.

Amateurs will differ from experienced politicians in four areas: their goals, their campaign strategies, their costs and benefits of running, and their information-gathering and -processing capabilities. The first assertion is based on the assumption that preferences derive from the individual's experience, education, and indoctrination.[52] The experiences of the career politician are likely to stimulate a continued involvement in politics. Black and Kernell both discuss the "investment" in a political career that fosters political ambitions and the reelection goal.[53] Using the economists' language of "rates of return" and "investment transferability," Black argues that the political career develops its own momentum and makes nonpolitical career alternatives less attractive. As the politician's sunk costs increase, his or her evaluation of political alternatives is likely to become increasingly positive.[54]

An extension of this reasoning, and a central assumption of most purposive models of political behavior, is that the primary goal of experienced politicians will be election or reelection. Amateurs, on the other hand, will have a mix of goals: election, policy, and other (e.g., to help their party, perform a civic duty, or pursue personal and nonpolitical career considerations). Experienced politicians will not share this same mix of goals because of their investment in their political careers. State legislators and city council members are not likely to be motivated to run for higher office primarily from a feeling of civic or party duty. They have too

52. James March and Johan P. Olsen, "The New Institutionalism: Organizational Factors in Political Life," *American Political Science Review* 78:3 (September 1984): 734–49.

53. Black, "A Theory of Political Ambition," 155–59; Kernell, "Emergence of a Political Career Structure," 7–10.

54. Black, "A Theory of Political Ambition," 159.

much at stake. Ambitious amateurs, those who are considering making politics their vocation, are in a similar position because a bad showing in an initial race will damage their standing as future candidates. Amateurs' campaign strategies diverge greatly from those of experienced challengers and incumbents. Incumbents rarely emphasize policy positions because the costs of pursuing a policy-oriented campaign, both in terms of potentially alienating voters and in actual costs of establishing and disseminating policy positions, are extremely high. Instead, they make highly personalized and general appeals to voters. Any issues that arise will be of the valence (Mom-and-apple-pie) or pork-barrel variety. Heavily favored open-seat candidates also eschew issues and rely on their partisan advantage to carry them into office.

Challengers and candidates in competitive open-seat races do not have this luxury. The consensus of the substantial literature on campaign strategies is that challengers must erode the incumbent's support while simultaneously establishing their own credibility and appeal.[55] Any candidate faces a difficult task on the first count, but it is the second point that distinguishes amateurs from experienced politicians. One of the most common strategies for establishing credibility—stressing previous political experience—is not available to amateurs.

The handicap of not having a political base can often be overcome by engaging in what Jeff Greenfield calls "political jujitsu": making a virtue of an apparent weakness. The claim of being "above politics" or running as a "citizen-politician" has strong appeal in some elections. Jimmy Carter, while not a complete amateur, had limited experience for a presidential candidate. Carter successfully ran against Washington by emphasizing that he was just a peanut farmer, not a political insider. The confidence of the people in their government was at an all-time low, so they were willing to give inexperience a chance. More commonly, amateurs overcome the handicap by demonstrating their competence and stressing the issues. Tom Atkins, the Republican nominee in Ohio's Second District in 1978, explains the charges made by his opponent and how he countered them:

> Stan's theme was that the party . . . had endorsed a rank
> amateur who wasn't qualified to serve in the Congress, not an

55. Louis Sandy Maisel, *From Obscurity to Oblivion: Running in the Congressional Primary*, rev. ed. (Knoxville: University of Tennessee Press, 1986), chap. 5; Jacobson, *Politics of Congressional Elections*, 77–86; Jeff Greenfield, *Playing to Win: An Insider's Guide to Politics* (New York: Simon and Schuster, 1980).

experienced legislator like himself who had . . . served the
people well. . . . I tried to show that my experience was the
relevant experience. I've been intimately involved with
national politicians and national issues.[56]

Ronald Reagan, of course, was the prototypical amateur in his initial
campaign for governor of California. To establish credibility, he combined the policy approach with the Carter approach of claiming amateurism as a virtue. Reagan's amateurism was a central issue in both the primary race against San Francisco mayor George Christopher and in the
general-election contest against incumbent governor Pat Brown. Brown
stressed his experience and ridiculed Reagan's background. Brown's ad-
vertisements featured Reagan in various movie roles and advertising slots
and ended with the punch line, "Vote for a real governor, not an acting
one," or "Over the years Ronald Reagan has played many roles. This
year he wants to play the role of governor. Are you willing to pay the
price of admission?"[57] Reagan's consulting firm, Spencer-Roberts,
knew experience would be an issue, and they were prepared. William
Roberts feared it would be difficult to overcome the charges because Reagan was not well informed on a broad range of issues. To counter this
problem the firm executed a brilliant plan that relied on both image and
issues:

> Our answer was to be very candid and honest about it, and
> indicate that Governor Reagan was not a professional
> politician. He was a citizen-politician. Therefore, we had an
> automatic defense. He didn't have to know all the
> answers. . . . A citizen-politician is not expected to know all
> of the answers to all of the issues. As a matter of fact, before
> the end of the campaign, he hit it so well and so hard that
> Governor Brown was on the defensive for being a professional
> politician.[58]

At the same time, Reagan emphasized the issues that would characterize
his future campaigns: the perils of big government, the need for morality
in government, and a belief in the free market. Reagan's campaign was
by no means centered around issues, but the candidate was able to convince the voters that the star of *Bedtime for Bonzo* had a vision.[59]

56. Maisel, *From Obscurity to Oblivion,* 85.
    57. Stephen A. Salmore and Barbara G. Salmore, *Candidates, Parties, and Campaigns*
(Washington, D.C.: Congressional Quarterly Press, 1985), 130.
    58. Greenfield, *Playing to Win,* 256.
    59. As noted above, professional politicians often recognize the value of running

The third area in which amateurs will differ from their experienced counterparts is in the assessment of the costs and benefits of running for office. An experienced politician has more at stake: a loss may end his or her career. One congressional candidate who carefully weighed his chances before entering the race stated, "If I lose, my political future is demolished. You can't afford a couple of losses, so this could be the last hurrah for me."[60] For an experienced politician, the benefits of running primarily involve the perpetuation of the political career. Obviously, most politicians also gain satisfaction from pursuing policy goals or they would not be in politics, but their policy advocacy is secondary to their electoral goals.

For amateurs, on the other hand, losing does not present an inherently costly situation. In fact, many amateurs run primarily for the publicity they receive for their business or law practice, without much regard to whether they win or lose. For others, the costs are lower because of the perception that it really does not matter if they lose. One candidate who ran in order to help his party said, "I am not concerned about getting a loser image because everyone expects me to lose, especially my own party. If I lose, no one will think the worse of me, and if I win, I'll be a hero . . . so I can't lose."[61]

While the costs of losing are generally lower for amateurs, the actual costs of running will be similar to those of the experienced candidate. Both must take time off from their current jobs to engage in distasteful fund-raising and time-consuming wooing of voters. The psychological costs may be greater for amateurs because they often do not know what to expect.

For amateurs with a chance of winning, the decision becomes more

---

"against the establishment." Reagan still considered himself a citizen-politician after eight years as governor of California and eight years in the presidency, often referring to "those people inside the Beltway." Amateurs clearly do not have a monopoly on this strategy, but their claims of being outsiders ring truer than the protestations of the Washington insiders. This strategy is more likely to be forced upon an amateur because he or she cannot use the alternative approach of stressing prior elective experience.

60. Fowler, "Cycle of Defeat," 65.

61. Ibid. Tip O'Neill describes the successful effort to win Democratic control of the Massachusetts state legislature in 1948. To recruit able candidates in districts that had been dominated by Republicans for years, he made a simple appeal: "We'd go into an area and talk with a young lawyer. 'You're just back from the war,' we'd tell him, 'and you're not allowed to advertise. Running for office is your golden opportunity to get known in the community. . . . We'll do all we can to help you win, but win or lose, you'll be better off than you were. Look at it this way: meeting all those people can only help your career' " (Thomas P. O'Neill, Jr., with William Novak, *Man of the House: The Life and Political Memoirs of Speaker Tip O'Neill* [New York: Random House, 1987], 57).

complex because it involves a choice between a political and a nonpolitical career, whereas experienced politicians have only a move to
higher office to contemplate. This difference can be expressed in terms of
opportunity costs.[62] The opportunity costs of moving to Congress are not
as high for experienced politicians. Typically, politicians at the state and
local levels serve only part-time in their political careers. The chance to
move to the House or Senate allows them to engage full-time in their
chosen profession. Serving in lower office has all the disadvantages of
holding public office (long hours, low pay, fund-raising activity, and
broad responsibilities) without the greater benefits of higher office (more
power, higher pay, greater visibility). Some politicians at the state and
local levels may prefer their dual-career existence; for them there are opportunity costs. But for most who have chosen politics as their vocation, a
move to the House or Senate is a "step up," and therefore their opportunity costs are not very high.

For amateurs, the transition to a political career involves a more significant change. Job security, possibly much higher pay, and an absence of
public scrutiny and responsibility are often sacrificed as the amateur takes
public office. Potentially high opportunity costs may explain why celebrity candidates and millionaires more often choose to run for the Senate
than for the House. The attractive life-styles they relinquish require substantial inducements in terms of power and prestige to justify a change;
House service apparently does not compensate for the opportunity costs
that are often present for amateurs. Therefore, officeholders will experience significant opportunity costs only if they lose, whereas amateurs
many incur such costs if they win!

The other side of the equation also is different for amateurs: the benefits of running for office are more diverse. Huckshorn and Spencer
suggest that most losers expect very modest benefits; "The reward is in
the running rather than in the winning."[63] Kazee provides anecdotal evidence for this point. Two unsuccessful challengers comment on their
experiences:

> I have nothing but good things to say about it. It was probably
> the most exciting, interesting, and challenging experience I
> have ever had.

62. Opportunity costs are the costs of doing something as measured by the loss of the
opportunity to do the next best thing instead with the same amount of time and resources. In
this context, opportunity cost refers to the job and income that a candidate would give up if
elected.

63. Robert J. Huckshorn and Robert C. Spencer, *The Politics of Defeat: Campaigning
for Congress* (Amherst: University of Massachusetts Press, 1971), 8.

Exhilarating . . . even if you lose, you come away a better person. You are better able to add to society. I don't know of a candidate like myself who is bitter.[64]

Amateurs' disproportionate involvement in seemingly hopeless races can be partly explained by their enjoyment of the process and lack of an overriding concern with the outcome. Other rewards include helping their political party, raising issues, and increasing name recognition, for both political and nonpolitical career benefits.[65]

The final area in which amateurs are likely to differ from their experienced counterparts is in the gathering and processing of information related to the decision to run for office. Leuthold observes that amateurs "often did not realize that they had no chance of winning" and finds that experienced candidates gave more serious and accurate consideration to their chances of winning.[66] Candidates with previous campaign experience have a better sense of their vote-getting ability, the strength of a challenger, and the proper strategies to pursue in coalition building.[67]

The net effect of these various differences between amateurs and experienced candidates is to create a set of decision-guiding conditions that is likely to produce very different outcomes for the various types of candidates. The lower costs and broader-based benefits associated with amateur campaigns lower the threshold that must be passed before the amateur will decide to run for office. Experienced candidates, who have much to lose and little to gain from running and losing, operate on an entirely different scale of costs and benefits and therefore must choose their races carefully. They may receive the same broad-based benefits as amateurs, but these are dwarfed by the benefits of winning and the costs of losing, and therefore hardly figure into the calculus of the experienced candidate. Amateurs who are less concerned with the outcome and more with the process of the campaign are more likely to run in a variety of situations. Furthermore, because amateurs may not have access to information concerning their chances for success, they may often appear to be

64. Kazee, "The Decision to Run," 82–83.

65. Of course, these candidates could be offering rationalizations for what objectively could be seen as a frustrating and difficult experience. However, in Fowler's sample, 42% of those involved in hopeless races cited "increasing name recognition" as a primary reason for running, whereas *none* in the advantageous races gave this as a reason (Fowler, "Cycle of Defeat," 62). Of course, increased recognition can be of benefit to experienced candidates as well. A stronger than expected first showing can be a valuable asset for future campaigns for ambitious amateurs and experienced politicians alike.

66. Leuthold, *Electioneering in a Democracy,* 22.

67. Kingdon, *Candidates for Office.*

less strategic in their behavior. One factor may limit the number of amateurs entering politics: the opportunity costs of entering politics may keep many amateurs from running for office, and may motivate others to run only for the Senate or for a governorship.

Amateurism in Congress

I maintain the traditional assumptions of rational-choice theory to explain amateurs' behavior in Congress, but assign different goals to amateurs and experienced politicians based on my theory of amateurism. Preferences are not external to the political system—they are formed by past experiences. Thus, the political amateur, whose experiences in the political world differ from those of the career politician, is likely to hold different goals and preferences in pursuing a political career.

Differences in goals influence behavior in the institution. I will test for differences in behavior in four areas: roll call voting, committee assignments, careers within the body, and floor activity. Ambitious amateurs and experienced politicians are expected to behave in a similar manner in all these areas, just as in the electoral arena. In pursuing reelection goals, this group of congressmen will seek assignments on the "reelection," constituency-oriented committees or on prestige committees that further the goal of achieving "power within the House."[68] The latter is expected to be more evident because experienced and ambitious politicians may be seen by the leadership as more deserving of prize committee assignments.[69] Constituency committees, such as Public Works, do not necessarily attract the politically ambitious even if they do further the reelection goal. Members of Congress have many other ways to maintain constituency ties—for example, through service or individualized "home styles" that appeal to specific pockets of voters.[70]

Experienced politicians and ambitious amateurs are not ideologically extreme in their roll call voting (relative to the district), but maintain moderate positions that appeal to the largest group of voters. They attempt to establish themselves in long careers in the House or Senate, and

68. Richard F. Fenno, Jr., *Congressmen in Committees* (Boston: Little, Brown, 1973), 1–14.

69. Burdett A. Loomis, "Congressional Careers and Party Leadership in the Contemporary House of Representatives," *American Journal of Political Science* 28:1 (February 1984): 192–93.

70. On constituency service, see Morris P. Fiorina, *Congress: Keystone of the Washington Establishment* (New Haven: Yale University Press, 1977); on home style, see Richard Fenno, Jr., *Home Style: House Members in Their Districts* (Boston: Little, Brown, 1978).

on average they have longer tenures than their amateur counterparts. Furthermore, they pursue and achieve leadership positions with greater frequency than the other members of Congress. Finally, they are more likely to be active on the floor (as measured by amending behavior) than their amateur counterparts.

The policy amateur is likely to have a different career. In their pursuit of policy goals, policy amateurs seek policy-committee assignments (such as Education and Labor). Their advocacies of specific policies make them more ideologically extreme, and their careers in the body are shorter and more focused. They are not as likely to climb to leadership positions, though some who balance the reelection and policy goals will seek power within the body. In general, they are less active on the floor across a broad range of issues. Instead, their activities are more focused around their specific policy concern.

Finally, the few hopeless amateurs who are swept into office combine aspects of the two types described above. The outstanding characteristic of hopeless amateurs is that they are not likely to have long careers in the body. Many who are swept into office on national partisan tides are swept back out in the following corrective election. As former Speaker John McCormack said, "A new member could be elected by accident, but [they are] seldom reelected by accident."[71] (Five of the nine Republican hopeless amateurs who were elected in 1980 were defeated in 1982.)[72] Some, such as Jim Jones (D-OK), manage to establish lengthy and productive legislative careers, but the hopeless amateur is generally assured of difficult races throughout his or her career. (Jones received only 54% of the vote in 1982, which was a good year for Democrats, and then received only 52% in 1984. In 1986, Jones decided to run for the Senate against Don Nickles and lost badly.) For this reason, the reelectoral or constituency goal will dominate his or her behavior in the attempt to transform a marginal district into a safe seat.

Some hopeless amateurs do not view politics as a career and do not have ambitions for higher office. In this way, they resemble Barber's "reluctants" or many of the city council members described by Prewitt.[73]

71. Quoted by Speaker Thomas S. Foley (D-WA) (transcript of a speech given at the National Press Club, Washington, D.C., 24 July 1989), 1.

72. The other four—Duncan Hunter (R-CA), Marge Roukema (R-NJ), Denny Smith (R-OR), and Jack Fields (R-TX)—may have had more trouble holding on to their seats, but they were aided by favorable redistricting in 1982.

73. Barber, *The Lawmakers;* Prewitt, *Recruitment of Political Leaders,* esp. chap. 8. Only about a quarter of the local politicians in Prewitt's study indicated an interest in higher office; voluntary retirement was frequent, and desire for lengthy careers in politics was relatively low. Thus, one central tenet of democratic theory—the accountability imposed by

Those who develop careers in the body will probably resemble the amateurs described in Leiserson's study of machine amateurs in the U.S. House:[74] they will not pursue policy goals, will be less active in floor debate, and will be primarily interested in serving their constituencies. The hopeless amateurs will be supportive of the president (or party) whose coattails they rode in on. Amateurs who were swept into office in 1964, 1974, and 1980 should be great supporters of the Great Society, post-Watergate reforms, and the Reagan revolution, respectively.

Conclusion

The theoretical traditions that underlie my research are the deductive approach of purposive theory and its assumptions of rational behavior, but there are some qualifications. After recognizing that preferences are not exogenous to the political system, one can specify the role that previous experiences and institutions play in shaping preferences. The behavior of amateurs in the electoral arena can be better understood by recognizing that their assessments of the costs and benefits of running for office, their opportunity costs, and their information-processing capabilities all differ from those of experienced politicians (with the exception of ambitious amateurs, who resemble their experienced counterparts). Once in Congress, ambitious, policy, and hopeless amateurs will behave differently, depending on the goals they hold.

---

regular elections—is not very apparent at the local level. Some politicians in Prewitt's survey made this very clear: "You don't always follow the majority; you shouldn't give a damn whether you get elected or not. Don't be afraid to be defeated." Hardly the musings of a Mayhewian member of Congress! This tendency becomes less pronounced as one moves up the career structure (Schlesinger, *Ambition and Politics,* chap. 1), but I argue that the tendency may still be observable in policy-oriented amateurs, who tend to have shorter, more focused careers.

74. Avery Leiserson, "National Party Organization and Congressional Districts," *Western Political Quarterly* 14 (September 1963): 633–49.

Three

Changes in Political Career Structures

The conventional wisdom holds that previous political experience is nearly a necessary condition for election to Congress and that the patterns of advancement are relatively fixed. Both of these points need revision. The view of stable career paths is accurate for normal electoral periods in the context of a given party system. The strategic calculus employed by politicians encompasses, among other things, the competitive position of the party and the relative success of others who have followed the same career path. In periods of electoral upheaval, most dramatically during partisan realignments, the expectations of the politically ambitious undergo significant change and the normal patterns of political careers are disrupted. After presenting the conventional understanding of political careers, this chapter will chart how career structures responded to changes in opportunities for the U.S. House from 1930 to 1986 and for the U.S. Senate from 1913 to 1986.

The Conventional Wisdom: Political Career Paths and Change in the Opportunity Structure

In _Ambition and Politics,_ Schlesinger argued that many politicians behave in a manner consistent with achieving higher office, and that ambition is the driving force to attain that goal. In chapter 1, I showed how ambition operates within the context of the career structure. While the "loose tangle" of political careers generally encourages movement up the tier of offices, some positions emerge as the favored route to higher office. These stepping-stones, which Schlesinger calls "manifest offices," are linked together by shared constituencies and functions.[1] Any political office has a constituency that overlaps to some degree with that of a higher office; therefore, the candidate moving, for example, from the state legislature to the House or from a governorship to the

---

1. Joseph A. Schlesinger, _Ambition and Politics: Political Careers in the United States_ (Chicago: Rand McNally, 1966), chap. 6.

Senate probably will have an advantage in name recognition. Similarly, those with previous legislative experience are able to claim that they are more qualified to serve in Congress because, as Schlesinger puts it, "The legislative function requires similar skills and talents whether in the City Council or the federal Senate."[2] The manifest conditions encourage a patterned movement among offices; if two offices are similar both in function and constituency, a clear stepping-stone is likely to emerge. (Thus in many states lieutenant governors often are elected governor, and House seats in small states make excellent stepping-stones to the Senate.) This tendency helps create the structure of political careers.

In sum, political ambitions provide the impetus, and manifest conditions form the structure, for a system of electoral advancement that generally encourages political experience. Indeed, in the period Schlesinger examines, only 8% of those elected to the Senate had no previous political experience. V. O. Key reaffirms the expectation that senators will be seasoned politicians:

> Commonly, nominations for the Senate go to men who have achieved eminence in the party of their state. By their performance in other public offices and by their ascent up the ladder of party status, men make themselves "available" for the senatorial nomination. . . . The natural processes of leadership selection tend to narrow the range of eligibles for senatorial nominations. In only a few states can the party organization cast the mantle of its nomination upon an unknown and thereby convert him into a potential Senator.[3]

In the House there is no consensus on prevailing levels of previous experience. Different measures have produced figures that range from more than 90% of incoming House members with previous experience, to roughly 80%, to a low of 64%[4] By my measures, three-fourths of all House members from 1930 to 1986 had previously held some public office (see appendix A for coding method). While, as these figures indicate, political experience is far from a necessary condition for election, it is still the dominant tendency.

2. Ibid., p. 99.
3. V. O. Key, Jr., *Politics, Parties, and Pressure Groups,* 5th ed. (New York: Thomas Y. Crowell Co., 1964), 436.
4. Michael R. King and Lester G. Seligman, "Critical Elections, Congressional Recruitment, and Public Policy," in *Elite Recruitment in Democratic Politics: Comparative Studies Across Nations,* ed. Heinz Eulau and Moshe Czudnowski (New York: John Wiley, 1976), 276–77; Walter J. Oleszek, "Congressional Career Patterns: 1910–1960" (Ph.D. diss., State University of New York at Albany, 1968), 197; Michael L. Mezey, "Ambition Theory and the Office of Congressman," *Journal of Politics* 32 (August 1970): 569.

The possibility that the expectation of prior experience may change is not considered in ambition theory. Change is antithetical to a theory that is based on a structure that guides men's ambitions through the very nature of its stability. "If a political system controls politicians' behavior," Schlesinger says, "political careers must be orderly enough to direct and guide the expectations of the politically ambitious."[5] Oleszek makes the assumption of stability clearer: "By the independent character of the system of political advancement we hypothesize that the public office experience associated with changes in House personnel will remain constant through time."[6]

Schlesinger recognizes that the opportunity structure is not completely fixed.[7] He notes that demographic trends, shifting partisan conditions, and wars all "have their observable impacts on political change," but asserts that most of these changes are slow and predictable. He concludes, "One might argue that the structure of political opportunities is one of the aspects of American life most resistant to change."[8] If the determinants of change are predictable, it is desirable to document those influences and assess their importance.

The Dynamics of Career Structures
Defining Change

Changes in the paths to political office may occur three ways: (1) by a shift in the most common stepping-stone to higher office, or in the jargon of ambition theory, in the use of the manifest office, (2) by the lateral entry of political amateurs into the structure, and (3) by changes in the temporal sequence of officeholding.[9]

5. Schlesinger, *Ambition and Politics,* 89.

6. Oleszek, "Congressional Career Patterns," abstract.

7. In a more recent article, Schlesinger examines the impact of partisan strength at different levels of the career structure on the career calculations of those at other levels in the structure. If Republicans are competitive for the presidency or governorship, ambitious Republicans may more seriously consider attempts for a House seat ("The New American Political Party." *American Political Science Review* 79:4 [December 1985]: 1167). While this notion addresses the impact of changing partisan conditions, it does not systematically examine the magnitude of changes in the career structure. See also n.47 in chap. 1 herein.

8. Schlesinger, *Ambition and Politics,* 20.

9. I will not address another type of change, a shift in differences among levels of the career structure, because the hierarchy of offices and the direction of movement within that hierarchy was already established for the period I examine. By the late nineteenth century, and certainly by the 1930s, the federal government was the center of policy-making and the locus of political power (Samuel Kernell, "Congress and the Emergence of a Political Career Structure," paper presented at the Project '87 Conference on Congress, Washington, D.C., 1–4 February 1981). At the same time, national offices clearly moved to the top of the career structure.

The best-documented change in the use of a manifest office is the shift from governor to senator in the presidential career structure in the 1960s and 1970s,[10] but, as I will show, changes have also occurred in the House and Senate. Why are such shifts of more than passing interest? First, a central tenet of ambition theory is that politicians respond to their office goals—that is, ambition influences behavior. Senators who catch the presidential bug are more likely to violate norms of the body and respond to different constituencies. Norms of legislative work and senatorial courtesy also are eroded by the increase in the number of presidential hopefuls in the Senate.[11] The same is true of House members who yearn for a chance at the Senate. David Mayhew observes that the standard practice of "credit claiming" is all but useless for representatives with higher aspirations: "It does little good to talk about the bacon you have brought back to the district you are trying to abandon."[12] Other evidence indicates that House members who run for the Senate alter their roll call voting to better match their new constituencies and become "virtual truants" in their participation.[13]

The shift may have secondary effects in the career structure, which in turn may have additional influence on behavior in the body. When the Senate become the primary stepping-stone to the presidency, more experienced and ambitious politicians aspired to that office. Peabody, Ornstein, and Rohde note, "A number of House members and small-state governors, frustrated at their inability to draw national attention, were further motivated to seek a Senate seat"—which in turn, they suggest, affected the operations of the body: "The resulting increased political experience among new senators in turn contributed to the breakdown of apprenticeship."[14] The same type of effect should be evident at lower levels of the structure. As the House surpasses governorships as the most

10. John H. Aldrich, "Methods and Actors: The Relationship of Processes to Candidates," in *Presidential Selection,* ed. Alexander Heard and Michael Nelson (Durham, N.C.: Duke University Press, 1987), 155–87; Robert L. Peabody, Norman J. Ornstein, and David W. Rohde, "The U.S. Senate as a Presidential Incubator: Many Are Called but Few Are Chosen," *Political Science Quarterly* 91:2 (Summer 1976): 237–58.

11. Peabody, Ornstein, and Rohde, "U.S. Senate as a Presidential Incubator," 253–54; Donald R. Matthews, *U.S. Senators and Their World,* 2d ed. (New York: W. W. Norton, 1973), 109–10.

12. David R. Mayhew, *Congress: The Electoral Connection* (New Haven: Yale University Press, 1974), 75–76.

13. John R. Hibbing, "Ambition in the House: Behavioral Consequences of Higher Office Goals among U.S. Representatives," *American Journal of Political Science* 30:3 (August 1986): 654–57.

14. Peabody, Ornstein, and Rohde, "U.S. Senate as a Presidential Incubator," 253.

common path to the Senate, more experienced and ambitious politicians should be attracted to the House. Similarly, state legislatures would be more attractive to the politically ambitious if they were the preferred route to the House.[15] As I will show below, these patterns evolve slowly, but they are also very sensitive to sudden changes in political opportunity.

The second type of change, the number of amateurs elected to Congress, also raises the possibility of institutional change and indicates changes in the shape of the political career structure. A large cohort of amateurs elected during a period of political change may bring with them a different view of politics and attitudes. I will discuss these important broader implications in the conclusion of this chapter.

The pattern of officeholding does not tell the complete story of change in career structures. I hypothesize that the temporal sequence of holding office will also change in two ways that have not been noted in previous work: (1) When perceived opportunities are greater at high levels in the structure, politicians accelerate their decisions to run for higher office, and (2) In periods of extreme change when the supply of experienced candidates cannot meet demand, many former officeholders reenter politics. These points are central not only to a theory of change in the career structure, but also to a discussion of political amateurism. Amateurs have limited access to the career structure in periods of normal office succession and greater access in periods of electoral instability, especially during realignments. If current officeholders respond to increased opportunity by accelerating their decisions to run for higher office, and if previous officeholders reenter politics in similar situations, opportunities for amateurs are restricted.

It is the argument of this chapter that all three types of changes in career structure will be evident in periods of increased opportunity. I define landslide or "high-opportunity" elections as those in which the partisan division of newly elected seats is at least 2 : 1 and the winning party captures a minimum of fifty new seats in the House. These years are 1930–

15. It is difficult to isolate any single factor, such as the value of the office as a stepping-stone, as the cause of changing characteristics of membership in a body. There are many other factors that determine the attractiveness of an office: powers of the office, compensation, size of the constituency, and potential for making a career of the office (the chance of electoral defeat and constitutional provisions). For the U.S. House, these factors have been relatively constant in the past several decades. The same cannot be said for the increasingly professionalized state legislatures. Sessions are longer, pay is higher, and more legislators are able to make politics their primary vocation. These factors are probably more important in attracting more experienced candidates than the increased value of the office as a stepping-stone. A multivariate test of these factors is beyond the scope of this study, but such a test is possible.

38, 1944–50, 1958, 1964, 1966, 1974, 1980, and 1982. "Low-opportunity" elections are these same years for candidates of the losing party. "Normal" elections are those in which the partisan ratio of new seats is less than 2 : 1 (1940–42, 1952, 1956, 1962, 1968–72, 1976, 1978, and 1986), or is greater than 2:1 but the winning party failed to capture fifty seats (1954, 1960, and 1984).

One possible criticism of this measure is that it takes account of the volume but not necessarily the *direction* of change (because proportions of new members who replace incumbents of the opposing party vary from year to year, depending on the number of open seats). This is a valid theoretical concern, but this measure identifies most of the landslide elections since 1930. In the fifteen high-opportunity years, the winning party gained an average of 44.7 seats, compared with an average of 13.1 seats in the fourteen normal years. In thirteen of the fifteen landslide years, the winning party gained more seats than in all but one of the normal years.[16] The extent of each type of change in normal and high-opportunity elections is outlined below.

Defining the Data Set

Senators and representatives are coded for their previous political offices held, age upon entry, party, total number of offices held, total number of years in political office (elective and appointive), and number of years between most recent office held and election to Congress. Including the number of offices held and the length of time in office provides a more comprehensive basis for describing the changing nature of the prior political experience of senators and representatives than has been available in previous work.[17] The sources for the data are the *Bio-*

16. The exceptions are 1934 and 1936, when Democrats won a net of ten and thirteen seats respectively (while meeting the conditions for a high-opportunity election as outlined above), and 1942, when Republicans picked up forty-five seats in the House, despite winning less than two-thirds of the new seats that year. Two truly high-opportunity years were 1934 and 1936, because they solidified the New Deal partisan realignment (Democrats gained ten and six seats in the Senate in those two elections respectively). Furthermore, even though the Democratic party's net gains were small in those two elections, many opponents of the New Deal agenda were replaced with FDR supporters (*New York Times*, 4 November 1936, 1). The 1942 election could be considered a landslide year (the net partisan shift was the ninth largest since 1930). If it were included, the results would be strengthened in three of the four areas outlined above (the percentage of amateurs, the temporal sequence of officeholding, and the "woodwork" theory).

17. The most common source of data on congressional careers, the Carroll McKibbin/Inter-university Consortium for Political and Social Research data, does not report total political experience (in either number of years or number of offices held). Due to data col-

graphical Directory of the American Congress and the 1974–88 editions of *The Almanac of American Politics.*[18]

The central concern in choosing the period for analysis was to encompass both periods of electoral change and periods of stability. The House data are from the years 1930–86, a time span that is adequately long to discover the established career patterns in the relatively stable 1950s and 1960s and contrast this period to the period of partisan realignment in the 1930s. The smaller numbers in the Senate allow the inclusion of all popularly elected senators (beginning in 1913). The study was not extended to the 1890s realignment because the data are less accurate for earlier periods. By limiting the analysis to a more recent period, there is more certainty that any changes in career structures that are uncovered are not artifacts of the available data.[19]

Two issues of coding merit brief mention. First, appointed senators are not included in the analysis even though they comprise nearly a fourth of all senators who served from 1913 to 1987.[20] One rarely can plan on being appointed to the Senate, and those who try, such as Wendell Anderson (D-MN) in 1976, almost always meet subsequent defeat. Therefore, this path cannot be considered part of one's strategic calculus. The second concern is the recency of experience. If someone held office early in his or her career, left politics for fifteen or twenty years, and then was elected to the House or Senate, would that person be an amateur? Jesse

---

lection problems for the nineteenth century, McKibbin records only the number of levels of government service; therefore, if a person held two offices at a given level, that additional experience would not appear.

18. *Biographical Directory of the American Congress: 1774–1971,* Senate Document 92-8 (United States Government Printing Office, 1971). *The Almanac of American Politics* was published by E. P. Dutton (New York) in 1973, 1975, 1977, and 1979, and by Barone and Co. (Washington, D.C.) in 1981, 1983, 1985, and 1987. Michael Barone and Grant Ujifusa edited the *Almanac* between 1973 and 1987, and Grant Matthews was a third editor between 1973 and 1979.

19. See Allan G. Bogue, Jerome M. Clubb, Carroll R. McKibbin, and Santa A. Traugott, "Members of the House of Representatives and the Process of Modernization: 1789–1960," *Journal of American History* 63 (September 1976), for a discussion of the problems associated with collecting and interpreting data on political careers from the nineteenth century.

20. Nearly 7% of the 677 senators who served between 1913 and 1987 were appointed and subsequently elected, 9% were appointed and then defeated in their attempted election, and 8% did not try to run for a full term. Including appointed senators who are subsequently elected would strengthen the results outlined below. See David. T. Canon, "Actors, Athletes, and Astronauts: Political Amateurism in the United States Congress" (Ph.D. diss., University of Minnesota, 1987), 133–37, for a more extended discussion of coding decisions.

Helms (R-NC), Terry Sanford (D-NC), and Howard Metzenbaum (D-OH) are examples of senators who followed this career path. The problems of determining the length of absence from office required before one is considered "inexperienced," combined with the assumption that prior experience has enduring effects, led me to code all previous political experience in the same manner, whether it occurred early or late in the pre-House or pre-Senate career.

Charting Changes in the Congressional Career Structure
Manifest Office and Deviations from the Preferred Path

One indicator of general stability or change in career structures is the frequency of use of the manifest office. Greater use of the most common path to higher office gives structure to ambitions and limits the openness of the career structure. Conversely, when common stepping-stones are used less frequently, career structures will be more open. Several questions will be raised here. Has the use of manifest offices for the House and Senate changed? What happens when use of the manifest office breaks down? Are certain types of candidates favored over others? Do alternative paths develop? Finally, can change be explained? I will show that paths to the House have become more structured, while the common route to the Senate is less predictable.

STEPPING-STONES TO THE SENATE

Governorships and seats in the House are the primary paths to the Senate. As can be seen in table 3.1, the percentage of senators who have served in the House has increased slightly since Schlesinger's writing, remaining close to 33% in the twentieth century.[21] Governors, on the other hand, have steadily become a smaller percentage of incoming Senate classes, falling to 13.7% in the last three decades from an average of 23.2% in the years 1913–59. This trend is especially pronounced among Republicans, who have elected only one governor to the Senate in the five elections from 1978 to 1986. The U.S. House, on the other hand, continues to be a popular stepping-stone for Republicans. More than a third of Republican senators elected in the last two decades came from the House. This trend continued in the 1988 Senate elections, when three of

21. This stepping-stone has become increasingly popular in recent years. Thirteen of the twenty senators elected in 1984 and 1986 came from the House. Seven other House members made unsuccessful bids for the Senate in 1986.

Table 3.1   Changes in the Manifest Offices: Proportion of Senators
Elected from Governorships and the House

Senators with Previous Service in	1913–59	1960–87	Totals
House of Representatives	32.7%	36.9%	34.0%
Governorships	23.2%	13.7%	20.3%
Total percentage of senators using manifest offices	55.9% (358)	50.6% (160)	54.3% (518)

NOTE: Number of cases from which percentages were calculated are in parentheses.

the five newly elected Republicans came from the House, and three of the five Democrats were governors![22]

While the decline of governorship as a path to the Senate represents an important change in the career structure, the overall proportion of senators coming from the manifest offices has not significantly decreased. Therefore, it is also important to consider the characteristics of candidates who deviate from the preferred path. Schlesinger paints a radically different picture of this group than is observed today:

> When the manifest office patterns break down, . . . the professional requirements appear to have taken precedence. Men without office experience and lesser officials can win the

22. The pool of potential candidates must be controlled in order to make conclusive statements about a shift in career paths. That is, a decline in the proportion of Republican governors relative to the proportion of Republican House members may account for the shift. Clearly there is no relationship between the size of the pool and the number of governors and House members elected to the Senate. The percentage of Republicans in governorships was 45.2%, 42%, 41.9%, and 40% for the 1950s, 1960s, 1970s, and 1980s, respectively, and the percentage of Republican senators who came from governorships was 17.2%, 28.6%, 9.7%, and 4.3% for those same decades; the percentage of Republicans in the House was 45%, 40%, 42%, and 41.3% for the 1950s, 1960s, 1970s, and 1980s, respectively, and the percentage of Republican senators who came from the House was 58.6%, 28.6%, 38.7%, and 34.8% for those same decades.

The percentages for the Democrats are much more stable: the proportion of governors moving to the Senate is 19.1%, 16.7%, 12.5%, and 15% for the 1950s, 1960s, 1970s, and 1980s, respectively (24% for the 1980s if the 1988 election is included). The percentages of House members making the move are 42.9%, 33.3%, 30.0%, and 55% for the four decades (the percentage of the 1980s falls to 44% if the 1988 election is included).

office of senator and win early, *not because they have become conspicuous in the public eye* but because they have a close association with the party organization or the organized elements capable of helping them to office.[23]

He concludes that the "office of governor is by far the more likely outlet for those whom the French call 'notables,' the Senate the more likely outlet for the career politician."[24]

Clearly, this distinction no longer exists. Amateurs *are* elected to the Senate, and often they run independent of party support; if they win, it is often precisely because they have "become conspicuous in the public eye." Celebrity candidates have name recognition that rivals that of their incumbent opponents, which contributes to their ability to run effective, well-financed campaigns. Thirty years ago, candidates were not required to be "conspicuous" because state party organizations were better able to secure the nomination for selected nominees. The contrast indicates that today's inexperienced senators may use their celebrity status or business contacts and personal wealth to acquire needed electoral resources through channels that are independent from party organizations.

How does this assertion square with the recent efforts of party officials to recruit celebrity candidates? Burt Reynolds, Harry Belafonte, Brooks Robinson, Charlton Heston, Roger Staubach, and Woody Hayes are just a few of the prominent people who have turned down chances to run for the Senate. But these were mostly races in which more experienced candidates also chose not to run. For example, Robinson, the former Baltimore Orioles star, was wooed by GOP officials to run in the 1986 Maryland Senate race. Prominent Republicans were reluctant to enter because it was almost certain to be a Democratic landslide. Similarly, in the 1986 New York Senate race, Alfonse D'Amato's huge campaign war chest deterred prominent Democrats such as Elizabeth Holtzman and Geraldine Ferraro from entering, leaving the door open for Belafonte (Ralph Nader activist Mark Green was the eventual nominee, by virtue of an upset over another amateur, businessman John Dyson).[25]

In sum, use of stepping-stones to the Senate has changed in two ways: a quantitative change—representing an erosion of one of the preferred

23. Schlesinger, *Ambition and Politics*, 186–87, emphasis added.

24. Ibid., 187.

25. This pattern is consistent with Linda L. Fowler's findings for House races in "The Cycle of Defeat: Recruitment of Congressional Challengers" (Ph.D. diss., University of Rochester, 1977), 192–94.

paths outlined by Schlesinger—and a qualitative change in the nature of senators who gain office through a route other than the manifest office.

STEPPING-STONES TO THE HOUSE

Previous work has demonstrated that career paths are less structured lower in the hierarchy of offices; therefore, the use of a manifest office has been more limited for the House than for the Senate.[26] However, two shifts in career paths have made the state legislature a true manifest office for the House. First, there has been a steady increase in the percentage of House members using state legislatures as stepping-stones. Table 3.2 shows that 30% of newly elected members used the manifest office in the 1930s and 1940s, while nearly half (49.3%) did so in the 1980s. Second, most state legislators are now moving *directly* to the House. In the 1930s and 1940s, it was common for state legislators to drop out of politics temporarily or hold another office before moving to the House.[27] Since 1970, 80% of all state legislators elected to the House moved directly from their state office; this proportion was about one-third in the 1930s and 1940s.

These trends can be largely explained by the increased professionalization of state legislatures, which has moved them onto a distinct level below the U.S. House in the career structure. Movement in pre-House careers is now largely in one direction. As career paths become more structured and state legislatures are viewed as direct stepping-stones to the House, ambitious politicians will move their careers in that direction, and the opportunities for amateurs may be limited. Party organization (especially the Republican Congressional Campaign Committee and the Republican National Committee), recognizing the growing talent of this pool, have recently increased their efforts to recruit state legislators to run in House races.[28]

There is significant and predictable variation within the trend toward increased use of the state legislature as a manifest office for the House.

26. Oleszek, "Congressional Career Patterns."

27. The last row in table 3.2 shows the proportion of legislators who were currently serving in state legislatures at the time of their election to the House. The pattern is nearly the same if nonpolitical interruptions to the legislator's career are included.

28. Bill Brock was instrumental in establishing this focus. In his tenure it became the RNC's "top priority" (Marjorie Randon Hershey, *Running for Office: The Political Education of Campaigners* [Chatham, N.J.: Chatham House Publishers, 1984], 133). In 1980, RNC staffers were involved in some four thousand races, helping candidates design and conduct surveys, analyze the data, and target precincts for fund-raising, registration, and get-out-the-vote efforts.

Table 3.2 Manifest Office Use in the U.S. House, 1930–86

	1930s	1940s	1950s	1960s	1970s	1980s	Total
Former House members who return to House	9.8% (613)	13.3% (555)	9.8% (379)	7.0% (374)	3.3% (389)	3.0% (270)	8.4% (2,580)
Those with previous state legislative experience	30.0% (613)	29.2% (555)	36.7% (379)	38.8% (374)	45.0% (389)	49.3% (270)	36.4% (2,580)
Those with some legislative experience who move directly to the House	37.0% (184)	33.9% (162)	54.0% (139)	71.0% (145)	84.0% (175)	76.7% (133)	58.0% (938)

NOTE: Number of cases from which percentages were calculated are in parentheses.

Fewer state legislators are elected to the House when their parties win landslide elections.[29] This pattern holds true in fourteen of the fifteen high-opportunity elections. In the partisan realignment of 1930–37, only 27.6% of all Democrats were elected from state legislatures, compared to 38.9% of the newly elected Republicans (differences significant at the .02 level). More recently, in 1980, when fifty-three Republicans swept into the House, 38.9% of them came from the manifest office, while Democrats followed that path 61.5% of the time (significant at the .03 level). High-opportunity elections in 1938, 1944–50, 1958, 1966, 1974, and 1982 follow the same pattern.[30]

This finding contradicts two arguments in existing theory. First, ambition theorists argue that proportionately *more,* rather than fewer, experienced politicians should be elected in high-opportunity elections because they are more likely to run when the chances for success are good.[31] Second, Schlesinger sees the use of manifest offices as unpredictable and idiosyncratic, with the only discernible patterns coming from differences among states. He says that "the breakdown in the use of manifest office need not direct our attention to external forces impinging upon the attainment of political office. Both competition and personal idiosyncrasies are enough to prevent perfect use of manifest offices."[32] The latter observation is correct, yet idiosyncrasies should not direct our attention away from patterns of partisan competition that indicate more general relationships: common stepping-stones are used less frequently in periods of

29. The same pattern is weakly evident for use of manifest offices for the Senate. In periods of high electoral opportunity, 19.1% of newly elected senators come from governorships and 33.3% from the House. This compares with 24.1% from governorships and 37.9% from the House in low-opportunity years. High-opportunity elections for the Senate are defined as those in which one party won more than ten new Senate seats: 1918, 1920, 1924, 1946, 1978, and 1980 for Republicans, and 1922, 1930–36, 1948, 1958, and 1986 for Democrats.

30. The data strongly support the conclusion. The use of the manifest office for the U.S. House by Democrats during high-opportunity elections was 30.2% (828), during low-opportunity elections was 43.1% (160), and during normal elections was 41.7% (472); use by Republicans during high-opportunity elections was 29.4% (340), during low-opportunity elections was 41% (244), and during normal elections was 39.6% (480); the total during high-opportunity elections was 30% (1168), during low-opportunity elections was 41.8% (404), and during normal elections was 40.7% (952). The differences between high- and low-opportunity years for both Democrats and Republicans are significant at the .005 level. Manifest office use in normal elections resembles use during low-opportunity elections.

31. Gary C. Jacobson and Samuel Kernell, *Strategy and Choice in Congressional Elections* (New Haven: Yale University Press, 1983). An extended discussion of this point is presented in the conclusion to this chapter.

32. Schlesinger, *Ambition and Politics,* 90.

high electoral opportunity. Although these findings about the use of manifest offices are important, a more broad-based test is needed that examines all politicians.

Changing Types of Prior Political Experience
CHANGING PRIOR EXPERIENCE FOR THE SENATE

The most distinctive trend in the Senate is the surge of amateurism between 1974 and 1982. This trend is observable with all measures of prior political experience. The basic measure is the number of offices held, both elective and nonelective. As table 3.3 shows, the level of experience, as measured in these broadest terms, declined dramatically in this period. The number of senators who had held no previous political office increased fourfold from 1974 to 1983 compared with the previous twenty years (14.1% versus 3.5%), and more than trebled the 4.6% average of the entire period of popularly elected senators.[33] Only 29.7% of all senators elected between 1974 and 1983 had more than ten years' experience in public office, whereas more than a majority from 1944 to 1972 achieved this level of experience. Patterns are similar when number of years in elective office is considered. Table 3.3 also shows the proportion of senators with previous legislative and executive experience. Twenty percent fewer senators had legislative experience from 1974 to 1983, and more than twice as many senators in this period had no major elective experience (36.6% versus 15.9%), as compared to the previous two decades.

These highly aggregated statistics ignore a central expectation of my theory of political careers—that structures change during periods of high electoral opportunity. As with the data on manifest offices, if only overall patterns are examined there appear to be minimal differences between the parties.[34] When specific elections are examined, it is clear that amateurs

---

33. I have chosen to present the discussion in terms of percentages of senators elected in a period rather than absolute numbers because percentages are a more accurate reflection of changes in the career structure over periods. At the same time, it would not be strictly accurate to say "a fourfold increase" if the numbers of senators elected in different decades were wildly different. In fact, the average for the entire period is seventy-one senators elected per decade, with a range from fifty-two to eighty-three. In the period 1974–82, which is the point of departure for much of the discussion, exactly the mean level of senators were elected.

34. However, differences have become more pronounced since 1960. From 1913 to 1959, 21.1% of all Republican senators had held no prior elective office, while for the Democrats the figure was 19.1%. Since then (1960–86), 25.3% of the Republicans and 16.5% of the Democrats had no elective experience.

Table 3.3 Number of Years in Office for Senators: Elected and Total Public

		1913–23	1924–33	1934–43	1944–53	1954–63	1964–73	1974–83	1984–87
Number of years in public office (%)	0	2.4%	6.5%	5.6%	6.0%	3.3%	3.8%	14.1%	0%
	1–5	18.3	18.2	20.8	12.0	14.8	15.4	15.5	15.0
	6–10	37.8	28.6	31.9	22.9	26.2	34.6	40.8	15.0
	≥10	41.5	46.8	41.7	59.0	55.7	46.1	29.7	70.0
Average (yrs.)		9.93	11.49	10.22	12.62	12.89	10.94	8.80	13.40
Number of years in elected office	0	13.4%	28.6%	26.4%	16.9%	11.5%	13.5%	32.4%	0%
	1–5	35.4	32.5	31.9	21.7	21.3	19.2	15.5	20.0
	6–10	34.1	15.6	20.0	27.7	27.9	40.4	32.4	30.0
	≥10	17.1	23.4	20.9	33.1	39.4	26.9	19.6	50.0
Average (yrs.)		6.48	5.98	5.78	7.98	8.92	7.75	6.59	11.35
No legislative experience		28.0%	42.0%	47.2%	44.6%	29.5%	28.8%	49.3%	25.0%
No legislative or executive experience		18.3	32.5	27.9	22.9	16.4	15.4	36.6	5.0
Column (n)		82	77	72	83	61	52	71	20

are disproportionately elected when their parties win national landslides. In 1932 and 1934, Democrats elected thirty senators, while Republicans managed to win only one seat (four Democrats and one Republican also were appointed in this period). Eleven of the thirty had no prior elective experience (35.5%), and three had no public experience (10%). The comparable figures for Democrats elected in all other elections from 1913 to 1986 are 16.1% and 3.2%. High-opportunity years for Republicans reveal similar patterns. In 1946, when an unprecedented twenty Republicans gained seats, more than a third had no elective experience, and three were complete amateurs. In 1980, when Republicans won control of the Senate by electing sixteen new members, Jeremiah Denton (AL), Frank Murkowski (AK), Mack Mattingly (GA), and John East (NC) all took office with no previous elective experience. In addition, Paula Hawkins (FL), Alfonse D'Amato (NY), and Don Nickels (OK) had less experience than is typical for Senate candidates.

Interestingly, four of this group did not return to the Senate in 1986 (Denton, Mattingly, and Hawkins were defeated; East retired for health reasons that eventually led to his tragic suicide in 1986). They were replaced by four Democrats who had fifty-nine years of public office experience among them. Two had served as governors for twelve years and the other two had been in the House for a total of eighteen years. It remains to be seen whether the 1984 and 1986 elections signal a shift back toward more traditional career paths and long apprenticeship in lower office for the Senate.[35]

CHANGING PRIOR EXPERIENCE FOR THE HOUSE

As in the Senate, amateurs and officeholders with less experience are elected to the House in proportionally greater numbers when their parties are strong at the national level. One other unexpected trend will be discussed first: a gradual but significant shift toward more elective experience and less appointive experience. The two trends are equal in magnitude, so that overall levels of total prior public experience have been relatively constant for the House since 1930. This may explain why previous research has assumed that career structures for the House are static. As can be seen in figure 3.1, there is a steady rise in the number of

35. The 1988 elections provide mixed signals. Three House members, three governors, and a former senator were among the freshman class of ten. On the other hand, Herbert Kohl (D-WI), a prominent businessman and owner of the NBA's Milwaukee Bucks, lavishly spent from his personal fortune to be elected to William Proxmire's old Senate seat. Conrad Burns (R-MT) used his fame as a broadcaster on the Northern Agricultural Network to upset Sen. John Melcher (though Burns was not a complete amateur—he had served for two years as a county commissioner).

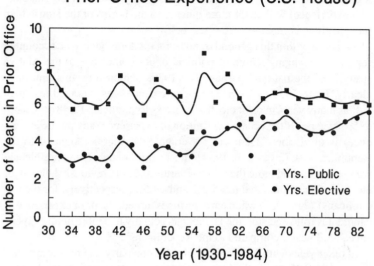

Fig. 3.1   Prior office experience (U.S. House)

years in prior elective office, from lows of under three years to averages of about six years in the recent period, while the average number of years in prior appointive office has fallen from about four years in the 1930s to less than one year in the 1980s. Ten percent of House members had previous appointive experience in the 1980s, down from an average of more than 40% for the years 1930–56. The increase in prior elective experience is attributable to the increase in state legislative experience outlined above. The decrease in appointive experience is more difficult to explain. Perhaps the increasing attractiveness of state legislatures lured ambitious politicians away from other traditional base offices, such as those in the legal system.[36]

The broader significance of this point is twofold. First, it indicates that the career paths to the House have become more structured, while just the opposite situation obtains for the Senate. Second, a greater proportion of House members with previous electoral experience has implications for behavior in the electoral and institutional arenas. Politicians who have been exposed to the electoral process will be more likely to be strategic in their decisions to run for higher office. They will be more aware of the demands of fund-raising and establishing a campaign organization. In the institution, socialization theory would hold that candidates with prior

36. Schlesinger, *Ambition and Politics,* 113–14.

legislative experience (who are the great majority of those with prior elective experience) will adapt more quickly to the norms of the House than those without comparable experience.[37]

Variation within this general trend is not random, but can be accounted for by the changing nature of political opportunities due to the relative strength of the national parties. The 1930s demonstrate this link most clearly. From 1930 to 1936, Democratic candidates averaged less than half as many years in prior elective office as Republicans (2.48 compared to 5.68 years). If the broader definition of experience (any public experience) is used, these Democrats average 5.18 years, compared to the Republicans' 9.72 years. In 1934 almost a third of the Democrats elected were amateurs and more than three-fourths had not previously held major elective office (compared to 15.2% and 48.5%, respectively, for the Republicans).[38] In 1938, when party fortunes turned, the prior experience of candidates followed suit: the Democrats actually had more public experience—6.3 years, compared to the Republicans' 5.8.

In other years with high opportunity for one party, the results are similar. In 1958, 22.4% of the Democrats were amateurs and 70.0% had not served in major elective office. The Republicans were much more experienced (12.0% and 40.0%, respectively). In 1974, when eighty-one Democrats were swept into office, their average level of prior elective experience was 4.1 years, compared to the Republicans' 5.9 years.[39] In 1980, when Republican congressional candidates enjoyed Ronald Rea-

<hr />

37. Herbert Asher presents limited evidence for this claim. In his small sample of freshmen, three state legislators claimed that they did not have to serve an apprenticeship because they already knew the ropes, and experienced freshmen showed more willingness to engage in logrolling. There was no general difference in attitude toward the apprenticeship norm between those with and those without legislative experience (Herbert B. Asher, "The Learning of Legislative Norms," *American Political Science Review* 67:3 [September 1973]).

38. The differences are even more dramatic if one controls for the South. Because the Democratic party was already dominant in the South, no change in the career structure would be expected during the realignment. More than a third (35.9%) of all Democratic representatives outside the South elected between 1930 and 1936 were amateurs, compared with 23.6% between 1938 and 1984. In 1932 and 1934, 42.1% (75 of 178) of the new nonsouthern Democratic members were amateurs! In contrast, 20.5% of southern Democrats elected between 1930 and 1936 were amateurs, compared with 22.1% between 1938 and 1984.

39. Some elections do not conform to the general pattern. In 1964 there was a sharp drop in experience for both parties. The high proportion of amateur Democrats (nineteen of seventy-four) is consistent with my theory. The unexpected surge for Republicans (eleven of twenty-two) can be explained by the extremist, nonmainstream nature of the Goldwater presidential campaign that attracted amateur candidates.

gan's landslide victory, they averaged only 4.2 years of prior experience, compared to the Democrats' 7.4 years. Almost 40% of the entering Republican class (21 of 54) had no previous public experience. This figure is nearly double the 20.3% Republican average (31 of 153) for the previous decade.

The pattern holds in other elections. In twelve of the fifteen high-opportunity elections, the winning party had more inexperienced candidates elected. Overall, in the high-opportunity years, 27.1% of the candidates were amateurs, 59.1% had not served in major elective office, and 48.2% had not served in any elective office. In low-opportunity elections the candidates were more experienced (21.5% amateurs, 51.5% without major elective office, and 42.3% without any elective office). Normal elections fall between the other two groups (23.5% amateurs, 51.5% without major elective experience, and 44.2% without any elective experience).

The Sequence of Officeholding
TENURE IN LOWER OFFICE

The disproportionate rate of election of amateurs during periods of high opportunity does not mean that current officeholders are immune to partisan tides. House members looking to move to the Senate and politicians at the state level who eye the U.S. House are sensitive to national electoral conditions. During normal electoral periods, junior House members (serving in their first or second term) are not likely to run for the Senate unless a seat opens, and relatively rarely even then.[40] It is very unusual for a House member to challenge an incumbent senator of his or her own party, and members of the opposing party are likely to challenge an incumbent senator only later, in mid-career (it is most common to run for the Senate in a fourth or fifth term in the House).[41] In periods of high political opportunity, especially during realignments, these typical pat-

40. The case of John McCain of Arizona illustrates this point. Described as "nothing short of a political phenomenon," McCain was seen to be a sure bet to rise in the Arizona Republican party (*Congressional Quarterly Weekly Report* 44 [22 February 1986]: 343). When Barry Goldwater announced his retirement, McCain was just beginning his second term in the House, but was widely perceived as Goldwater's successor. McCain clearly would not have run for the Senate had the seat not been open (challenging Goldwater would not have been a good move for a rising Republican star).

41. Data gathered by the author. this argument is consistent with Paul R. Abramson, John H. Aldrich, and David W. Rohde's analysis of senators who run for president ("Progressive Ambition among United States Senators: 1972–1988," *Journal of Politics* 49:1 [February 1987]: 3–35).

terns do not persist as politicians accelerate their decisions to run for higher office.

Timing of Moves to the Senate

During the New Deal realignment, the same forces that created new opportunities for amateurs also whetted the ambitions of New Dealers, who swept into the House starting in 1930. Spurred by the disequilibrium between supply of and demand for experienced candidates for the Senate (which continued for the first few years of the realignment), many New Deal Democrats in the House perceived the opportunity to move quickly up the career ladder. From 1932 to 1936, of the twelve House members elected to the Senate, eleven were Democrats who had an average of slightly more than three years' experience in the House.[42] No other period in the entire history of popularly elected senators demonstrates this rapidity of movement from the House to the Senate. In fact, the average tenure of House members elected to the Senate for the remainder of the years 1913–86 is 8.21 years.

The unusually rapid rise of New Deal House members to the Senate is further documented by noting the rarity with which one term in the House is viewed as adequate seasoning for service in the upper chamber. From 1913 to 1986, excluding the 1932–36 elections, 141 of the 476 popularly elected Senators came from the House; only 11 were House members who had served one term. From 1932 to 1937, half of the House members who were elected to the Senate had served only one term (six of twelve; overall, forty-six Democrats were elected to the Senate in this period). The manner in which these six House members gained their Senate seats reveals more about their ambitions. Three defeated incumbent Republicans, two defeated incumbents of their own party in primary elections, and one took an open seat vacated by the death of a Republican senator.

Timing of Moves to the House

A broader test of this aspect of change in the opportunity structure must come from the House. This test was conducted by examining members who were current officeholders at the time of their election to the House.[43] As with movement to the Senate, politicians who aspired to the House accelerated their career decisions to the greatest extent in the

42. Six served one term, four served two terms, and one senator who was elected in a special election in 1937 had started to serve in his fourth term after being elected to the House in 1930. Ernest Lundeen (MN) actually was a member of the Farmer-Labor Party, but he caucused with the Democrats.

43. I define "current officeholder" as any politician who has served in office anytime in

1930s. From 1930 to 1936, Democrats who had previous elective experience averaged less than three years in prior office, while Republicans averaged almost seven years.

Shorter tenure in prior offices is also evident in other years in which one party won a disproportionate number of seats. If the three World War II elections are excluded (which is reasonable because the war interrupted political careers and changed the nature of opportunity), eleven of the twelve high-opportunity years confirm the hypothesis that politicians accelerate their decisions to run for higher office in periods of high opportunity. In these eleven elections, politicians responded to the increased opportunities by running for the House after serving for an average of only 4.43 years in elective office ($n=401$). Candidates in the party winning fewer seats in those eleven elections had an average of 6.26 years of elective experience immediately preceding their election to the House ($n=160$). The pattern in the fourteen normal elections was the same, though the differences were statistically insignificant (6.15 and 6.75 years of prior experience for the party winning more and fewer seats, respectively; $ns=340$ and 248).

THE WOODWORK HYPOTHESIS

The second aspect of the temporal sequence of officeholding concerns the continuity of the political career. Politicians often do not progress easily up the tier of political offices. Careers are interrupted by defeat or voluntary shifts away from politics. Some politicians retire, only to be drawn in again by opportunities for election to higher office. For example, in 1986, after being out of politics for twenty years, former North Carolina Governor Terry Sanford was elected to the Senate seat vacated by the retirement of John East. Other prominent Democrats, such as former governor Jim Hunt, declined to run, leaving the opportunity open for Sanford. Others never lose the political bug when they leave office. Howard Metzenbaum (D-OH) is probably the best example of this type. Metzenbaum served in the Ohio state house from 1943 to 1947 and then in the state senate from 1947 to 1951. He left public office and became a very successful businessman and lawyer, but remained active in politics. After twenty-five years of managing other candidates' campaigns, losing two general elections for the Senate, and serving a brief stint as an appointed senator, Metzenbaum was elected in his own right to the Senate in 1976.

the year prior to the election. Sixty-seven percent of the House members elected from 1930 to 1986 with prior experience fall under this category.

I assert that the continuity of officeholding is not random or idiosyncratic, as the above anecdotes may suggest, but follows patterns of broader changes in career structures. In periods of heightened political opportunity, politicians of the first type, such as Terry Sanford, will be drawn back into politics, while the Metzenbaums, who have been waiting for the right moment to reenter politics, will also run for office. These patterns of succession suggest a "woodwork hypothesis" of political careers, in which aspiring candidates "come out of the woodwork" when new opportunities become available. I will use two measures of the continuity of careers: (1) the reentry of politicians who have been out of politics for at least ten years, and (2) the average length of time between the most recent office held and election to Congress. For the Senate I use only the former measure, because means are strongly skewed due to small *n*s. For example, Jesse Helms (R-NC) served on the Raleigh city council from 1957 to 1961, but then was out of office for twelve years before being elected to the Senate (achieving notoriety as a radio announcer in the interim). Helms's twelve-year absence accounts for more than half of the total years out of office of the fourteen senators elected in 1972.

The Woodwork Hypothesis in the Senate

Of the 488 popularly elected senators with some previous political experience (1913–86), only 43 were out of office for more than ten years before being elected to the Senate.[44] As expected, a disproportionate number of them were attracted back into politics during periods of high opportunity. Fourteen of the forty-three were Democrats in 1930 and 1932! No more than two of the forty-three were elected in any other election. Only a *third* of the twenty-eight Democrats elected to the Senate in 1930 and 1932 came directly from some previous public office. The average for all non–high-opportunity elections is close to 80%. Patterns are similar for Republicans in their best Senate elections. Overall, only 57.5% of the newly elected senators in high-opportunity elections came directly from prior office, compared to 81% in low-opportunity elections (and 77.5% in normal elections). More than a fourth had been out of office for more than five years (compared with 12.9% in other elections).

---

44. This includes four of the House members mentioned above who were elected to the Senate after serving one or two terms in the lower chamber and who had been out of politics for more than a decade before their election to the House in 1930. They responded to the new opportunities of the 1930s by *both* entering Congress initially after a long hiatus and then accelerating their decisions to run for higher office.

Clearly, former officeholders respond to increased opportunity by running for the Senate.

The Woodwork Hypothesis in the House

The same pattern is evident in the House. Of the 1,971 House members with some previous political experience elected between 1930 and 1986, 148 had been out of office for ten years prior to their election to the House. Of these, forty-three (29.1%) were Democrats elected from 1930 to 1934; no more than four were elected from one party in any other election. The patterns of succession are very different for the two parties in periods of electoral upheaval. For example, in 1930, only 38% of the Democrats—but 76% of the Republicans—came directly from a previous office. The average time out of office for the Democrats elected from 1930 to 1934 who had some previous political experience was 4.51 years, compared with a Republican average of only 2.93 years. For 1938, when the Republicans made significant electoral gains, the reverse pattern holds: Republicans averaged 3.47 years out of office, while thirty of the thirty-nine Democrats elected moved directly from a preceding office, for an average of less than a year for the entire group. Elections in 1958, 1974, 1980, and 1984 all had significantly larger numbers of candidates who were attracted back into politics by the promise of electoral victory in their parties.

A general relationship between high opportunity and lower office continuity is evident. In twelve of the fifteen high-opportunity elections from 1930 to 1986, the mean time out of office before election to the House was higher for the winning party than the losing party (2.46 years, compared to 1.63 years, in the twelve election; the mean was 1.42 years in normal elections). Only 63.3% of all House members who were elected in high-opportunity elections with some previous political experience came directly to the House from a previous office. The comparable figure for those elected in low-opportunity elections if 70%, thus showing greater office continuity (normal elections show even more regularity, with the figure at 77.6%).

One type of candidate who reenters politics in periods of high opportunity is noteworthy. Prior to 1968, former House members who recaptured their seats comprised up to 20% of entering freshman classes (see table 3.2 for the trend by decade). These politicians were especially sensitive to national partisan tides. For example, 28.9% of *all* former Democratic congressmen reelected to the House from 1930 to 1986 were elected in the landslides of 1930 and 1948 (63 of 218). Similarly, large numbers of Republicans were elected in their good years of 1946, 1950, and 1966 (36.2% of the Republican total). Recently this career path has all but disappeared. From 1976 to 1986, only 11 of 420 new members had previously served in the House (2.6%).[45] The disappearance of ex-incumbent challengers has a potential impact on the career structure. Former members are inherently formidable challengers: they have great name recognition and access to former campaign organizations and fundraising sources (on the other hand, they do have the liability of having lost a House race). As this pool of candidates shrinks, or indeed disappears, more opportunities for other experienced or amateur challengers become available.

The temporal sequence of officeholding suggests that politicians are very sensitive to the changing nature of political opportunities. The changing patterns of succession to higher office are significant for two reasons. First, they are further evidence that the assumption of the stability of career structures is not valid in periods of partisan change. Second, as with the election of amateurs and shifts in the use of manifest office, changes in the temporal sequence of officeholding may have consequences for the operation of Congress. The group of highly ambitious New Deal Democrats who were elected to the Senate after brief service in the House may have served as a core of support for the policy changes that swept through the Senate in the years 1932–36. On the other hand, intraparty tensions may have been generated by the election of large numbers of politicians who had been out of office for more than ten years (fourteen senators in 1930 and 1932 and forty-three representatives from 1930 to 1934). Although this assertion is highly speculative, an "old guard/new guard" tension may be generated by conflict between the seasoned politicians who are attracted back into office and the amateurs and ambitious ladder climbers who are swept in on the partisan tides.[46]

Explaining Change in the Congressional Career Structure

I have shown that career structures for the Senate and House are not static and that changes can be explained. Shifts in political careers can be traced

45. The trend can be explained by decreased turnover in the House, longer service, and more voluntary retirements. Decreased turnover reduces the size of the pool of former House members who might like to regain their seats. Age becomes a limiting factor as longer careers reduce the likelihood that a member will seek to reenter the body after retiring or being defeated. Finally, increased voluntary retirement obviously would reduce the number of members interested in returning to the body (John R. Hibbing, "Voluntary Retirement from the U.S. House: Who Quits?" *American Journal of Political Science* 26:3 [August 1982]: 467–83; Stephen E. Frantzich, "Opting Out: Retirement from the House of Representatives, 1966–1974," *American Politics Quarterly* 6 [1978]: 251–76).

46. I thank David J. Sousa for this insight.

to the nature of political opportunities facing career politicians and potential candidates. Changes in the use of the manifest office, in levels of amateurism and major elective experience, in the patterns and timing of succession from lower office, and in the return of former politicians create a markedly different opportunity structure in periods of electoral flux (especially in realignments, but to a lesser extent in any high-opportunity election).

The shift away from politically experienced candidates toward amateurs and less seasoned politicians in times of electoral opportunity creates a paradox for the theory of ambition and strategic behavior. Current theory predicts that in times of great political opportunity the most experienced politicians will run for office. The strategic-politicians hypothesis asserts that current officeholders time their attempts at gaining higher office with the conditions that are most likely to lead to victory. Why then are proportionately *fewer* experienced politicians elected in the periods of greatest opportunity? I suggest that the individual-level understanding of office-seeking is an accurate description of careers in "normal" electoral periods, but when career structures change, one must look to other factors to explain patterns of political careers.

Ideally, more complete evidence for this claim would be provided by data on *all* candidates, not just winners. Unfortunately, it is extremely difficult to obtain reliable information on the backgrounds of all challengers in pre-1950s congressional elections. However, the notion that amateurs benefit disproportionately from periods of high electoral opportunity is supported by evidence from House races from the years 1972–84. Although there is a steady increase in the proportion of experienced challengers as the chances for success improve from low-opportunity to normal to high-opportunity years, this is not reflected in the success of candidates (see table 3.4). In high-opportunity years, 8.1% more of the challengers and 4% *fewer* of the winners have previous experience, as compared with low-opportunity years.

Thus, examining the pool of challengers presents an even more interesting paradox. Existing theory predicts that experienced candidates should benefit disproportionately from national forces because they are more likely to behave strategically.[47] At a minimum, the national forces

47. It may be argued that ambition theory is primarily concerned with the calculus of office-seeking and says little about the *outcomes* of elections. While this is generally true, my interpretation of ambition theory's predictions for the outcomes of elections follows directly from the logic of the strategic-politicians hypothesis. Furthermore, given the expectation within existing theory that more experienced politicians run for office during periods of high electoral opportunity, the theory cannot explain why proportionately more amateurs win in these elections.

Table 3.4   The Strategic-Politicians Hypothesis in House Races, 1972–84

| | | Type of Race | | | |
		High opportunity	Neutral	Low opportunity	Total
Challengers	Experienced	41.0%	37.9%	32.9%	37.7%
	Total n	(1,057)	(1,267)	(761)	(3,085)
Winners	Experienced	67.6%	74.8%	71.6%	71.0%
	Total n	(241)	(202)	(67)	(510)
Winners as	Amateurs	12.5%	6.5%	3.7%	7.7%
proportion of	Total n	(624)	(787)	(511)	(1,922)
candidate pool	Experienced	37.6%	31.5%	19.2%	31.1%
	Total n	(433)	(480)	(250)	(1,163)

NOTE: The table includes all races, open and incumbent, from 1972 through 1984. Neutral years are 1972, 1976, and 1978. Years 1974 and 1982 are high-opportunity races for the Democrats and low-opportunity years for Republicans. Years 1980 and 1984 are high for the Republicans and low for the Democrats. Entries are the percentage in each category. Numbers of cases are in parentheses.

in high-opportunity races should have an equal impact on all challengers within a party (the rising tide lifts all boats). In fact, *amateurs* benefit disproportionately—their success rate as a proportion of the candidate pool increases more than threefold in high-opportunity years, while experienced candidates' success rate is not even doubled.[48] In the 1930s, when the proportion of winning amateurs was dramatically higher, either the pool of experienced candidates was smaller (due to inadequate supply) or amateurs won a greater proportion of the races. Either way, this is an interesting theoretical paradox and indicates that amateurs are indeed agents of electoral change in periods of electoral upheaval.

What can explain the relative success of amateurs? Shifting career structures are caused by a change in the nature of opportunities facing politicians and potential candidates—a change triggered by changes in the determinants of career structures discussed in chapter 1: the rules of the game, the role of political parties, the extent of political participation,

48. The same pattern is evident in primaries. Only thirty-four amateur nominees beat experienced candidates in Democratic primaries that determined the challenger to Republican incumbents from 1972 to 1984; thirteen of those were in 1974! Amateurs who win in periods of high electoral opportunity by defeating experienced candidates in the primary will be stronger and more able candidates than the typical amateur challenger. See David T. Canon, "Contesting Primaries in Congressional Elections: 1972–1988" (paper presented at the annual meeting of the American Political Science Association, Atlanta, Georgia, 31 August–3 September 1989).

and the desirability of office. Thus a major change in the rules of the game, such as a four-year House term and an eight-year Senate term would probably affect the types of candidates who would run for those offices. Actual rule changes, such as the Seventeenth Amendment and other reforms in the nominating system, also affect the recruitment process. In the period I examine, the constitutional rules of the game have been stable, the lengths of terms have not changed, and the nomination systems have been relatively constant. Nor are different rates of participation (for example, between midterm and presidential elections) an important determinant of change in career structures in this context. However, these points are still important to a theory of change in career structures and would be relevant for comparative studies or work that traces longer historical periods.

The other two factors, the desirability of office and the role of political parties, are more promising avenues for exploration. The desirability of an office clearly has an effect on the type of candidate recruited to that office. (Some evidence of the changing nature of the relative prestige or desirability of an office was presented earlier). More ambitious politicians were attracted to the Senate when it became a "presidential training ground."[49] When a body is perceived less favorably, recruitment effects also may exist. The recent "identity crisis" in the Senate may be undercutting its ability to attract good new people. "The Senate is no longer necessarily the place to be. . . . It can no longer count on a steady stream of people coming in, on being the coveted institutional spot in the system," Norman Ornstein says.[50] Indeed, six popular governors decided not to run for the Senate in 1984, despite good probabilities of success. Recent research pinpoints growing frustration with the nature of House service as one of the causes of increased voluntary retirement through the 1970s.[51]

Other factors can also influence the relative desirability of offices. These include supply rather than demand forces and changing rules of the game. The increasing professionalization of state legislatures, which has created a whole new pool of potential ambitious politicians, is an example of the former (though, as noted below, this can cut both ways). Changing governors' terms from two to four years and making them coincide with off-year elections is an example of the latter. The effect of these

49. Matthews, *U.S. Senators and Their World.*

50. Quoted in Helen Dewar, "Senate Faces Institutional Identify Crisis," *Washington Post,* 26 November 1984, A11.

51. Frantzich, "Retirement from the House"; Hibbing, "Voluntary Retirement from the U.S. House."

changes may be to recruit more candidates with ambition for higher office. The evidence for this point is mixed: proportionally more state legislators have been elected to the House in the past two decades, but fewer governors have gained Senate seats. Furthermore, the evidence on the relationship between the professionalization of state legislatures and progressive ambition is unclear.[52] Given the mixed explanatory value of the desirability of office, change in career structures can best be explained by the role of political parties. Two aspects are central: the strength of the political party and the control that the party has over nominations.

Change in a party's success at the polls is the surest way to alter the nature of political opportunity. Deviations in the partisan balance can be regional or national, gradual or sudden. The growing Republican strength in the South has created a new source of opportunity for amateurs because there are virtually no Republican politicians in many southern districts and states.[53] For example, Jeremiah Denton, who had never held public office, won as a Republican in Alabama, a strongly Democratic state. Opportunities open more suddenly along regional lines during partisan realignments, as in the 1930s.

A more general understanding of how the changing strength of parties can influence career paths can be seen in a supply-and-demand theory that points to a depleted supply of political talent unable to meet the electoral demands of the new majority party. The Democrats in the 1930s had not elected great numbers of candidates to any level of political office for more than thirty years; the same was true for the Republicans in the South in the first half of the twentieth century. When new opportunities opened up, amateurs and politicians who had been out of politics for many years were better able to compete and were more successful in winning office.

52. Linda L. Fowler and Robert D. McClure argue that there may be a new tendency for members of professionalized state legislatures to stay at home rather than run for the House (*Political Ambition: Who Decides to Run for Congress* (New Haven: Yale University Press, 1989), 74–100, esp. 99–100). However, Peverill Squire finds that generalizations cannot be made from the New York experience. For example, California is highly professionalized, but the institution serves as a springboard to higher office (see "Career Opportunities and Membership Stability in Legislatures," *Legislative Studies Quarterly* 13:1 [February 1988]: 65–82).

53. In Mississippi, for example, Democrats held 122 of 129 state House seats in 1987. Other states are Texas, with 150 of 156; Alabama, with 105 of 121; Louisiana, with 103 of 125; and Arkansas, with 100 of 109 (David T. Canon and David J. Sousa, "Realigning Elections and Political Career Structures in the U.S. Congress" [paper presented at the annual meeting of the American Political Science Association, Chicago, 3–6 September 1987], 25).

Another factor complements the supply-and-demand theory of candidate emergence during realignments. Periods of electoral upheaval are often accompanied by significant and rapid policy change. The young "new breed" of candidate in the emerging majority party replaces the prior requirement of political experience with the simple qualification of identification with the new trend, i.e., "I am an FDR man."[54]

The second aspect of the importance of parties in explaining change in the career structure concerns party control over nominations. The changing electoral environment has created an independent base for candidates who run for office with no previous political experience. Earlier in the century, elective office was the best way to achieve name recognition and gain the support of the party organization—support which was then critical for success. With the advent of sophisticated voter targeting and massive media campaigns, party support is no longer so important. The diminished role of parties in nominating candidates may have contributed to the increased levels of amateurism in the Senate. This same pattern is not evident in the House, perhaps because the media and money have not yet had as great an impact on House elections.

As I noted earlier, celebrity amateurs have been recruited by party officials, especially in Senate races, yet these cases are typically limited to races against popular incumbents or to the minority party that does not have a large pool of experienced politicians from which to draw challengers. When there is a good chance of defeating an incumbent, or if the seat is open, amateurs often must run against a party favorite in the primary. Gordon Humphrey (R-NH), Jeremiah Denton (R-AL), Bill Bradley (D-NJ), John Glenn (D-OH), and Orrin Hatch (R-UT) all defeated handpicked party candidates in their party's primary. Denton, Bradley, and Glenn had extensive name recognition coming into their races, while Humphrey, an airline pilot, and Hatch, a lawyer, did not. Denton, a Vietnam War hero, swamped party choice and former U.S. Representative Armistead Selden in the primary and narrowly won the general election. Bradley defeated Gov. Brendan T. Byrne's candidate, former state treasurer Richard T. Leone, while Glenn beat favored Howard Metzenbaum in a rematch of their 1970 primary, which Glenn had lost by a few thousand votes. Humphrey and Hatch were even more independent of the party organizations. Both relied extensively on New Right money from

---

54. See Robert A. Caro, *The Path to Power: The Years of Lyndon Johnson* (New York: Alfred A. Knopf, 1982), chap. 21, for a description of Johnson's unabashed promises of commitment to the Roosevelt agenda.

outside of their states. Alan Ehrenhalt, reporting on Humphrey's campaign, said:

> Few New Hampshire politicians took the challenger seriously. . . . The primary provided the first clue to what a stranger could do in New Hampshire politics if he had ideological loyalists, money and skill. Humphrey drew more than twice as many votes as either of his moderate Republican rivals, a former mayor of Keene and a veteran state senator.[55]

Humphrey's independent and ideological style brought him into conflict with his state's Republican leaders. Even the *Manchester Union-Leader* blasted him as "the meddling junior senator" when he failed to support the paper's choice in the 1980 GOP Senate primary.[56] Since then he has attempted to mend his ways, but he still maintains his image of independence.[57]

Orrin Hatch explicitly used his amateur status to advantage. Ehrenhalt reports:

> a political neophyte, Hatch mounted a Senate candidacy that represented as pure an example of anti-Washington politics as the nation has seen in recent years. Hatch's lack of government experience at any level almost certainly helped him. In his private legal practice, he had represented clients fighting federal regulations.[58]

Hatch ran against Jack Carlson, a candidate with considerable experience. Carlson was a former U.S. assistant secretary of the Interior and also had served in the Office of Management and Budget, on the Council of Economic Advisors, and in the Defense Department. Carlson's extensive experience made him the party's endorsee and front-runner. The voters saw it differently, giving Hatch a 2 : 1 victory in the primary and a general-election win over incumbent Frank Moss.

Partisan conditions and party control over nominations go a long way toward explaining why career paths change, though the relationship be-

<hr>

55. Alan Ehrenhalt, *Politics in America: Members of Congress in Washington and at Home,* 1984 (Washington, D.C.: Congressional Quarterly Press, 1983), 928.

56. Ibid.

57. On 6 March 1989, Humphrey announced that he would not seek reelection for a third term, fulfilling his campaign promises in 1978 and 1984 that he would be a "citizen-legislator." Humphrey said, "I don't believe people should make a career in Congress" (Rhodes Cook, "New Hampshire Conservative to Quit in 1990," *Congressional Quarterly Weekly Report,* 11 March 1989, 544).

58. Ibid., 1531.

tween party recruitment efforts and amateur candidacies still requires systematic study. A full understanding of career paths must also incorporate the individual-level theory that examines decisions to run for office. Ambition theory's picture of the static opportunity structure that changes very gradually in response to demographic, partisan, and economic conditions is reflected in individuals' calculations. These are the conditions that candidates face when they are making the decision to run for office: Is the position open or occupied by an incumbent? If there is an incumbent, is he or she vulnerable or popular? What is the state of the economy? Has the incumbent been involved in a scandal? The answers to these questions provide a map through the minefield of potential defeat for ambitious amateurs and career politicians attempting to advance their political careers. The next chapter systematically examines these factors for all congressional candidates from 1972 through 1988.

Four

Political Experience and Elections

Little is known about amateurs' campaigns for Congress. Are amateurs pushed out of political campaigns when experienced candidates choose to run? Must ambitious amateurs challenge experienced candidates who are preferred by the party in primaries? Which district-level and national conditions influence ambitious politicians in their decisions to run for Congress? Are amateurs as successful as experienced candidates in similar electoral contexts? Answering these questions will provide a preliminary understanding of the differences between amateurs and experienced candidates in congressional campaigns.

Political Experience in Primary Elections
Pushing Out the Amateurs

An implicit assumption of previous theory is that amateurs are pushed out of a campaign when experienced politicians choose to run *or* that amateurs enter electoral contests only when conditions are not promising enough to attract an experienced candidate. To test this assumption I will present the patterns of challenges in primary elections to see if amateurs are faced with a systematically different set of opportunities. While I expect hypotheses derived from this assumption to be generally confirmed, I do not expect all amateurs to behave nonstrategically simply because they do not have previous political experience. (I will outline the basis for identifying strategic amateurs later in this chapter.) *In general,* amateurs will behave differently because they start the decision-making process from a different point in terms of their costs and benefits of running for office and the goals they hold.

The assumption that amateurs are pushed out was stated by Robert Dahl in the context of races for governorships: "The pattern varies somewhat with region, time, and party system, but it is there; and the intrepid amateur without experience in public life . . . will probably fall flat on his face, as he deserves."[1] That amateurs are disadvantaged in their attempts for office can be stated in two hypotheses: (1) When experienced candidates choose to run, amateurs generally will not enter the race, or they will drop out, and (2) When experienced candidates choose to run and an amateur enters the primary, the experienced candidate will usually win. These two hypotheses can be thought of respectively as "passive" and "active" removal of amateurs from the electoral process. The implication of these hypotheses, if they hold true, is that amateurs have a tough row to hoe on their way to Congress.

One assumption of existing theory is that information is readily available for candidates to make rational and strategic decisions. In fact, there is a great deal of uncertainty surrounding the decision to run. Only 40% of the 251 candidates polled in a 1978 survey knew when they decided to run who their eventual opponents would be.[2] Some candidates reveal that they probably would have chosen not to run had they been fully informed. Others indicate that they dropped out of the race when the field became crowded with qualified candidates. Given this uncertainty, one cannot be completely confident in ascribing motives to a specific decision to run.

Despite the uncertainty, broad patterns are clear. Given imperfect information, candidates rely on past experiences and historical patterns.[3] A fair chance of success will attract many qualified candidates, and all reasonably astute candidates know this. The result is the passive or active elimination of amateurs from political campaigns. Often left with no alternative, amateurs run where there is little hope of winning, which creates a residual amateur base. Amateurs themselves often recognize this fact. Fowler reports:

> [C]hallengers in disadvantageous [elections] indicated that
> they had obtained the nomination because more experienced
> politicians had rejected it. It was frequently reported that, "If
> this race were winnable, then _____ would have taken it."[4]

1. In the foreward to Joseph A. Schlesinger, *How They Became Governor: A Study of Comparative State Politics, 1870–1950* (East Lansing: Governmental Research Bureau, Michigan State University, 1957), 3.

2. Louis Sandy Maisel, *From Obscurity to Oblivion: Running in the Congressional Primary*, rev. ed. (Knoxville: University of Tennessee Press, 1986), 21–22.

3. See Linda L. Fowler and Robert D. McClure, *Political Ambition: Who Decides to Run for Congress* (New Haven: Yale University Press, 1989), chaps. 2 and 3, for an excellent discussion of the importance of context and the problems of uncertainty in the decision to run.

4. Linda L. Fowler, "The Cycle of Defeat: Recruitment of Congressional Challengers" (Ph.D. diss., University of Rochester, 1977), 64–65.

The results of this "pushing-out" process are clear, but the mechanics are difficult to pin down. The process derives from a combination of voter preference, the relative campaign skills of the candidates, and the expectations of amateur and experienced politicians. In other words, voters tend to prefer experienced politicians and amateurs tend to be less effective candidates, causing the "active" removal. The resultant expectations held by amateur candidates produce "passive" exclusion through amateurs' reluctance to challenge experienced candidates.

Primary voters are especially important in this chain of events. The candidacy of self-made millionaire Gene Solomon in the 1978 Republican primary to face Abner J. Mikva (D-IL) illustrates the point. Party regulars viewed Solomon with some resentment as an "opportunist" trying to buy a nomination. Maisel says:

> A high percentage of those voting in a primary are party
> activists. If these people do not know anything about a
> candidate at all, not even his or her party affiliation, it is
> unlikely they will support that candidate against known and
> respected competitors.[5]

In sum, amateurs have a more difficult path to the House because career politicians are able to keep the paths clear for their own quests for higher office.[6] The expectations of primary voters who favor seasoned politicians help create this scenario.

I will test the two hypotheses of active and passive exclusion in three types of contested races in the years 1972–88: (1) opposing-party primaries to face an incumbent in the general election (referred to in this chapter, for simplicity's sake, as "opposing-party primaries"; for example, the Democratic primary when there is a Republican incumbent), (2) open-seat primaries, and (3) challenges to an incumbent within a party's primary. I will also present a test of the strategic-politicians hypothesis, expecting that more experienced Democratic challengers will have contested primaries in 1974 and 1982, and more experienced Republican challengers will have appeared in 1972, 1978, 1980, and 1984.

OPPOSING PARTY PRIMARIES—U.S. HOUSE

The 98% reelection rate of incumbent House members in 1986–88 indicates the formidable odds facing a prospective challenger. Not sur-

---

5. Maisel, *From Obscurity to Oblivion*, 89.
6. While it is clearly advantageous for most candidates to restrict the size of the field, they typically cannot do much to achieve this end. The presence of a strong candidate is

prisingly, from 1972 to 1988, fewer than one-fifth of challenged incumbents faced an opponent with elective experience, and only 27.1% had opponents with any public experience at all. Incumbents have an impressive array of resources at their disposal and many ambitious politicians do not attempt to beat the odds. The recent increase in the number of unopposed incumbents in general elections indicates that the already limited number of competitive races is shrinking further. (In 1986, seventy districts had no major-party challenger.) Abramson, Aldrich, and Rohde wryly comment, "It is difficult to defeat an incumbent whose challenger has no political experience and no money, and it is particularly difficult to defeat an incumbent with no opponent at all."[7] Yet experienced candidates do run. What happens to amateurs in these races?

The pushing-out hypotheses are confirmed.[8] When experienced candidates chose to run, amateurs were pushed out in more than 90.4% of the races (35.5% actively and 54.9% passively; see table 4.1). The proportions were almost identical for both parties. In primaries to face Democratic incumbents, amateurs won only 42 of 427 races that experienced candidates entered. In Democratic primaries to face a Republican incumbent, amateurs won 45 of the 483 races; interestingly, thirteen amateurs won in 1974, a year in which experienced candidates were especially eager to run because of the Watergate scandal, which had Republicans running for cover. Amateurs wanting to run in highly valued races had an initial hurdle to overcome.

---

often not enough to deter the ambitious amateur or the frivolous candidate. Occasionally, candidates will try to take matters into their own hands. (Rep. Bobbi Fiedler's [R-CA] campaign for the 1986 Republican nomination for the Senate was damaged by allegations that she had offered money to one of her competitors if he would drop out of the race.) Party organizations, another potential source of influence, rarely have great power in congressional districts, but they may attempt to deter challenges to their preferred candidate (Fowler and McClure, *Political Ambition,* 44–49, 170–73).

7. Paul R. Abramson, John H. Aldrich, and David W. Rohde, *Change and Continuity in the 1984 Elections,* rev. ed. (Washington, D.C.: Congressional Quarterly Press, 1987), 325.

8. In this part of the chapter, hypotheses are stated and evidence is presented, but not in standard "null hypotheses/alternative hypothesis" form. One reason is that the null hypothesis could take many forms. Is the null hypothesis for the pushing-out test that the distribution of amateur and experienced candidates is 50:50, or 60:40, or 70:30? "Pushing out" implies something stronger than this, but complete exclusion is not reasonable. The same is true of other hypotheses in this section. I believe it best to present the evidence and let the reader decide. Throughout the discussion of primary challenges, "frivolous" candidates (defined as those who receive less than 5% of the vote) are excluded. One additional complexity concerns races in which an experienced candidate wins the primary, an amateur finishes second, and another experienced candidate finishes third. In such cases amateurs are considered "pushed out," even though they defeat an experienced candidate.

Table 4.1   Amateurs in U.S. House Elections, 1972–88: The Pushing-out Hypotheses

	Opposing Party Primaries		Open-Seat Primaries		Incumbent Primaries	
	Dems.	Reps.	Dems.	Reps.	Dems.	Reps.
Passive	52.0%	58.3%	60.7%	54.3%	54.5%	80.5%
pushing out[a]	(251)	(249)	(202)	(151)	(91)	(33)
Active	38.7%	31.9%	25.2%	32.4%	38.3%	14.6%
pushing out[b]	(187)	(136)	(84)	(90)	(64)	(6)
Amateur defeats	9.3%	9.8%	14.1%	13.3%	7.2%	4.9%
of experienced	(45)	(42)	(47)	(37)	(12)	(2)
candidates						
Totals	100.0%	100.9%	100.0%	100.0%	100.0%	100.1%
n	(483)	(427)	(333)	(278)	(167)	(41)

NOTE: All of the contests in this table are races involving experienced candidates. These races comprise 30.9% of all opposing-party primaries to face an incumbent in the general election, 78.7% of all open-seat primaries, and 19.4% of all contested-incumbent primaries. Amateurs defeat amateurs or run unopposed in the other races. Table entries are the percentage in each category. Number of cases are in parentheses.

[a]Races in which an experienced candidate runs unopposed or when two or more experienced candidates face each other.

[b]Races in which an experienced candidate defeats an amateur.

In general, opposing-party primaries are not competitive (the average margin of victory is greater than 25%), but results are even more lopsided when the nominee defeats one or more amateurs (rather than an experienced candidate). If a winning amateur's only opponent is another amateur, the margin of victory is 6.2% greater than when he or she defeats an experienced candidate in the primary (25.0% compared with 18.8%), whereas experienced candidates fare 10.9% better against the weaker amateurs than against an experienced challenger (32.5% and 21.6% margins of victory; differences significant at the .001 level). The differences are similar when party is controlled, but Republican primaries are less competitive by about a 3% margin.

Evidence also supports the strategic-politicians hypothesis that more experienced candidates run in years in which their party fares well. In the Democratic years of 1974 and 1982, 55.2% of all primaries to face Republican incumbents involved experienced candidates, while in less favorable years, 32.6% of these primaries had experienced candidates (differences significant at .0001). For the Republicans, 1982 is the only exception to the rule. A strong recruitment effort by the RNC in 1982 helped place experienced candidates in 27.5% of the primaries, despite dismal prospects for their party in the fall. In the years that do conform, experienced candidates ran in 25.7% of primaries to face Democratic incumbents in Republican years (1972, 1978, 1980, and 1984), while only 17.9% were experienced in 1974 (differences significant at .01). Furthermore, *no* primaries in 1974 involved two experienced Republican candidates (there were eleven such Democratic primaries in that year).

A simple regression shows that the relationship between the fortunes of the party and the proportion of experienced candidates is significant for the Democrats but not for the Republicans. Regressing the percentage of Democratic candidates with previous experience on Democratic seat loss or gain yields a surprising R^2 of .62 and a coefficient of 2.2 (significant at the .025 level). That is, for every percent increase in the proportion of Democratic candidates with previous experience, the Democrats gain about two seats in the House. For Republicans the model yields an R^2 of only .21 and a B of -3.39 (not significant).[9]

A picture of the primary process emerges in which amateurs respond to conditions and choices that are generally more constrained than those facing experienced politicians. When experienced candidates choose to run, they usually deter challenges, or they defeat amateur challengers in the primary. On the other hand, when amateurs enter races that they have a chance of winning, they must face experienced candidates, and usually they lose. Occasionally an ambitious amateur can raise a significant campaign war chest that deters possible competition, but this is rare.

PRIMARY ELECTIONS IN OPEN-SEAT RACES—U.S. HOUSE

Open-seat primaries provide candidates with a different set of conditions. The absence of an incumbent ensures the presence of strong and well-financed candidates in both parties. Candidates in the incumbent's party often wait many years for the opportunity to run, while the opposition party views the open seat as the best chance to regain control of the

9. The data for this regression are from the years 1972 through 1984. The best fit is given by the difference between the percentage of Democratic and Republican candidates with previous experience. This relative measure regressed on Democratic seat loss yields at R^2 of .68 and a coefficient of 2.00. The difference in percentage of challengers who have held elective office is still significant in a more fully specified model (Gary C. Jacobson, *The Politics of Congressional Elections* 1st ed. [Boston: Little, Brown, 1983], 148–49). Previous experience and party explain 70% of the variance in all elections from 1946 to 1984 (Gary C. Jacobson, *The Politics of Congressional Elections*, 2d ed. [Boston: Little, Brown, 1987], 160).

district.[10] Amateur candidates are likely to face stiff competition in pursuing this path to Congress. Far fewer will be unopposed in open-seat primary elections than in either of the other two types of primaries. At the same time, more amateurs who win primaries must defeat an experienced candidate before moving on to the general election. The pushing-out rule will still apply in a preponderance of cases, but experienced politicians will not be sensitive to national conditions because the absence of an incumbent will induce ambitious politicians to run, regardless of the state of the economy or other national tides. Finally, experienced candidates are more formidable challengers than amateurs, which should be reflected in victory margins and rates of success.

These expectations hold (see table 4.1). More than three-fourths of the primaries in open-seat races from 1972 to 1988 involved a candidate with some political experience (611 or 776). In these races, amateurs did not enter 57.7% of the races (passive pushing-out) and were defeated in 28.5% of the races (active pushing-out). Amateurs rarely run unopposed (10.8% of all races), but they defeat experienced candidates more frequently than in opposing-party primaries (13.8% of the races contested by experienced candidates, compared with 9.8%).

Democratic primaries are won more frequently by experienced candidates than are Republican primaries, but this appears to be a recent development. In 1972, 62.3% of Democratic open-seat primaries were won by experienced candidates, compared with two-thirds of Republican primaries. The proportion of Democratic experienced winners grew by 5% a year until 1980 when it reached 83%, while it remained between 60% and 65% in Republican primaries. Recently, Democratic amateurs have been somewhat more successful, with experienced candidates winning 73.5% of open-seat primaries from 1980 to 1988. In the same period, Republicans fielded more experienced candidates than they had in the previous decade, cutting the gap between the two parties to 7.3%.

The electoral advantage held by experienced candidates over amateurs is greater in open-seat primaries than in primaries to face incumbents. The average margin of victory is nearly twice as large for experienced candidates who defeat amateurs rather than other experienced challengers (31.0% and 16.3% respectively), while amateurs fare 12.6% better when they face another amateur (25.6% and 13.0% respectively; both differences significant at .0001).

10. See Jacobson, *Politics of Congressional Elections*, 2d ed., 92–93, for a general discussion of candidates in open primaries; see also Harvey L. Schantz, "Contested and Uncontested Primaries for the U.S. House," *Legislative Studies Quarterly* 5:4 (November, 1980): 545–62.

Experienced candidates of both parties do not appear to be sensitive to national tides in open-seat primaries. As expected, the advantage of running without an incumbent in the race overwhelms other considerations. However, there are a few years in which candidates exhibit strategic behavior. Only 4.4% of experienced Democratic candidates were unopposed in 1974, compared with the twelve-year average of 11.9%, and the 1980 and 1984 elections have the greatest proportion of primaries in which two experienced Republican candidates run, indicating the greater competitiveness and value of those races. A more complete test of the strategic-politicians hypothesis in open-seat primaries will be presented in the next section.

PRIMARY CHALLENGES TO INCUMBENTS—U.S. HOUSE

Experienced candidates are usually unwilling to challenge an incumbent in a primary because an unsuccessful attempt could alienate party leaders and elites, undermining future attempts to gain the seat. This cautiousness may open opportunities for the ambitious amateur. Jerry Huckaby (D-LA) is one amateur who took advantage of such a situation:

> While ambitious young politicians waited for veteran Rep.
> Otto Passman to retire, Huckaby took the risk of challenging
> him in 1976, defeated him in the Democratic primary and won
> the seat. It was Huckaby's first campaign. But the wealthy
> dairy farmer mounted an aggressive, well-financed challenge
> that capitalized on Passman's advanced age (76) and political
> problems. . . . Some Democratic politicians within the district
> were annoyed that the upstart Huckaby had taken the prize so
> many of them had been waiting for. One of them, state Sen.
> James H. Brown Jr., challenged Huckaby in 1978. But
> Huckaby spent nearly $400,000 and won by more than 25,000
> votes. He has faced minimal opposition since then.[11]

Three specific expectations can be derived from the general pattern of strategic behavior: (1) There will be relatively few challenges of incumbents by experienced candidates because an incumbent must be perceived as very vulnerable (usually as indicated by a scandal or a weak showing in the previous election) before an experienced candidate will enter a race (in these cases, the pushing-out rule will apply); (2) Challenges by amateur candidates will be more frequent because most amateurs challenge incumbents with little hope of success (the rare victories are considered

11. Alan Ehrenhalt, *Politics in America: Members of Congress in Washington and at Home, 1984* (Washington, D.C.: Congressional Quarterly Press, 1983), 622.

upsets); and (3) As a result of 1 and 2, experienced candidates will have a higher success rate against incumbents of their own party than will amateurs, as measured in terms of both victories and percentage of the vote received.

It is unusual for experienced candidates to challenge an incumbent of their own party: only 7.7% of Democratic incumbents and 3.0% of Republicans faced such challengers. The pushing-out hypothesis is confirmed in 93.3% of the races. Of the 208 experienced candidates who challenged incumbents, 124 faced the incumbent alone or with minimal opposition, 70 defeated amateur candidates who received at least 5% of the vote, and only 14 were defeated by an amateur (see table 4.1). The second expectation is also confirmed. Amateurs were more willing to enter incumbent primaries (31.6% and 12.8% for Democratic and Republican incumbents, respectively).[12] While it is impossible to prove with these data that amateurs enter races without the expectation of winning, this seems a reasonable assumption, given that an average of only two incumbents a year are defeated by amateurs in primaries.

The experienced candidates' strategic behavior and the amateurs' relatively indiscriminate choice of races should be evident in the electoral results. Almost a third of all incumbents had contested primaries, but challengers received more than 25% of the vote in only a third of these races. Only about a fifth of the amateurs and two-thirds of the experienced candidates reached this minimal level of competitiveness (with averages of 18.1% and 29.9% of the vote, respectively).[13] Experienced candidates also won a greater proportion of their races (11.7%, compared with only 1.7% of the amateurs).

The impact of national conditions on the strategic calculus of candidates in primary challenges to incumbents is not clear. The analytical problem for the researcher attempting to sort out various considerations—and for the strategic politician whose career may hang in the balance—is that the prospect for success in the general election cuts both ways. That is, unfavorable national conditions that make the incumbent

12. Democratic incumbents' primaries are contested more than twice as often as Republican primaries, which is consistent with Schantz's study of primary elections from 1956 to 1974 ("Contested and Uncontested Primaries," 550) and with my findings (David T. Canon, "Contesting Primaries in Congressional Elections, 1972–1988" [paper presented at the annual meeting of the American Political Science Association, Atlanta, Georgia, 31 August–3 September 1989]).

13. Experienced candidates running against incumbents who are unopposed in the fall fare even better, receiving an average of 37.7% in the twenty-two such cases from 1972 to 1988. In the 111 such cases involving amateurs, the average is virtually identical to the mean for all amateur challenges of incumbents (18.0%). These figures reflect the average vote for the second-place finishers in the primary.

more vulnerable in the primary also decrease the successful challenger's chances of winning in the fall. For example, a Republican challenger in 1974 may have perceived a Republican incumbent to be vulnerable, but may have chosen not to run, fearing subsequent defeat. Alternatively, when national forces make the general election a safer bet, the incumbent is more likely to be invincible. Because of these contradictory forces, I expect that primary challengers to incumbents will not be very sensitive to the prospects for success in the fall.[14]

The evidence on this point is indeed mixed. Republicans tend to respond more to the short-term rewards of defeating the incumbent in the primary, without much consideration for their chances of winning in the fall, and Democrats tend to behave in the opposite manner, but neither tendency is very strong. In 1974 and 1982, fourteen experienced candidates challenged Republican incumbents (4.2% of the total), while only seventeen of them challenged incumbents in the more favorable years of 1972, 1978, 1980, and 1984 (3%). Patterns are similar for Republican amateurs, with 16.0% and 13.1% challenging incumbents in the bad and good years respectively. On the other hand, 8.2% of the Democratic incumbents faced experienced challengers in their primaries in 1974 and 1982, while only 6.7% did in 1978, 1980, and 1984 (1972 is an exception, with 14.6%). Democratic amateurs reveal no consistent patterns.

National forces are, at best, of mixed value in understanding why some incumbents are challenged in their primaries and others are not. It is more helpful to examine the conditions under which incumbents actually are defeated. Experienced candidates attempt to choose races in which the incumbent is "ripe for the picking"; while amateurs are less discriminating in their choices of races, those who do win often have devised a creative plan of attack. In ten of the twenty-five races from 1972 to 1988 in which an experienced candidate defeated an incumbent, the incumbent was involved in scandal. In five of the remaining races, the incumbent was hurt by redistricting in three of the cases and fell victim to party infighting in the other two.[15] In only two of the fifteen races in which an

14. Though it is impossible to discover how many potential candidates decided not to challenge an incumbent in the primary due to poor prospects for their party in the fall, it is instructive to examine the cases in which challengers won the primary, but lost the general election. From 1972 to 1988 there have been eight such cases. In six of them, the successful primary challenger lost in the fall partly because of unfavorable national tides.

15. The two cases of party squabbles involved Katie Hall (D-IN) in 1984 and John Fary (D-IL) in 1982. Hall, the first black member of Congress from Indiana, became embroiled in a controversy when Rep. Adam Benjamin died two months before the 1982 election. Gary mayor Richard Hatcher appointed Hall to run for the seat over the objections of other prospective candidates, who wanted him to appoint Benjamin's widow. Hall narrowly won in 1982, but in 1984 Peter Visclosky won an incredibly close three-way primary with 35%

amateur defeated an incumbent was the incumbent handicapped by a district-specific factor. One of these cases involved Richard Kelly (R-FL), a central subject of the FBI Abscam investigation in the spring of 1980. Bill McCollum, a lawyer and political amateur, already had his campaign under way when the scandal broke. State Sen. Vince Fechtel entered the race in April, but McCollum narrowly won the initial primary, in which Kelly received only 18% of the vote, and then won the runoff with 54%.[16]

When amateurs defeat an incumbent, they occasionally have to fight off other challengers.[17] More typically, they must defeat the incumbent one-on-one with creative campaign strategies. Paul Kanjorski (D-PA) defeated first-term representative Frank Harrison by a 4% margin in 1984. *Congressional Quarterly* reported, "The outcome capped a stunning charge by Kanjorski, who entered the race in spite of the fact that his own poll showed him trailing Harrison by a margin of 61 to 9 percent."[18] Kanjorski used a largely self-financed $100,000 media blitz that criticized the incumbent for taking junkets and neglecting the needs of the district. His most effective advertisements attacked Harrison for taking a trip to Central America while his constituents were in a panic over the contamination of the district's water supply (they had to boil the water to make it drinkable). One ad showed a Costa Rican beach and mentioned that Harrison had visited there, and then the scene switched to a pot of boiling water, with a voice-over saying, "Where's Frank?" A similar ad concluded, "Isn't it enough to make you boil?" Not very sophisticated, but effective.

I do not want to overstate the case that experienced candidates are handed their primary wins on scandal-laden silver platters and that amateurs must claw their way to victory through skill and cunning. Yet fifteen of the twenty-four incumbents defeated by experienced candidates were weakened, while amateurs had this advantage in only two of their fifteen wins.

One final point concerns the size of the primary field. Incumbents are often advantaged by split opposition, especially when an experienced challenger enters the race. Almost 40% of the primary challenges to in-

---

of the vote. In the other case, three-term representative John Fary fell victim to the machine that he had supported for more than thirty years. A group of South Side Democrats led by Cook County State's Attorney Richard M. Daley, son of the later mayor of Chicago, decided that it was time for the seventy-year-old politician to step aside and make room for one of the machine's younger lieutenants, William Lipinski. Fary managed only 36% of the vote in his attempt to hang on to his seat.

16. Ehrenhalt, *Politics in America, 1984,* 305–6.

17. Four of the fourteen races in which an amateur defeated an incumbent were multi-candidate races.

18. *Congressional Quarterly Weekly Report* 42 (14 April 1984): 871.

cumbents by experienced candidates were multi-candidate races (82 of 208), while only one-fifth (161 of 858) of such races involved more than two candidates when the primary challenger was an amateur.[19] Thus it does not appear that experienced candidates are able to exclude the amateur who may siphon off enough votes to alter the outcome of the election. In fact, in eleven of the eighty-two races involving experienced candidates with additional candidates, the incumbent won with a plurality of the votes, with a third-place amateur playing the role of the potential spoiler. For amateurs the comparable figures are 6 of 161.[20]

PUSHING OUT AMATEURS—U.S. SENATE PRIMARIES

That Senate elections are more competitive than House elections was demonstrated with a vengeance in 1986. Following the 1982 and 1984 elections, in which more than 90% of incumbent senators were reelected in successive elections for the first time since World War II, it appeared that Senate seats were becoming less vulnerable. But in 1986, more incumbent senators (seven) than representatives (six) were defeated in the general election for the first time in the twentieth century (two House members and no senators were defeated in primaries).

A standard explanation for the greater competitiveness of Senate elections points to differences between districts and states. The greater homogeneity of House districts makes it easier for House members to appeal to a majority of the voters, while voters at the state level are likely to be split more evenly between the two parties. Other theorists cite the role of the challenger.[21] Senate races, by their very nature, receive more attention than House races and therefore are more likely to attract more

19. Only one-tenth of Republican primaries with an amateur challenger have more than two viable candidates, while the comparable rate for such Democratic primaries is almost one-fourth. With an experienced challenger, the figures are 17% for the Republicans and 45% for the Democrats involved in multi-candidate primaries. Overall, Republican incumbents have fewer primary challenges, but a larger proportion of them are two-candidate races (89.5% for Republicans, compared with 72.8% for Democrats).

20. This difference can be explained by the more competitive nature of the primaries contested by experienced candidates. The typical split of the vote is a multi-candidate primary contested by an amateur is 85, 10, 5, with the incumbent winning an easy victory, while the experienced candidate's primary is more likely to have a vote like 53, 43, 6, or, as in the eleven cases mentioned above, 40, 35, 25.

21. Jacobson, *Politics of Congressional Elections*, 2d ed., 93–94; Alan I. Abramowitz, "A Comparison of Voting for U.S. Senator and Representative in 1978," *American Political Science Review* 74:3 (September 1980): 633–40; Lyn Ragsdale, "Incumbent Popularity, Challenger Invisibility, and Congressional Voters," *Legislative Studies Quarterly* 6:2 (May 1981): 201–18; Barbara Hinckley, "House Reelections and Senate Defeats: The Role of the Challenger," *British Journal of Political Science* 10:4 (October 1980): 441–60.

campaign resources and stronger candidates.[22] Challengers in Senate races are more likely to have some previous political experience; all the winners in the 1986 Senate races had either House or statewide elective experience. In general, about two-thirds of Senate challengers have some previous experience. The link between Senate-race competitiveness and challenger strength may be exaggerated somewhat by the biased 1978 national election survey, which overrepresents large states and competitive Senate races. Only half of the Senate races from 1972 to 1980 are hard-fought races that fit the description outlined above.[23]

Yet, when compared with House races, Senate races *do* have more experienced, better financed, and more visible challengers. The implication for amateurs is that fewer make it to the general election. Of those who do, many use personal wealth or celebrity status to compensate for their deficiencies in campaign experience and name recognition. Do amateurs in Senate races get pushed out of campaigns like their House counterparts, or does the competitiveness of Senate elections make the amateurs' path even more difficult?[24]

Senate primaries from 1972 to 1988 are contested mostly by experienced candidates. Opposing-party primaries to run against Republican incumbents are generally more sought-after by experienced candidates than those to face Democrats (87.7% versus 72.2%). Thirty percent of the former had two experienced challengers, while only 14.3% of the latter were so hotly contested. Furthermore, eight Democratic incumbent senators faced no general-election opposition from 1972 to 1988, but no Republicans were so fortunate. Both parties' primaries exhibited the pushing-out of amateurs, with only 8.2% of amateurs winning races that are contested by an experienced candidate. Open-seat primaries exhibited similar patterns, although an even greater proportion of candidates in these races had previous political experience.

Primary challenges to incumbents occurred much more often in Senate races than in House contests. Only half of the Senate incumbents from 1972 to 1988 were unopposed in their primaries, compared with almost 70% of House incumbents (there are substantial differences between the parties—only 43.1% of Democratic senators were unopposed, while

22. Thomas E. Mann and Raymond E. Wolfinger, "Candidates and Parties in Congressional Elections," *American Political Science Review* 74:3 (September 1980): 622.

23. Mark C. Westlye, "Competitiveness of Senate Seats and Voting Behavior in Senate Elections," *American Journal of Political Science* 27:2 (May 1983): 279.

24. One characteristic of Senate elections that confounds the simple characterization of amateurs being "pushed out" is that races are more commonly multi-candidate affairs. Thus a House member may defeat an amateur who was a close second, with a former governor in third place. Such cases will be noted below.

61.5% of their Republican counterparts did not have a primary election opponent). As in House races, experienced candidates are reluctant to challenge an incumbent unless they have a reasonable chance of success. This cautiousness is reflected in the election results: experienced candidates received at least 25% of the vote in twenty-two of the thirty-two races they entered, winning nine of those races. Amateurs, on the other hand, won only two of the eighty-nine primaries they entered, receiving at least 25% of the vote in only eleven other races.

Differences between amateurs and experienced candidates are also evident when the path to office is considered. Amateurs who are elected to the Senate generally come by the more difficult routes. The preferred path, an open seat, is the domain of the experienced candidate; more than half of the experienced candidates who were elected did not have to defeat an incumbent, while the figure is only 20% for amateurs. All three of the amateurs elected in open-seat races from 1972 to 1988 had to defeat experienced candidates in their primary and in the general election. Most successful amateurs must defeat an incumbent in the primary or general election.

Some amateurs benefit from being in the right place at the right time. Five candidates with little or no previous political experience won election after the incumbent was defeated in the opposing party's primary.[25] Experienced candidates, who are not as willing to challenge incumbents, were not available to take advantage of the changed political stakes. In fact, no candidates with extensive political experience have been elected to the Senate in this manner since 1972.

Identifying Successful Amateurs

While the pushing-out hypothesis is largely confirmed, one must still explain the anomaly referred to above: contrary to the common wisdom, approximately one-fourth of the members of Congress *are* amateurs. It is unlikely that all amateurs elected to Congress are from this residual base. The challenge of a comprehensive theory of ambition and careers is to predict these cases. To make such predictions, one must have a method of making distinctions among amateurs prior to the general election. I will suggest such a method and then test the validity of the distinctions by examining the conditions under which amateurs *are* elected to the House and Senate.

25. Bill Bradley (D-NJ) and Jeremiah Denton (R-AL) are the only complete amateurs in the group. Paula Hawkins (R-FL) and Frank Murkowski (R-AL) served as state commissioners, and Jesse Helms (R-NC) served as a city councilman. Both Murkowski and Helms reentered politics after a ten-year hiatus; their nonpolitical careers were in banking and broadcasting, respectively.

It is clearly more difficult to model the initial decision to run for office than to model subsequent decisions to run. Ideally, a theory could provide a basis for predicting which amateurs would be elected. Prediction of the career advancement of experienced politicians is a more certain enterprise because ambition theory and the strategic-politicians hypothesis provide a sound basis for understanding the process by which politicians seek higher office. Current officeholders have already given some indication of their political ambitions and risk-taking propensities. They are sensitive to the opportunities facing them because of the central goal of perpetuating their political careers. Political neophytes, on the other hand, have no such obvious set of incentives and patterns of observable behavior. Furthermore, there is no comparable theory to guide the search.

My theory provides for identification of those factors that make it more likely that an amateur will behave in a strategic manner, which in turn allows predictions of success in the general election. The key intervening factor here between the candidate and success in the election is strategic behavior. Amateurs who are more sensitive to the nature of the opportunities they face (the ambitious amateurs described in chapter 2) will choose to run in races in which there is a greater likelihood of success. Ambitious amateurs can be identified on the basis of three factors: celebrity status, previous serious attempts for a congressional seat, and risk-taking in the primary election (a fourth consideration, the candidate's age, will also be discussed).[26] The reasoning here is simple. An amateur who challenges a secure and scandal-free incumbent who received 80% of the vote in the previous election cannot possibly be a serious politician. The ambitious amateur who has made a previous serious attempt at a House seat or who defeats a state legislator in a primary fight is more likely to have a future in politics.

Celebrity candidates (well-known business leaders and TV-news an-

---

26. Another factor that may seem like an obvious way to help draw distinctions among amateur candidates is their relative levels of campaign spending. This possibility, while attractive due to readily available data, was rejected for theoretical reasons. Rather than getting at strategic behavior, campaign money measures something else—the quality of the candidate. Furthermore, campaign money flows in a strategic manner; contributors do not like to waste money on a lost cause. Therefore, the argument would become tautological if campaign money were used to make distinctions among amateurs. Amateurs who have large campaign war chests are almost certainly involved in races they have a significant chance of winning. I am attempting to *predict* on some independent basis who those amateurs will be. Also, complete campaign-spending figures are not available until after the election, thus damaging the predictive capability of the theory. Policy amateurs will be identified only for the analysis of institutional behavior, due to the difficulty of gathering information on the policy goals of all congressional candidates.

chorpeople, as well as actors, athletes, and astronauts) differ from their counterparts who have no previous political experience in two ways: broad name recognition and established, successful careers. Strong name recognition before the start of a campaign is a tremendous advantage for any candidate, but it is an especially valuable commodity for amateurs, who typically start at a marked disadvantage in this regard. (A state representative or local politician will have high recognition in at least a portion of the district, but a potential challenger with no previous experience may be virtually unknown.) This stronger starting point allows celebrity candidates to seriously consider entering races in which there is some chance for success.

While greater name recognition permits celebrities to enter more highly valued races, their established careers may force them to exercise more caution, making it less likely that they would enter a hopeless campaign. As mentioned in chapter 2, many celebrities, such as Burt Reynolds, Brooks Robinson, and Roger Staubach, have been recruited to run for the Senate but have declined to do so. In many cases, the uncertain world of politics is not attractive to celebrities. Those who have had great success in one career are not likely to subject themselves to potential humiliation "for the good of the party" as sacrificial lambs. They are likely to run only when there is a reasonable chance of success, as are their politically experienced counterparts. In this sense, celebrity status plays the same function as the base office for a career politician: a resource for gaining higher office and a stake that is not casually risked.[27]

A previous political campaign that met with some success also indicates an amateur who is likely to share the experienced candidate's office-seeking goal and who will probably be more strategic in his or her behavior than the typical amateur. Just as the politically experienced candidate has demonstrated some level of political skill by being elected to lower

27. Gary C. Jacobson and Samuel Kernell make this point for current officeholders (*Strategy and Choice in Congressional Elections* [New Haven: Yale University Press, 1983], 22). In a whimsical piece on Brooks Robinson's potential candidacy, entitled "Brooks, Keep a Grip on Integrity by Not Running for U.S. Senate," Michael Olesker points to the tarnishing of one's image that may result from entering politics. Olesker speculated on what Brooks had to lose, and what the Maryland Republican Party had to gain, from his candidacy: "Clearly, the Republican Party of Maryland is not interested in you because of any political expertise. . . . They are bankrupt of legitimate candidates, and in their desperation are looking at people who are potential vote-getters for reasons not necessarily connected with experience in government" (*Baltimore Sun,* 3 November 1985, 1C, 4C). Other amateurs who are not celebrities may also be more strategic in their behavior due to potential career and income sacrifices they would have to make, but this group is too difficult to identify systematically.

office, amateurs who make a viable run for Congress show their ambition and interest in a political career.

William Gray (D-PA) is an example of this type of amateur. Using a church as his political base, Gray was successful in his second attempt to unseat Rep. Robert N. C. Nix, Jr., in the Democratic primary. A third-generation minister of the 3,000-member Bright Hope Baptist Church in North Philadelphia, Gray was able to cultivate the traditional connection between politics and church that exists in many black urban areas. His first attempt in 1976 fell 339 votes short, but two years later he swept past Nix with 58% of the vote. *CQWR* noted:

> Gray learned the lessons of his losing 1976 effort, starting
> early, putting together an effective campaign organization, and
> getting adequate funding. Nix's reliance on his congressional
> seniority and backing by the organization was not enough to
> overcome Gray's well-coordinated efforts.[28]

Gray has been coded as an ambitious amateur in his second attempt for office.[29]

Sometimes the strategy is more explicitly a two-race attempt for office, rather than a realistic chance of winning the first time, as in Gray's case. Jacobson notes:

> Challengers sometimes enter a contest knowing that their
> candidacy is hopeless in order to build momentum for a
> second, more formidable try in the following election. The
> first campaign is used to gain recognition, experience, and
> supporters for the second.[30]

Not all repeat candidates will fit this mold; it is important to distinguish between the party-loyalist sacrificial lambs or Harold Stassens and the strategic candidates that Jacobson describes. The two major studies of "rematch" congressional elections show that only one-third of rematch elections from 1946 to 1984 were competitive.[31] I define serious candi-

---

28. *Congressional Quarterly Weekly Report* 36 (20 May 1978): 1227.

29. Gray appears to be electorally secure, but he has been vulnerable to challenges from the left. Black activists claimed that he had become too comfortable with the "white establishment," and in 1982 State Sen. Milton Street challenged Gray as an independent in the general election. Street sent Gray a letter stating, "Your religious-acting, righteous-speaking soul may belong to Jesus, but your ass belongs to me." The voters disagreed, returning Gray to the House by a 76% to 22% margin.

30. Gary C. Jacobson, *Money in Congressional Elections* (New Haven: Yale University Press, 1980), 110.

31. Thomas A. Kazee, "Congressional Elections and the Rerun Phenomenon: A Study of Candidate Recruitment and Incumbency Advantage" (Ph.D. diss., Ohio State University, 1978); Eugene R. Declercq and James Costello, "When Old Friends Meet:

dates as those who receive at least 40% of the vote in a primary challenge to an incumbent or in the general election.[32]

The final factor that helps to make distinctions among amateurs is their risk-taking and success in the primary election. If an amateur defeats an experienced candidate in the primary, the nominee is probably not a typical sacrificial lamb. First, the race was valued highly enough to attract an experienced challenger, which means that the prospects for the November election were not completely dismal. Second, the amateur had enough political knowledge and support to defeat an experienced candidate.

Any attempt at high political office involves the confluence of ability, desire, and resources. Ability is measured to some extent by previous attempts at a House seat and success in the primary. Celebrity status is a resource. But what of desire? Schlesinger sees age as a primary indicator of desire for a political career. "The younger a man is when he enters politics," he says, "the greater the range of his ambitions and the likelihood of his developing a career commitment to politics."[33] Schlesinger discovers that only one-fourth of state political leaders begin their political careers after the age of forty. I initially expected that age would help distinguish among amateurs in two ways. First, amateurs who are elected to Congress at age thirty or younger should be likely to make politics their career. Second, amateurs who enter politics at age fifty are not likely to view their political careers in the same manner. Hain finds that progressive ambitions among politicians steadily drop with age,[34] and Schlesinger shows that the chances of being elected governor or senator as an initial office decrease greatly past age fifty and become remote past age sixty.[35] Despite the strong theoretical reasons and some empirical ev-

Congressional Rematches, 1946–1984" (paper presented at the annual meeting of the American Political Science Association, New Orleans, 29 August–1 September 1985).

32. While any definition of a credible challenger is somewhat arbitrary, Jacobson finds that candidates who receive less than 40% of the vote in an initial attempt are seriously underfinanced in a second race. He says, "They appear to be inordinately willing sacrificial lambs enduring another drubbing for the sake of the party" (*Money in Congressional Elections,* 112).

33. Joseph A. Schlesinger, *Ambition and Politics: Political Careers in the United States* (Chicago: Rand McNally, 1966), 176.

34. Paul L. Hain, "Age, Ambitions, and Political Careers: The Middle Age Crisis," *Western Political Quarterly* 27:2 (June 1974): 267.

35. Schlesinger, *Ambition and Politics,* 175–87. Tip O'Neill tells a great story about the House's oldest freshman, Jim Bowler of Chicago. When asked why he came to Congress at the age of eighty-six, he responded, "Fifty-two years ago, when I was just a young fellow, I served on the city council with Al Sabath. When a seat opened up in Congress, we took a vote to see which one of us would run. I received ten votes, so did Al. We must have gone through twenty ballots, but it was still tied. Finally, we decided to flip a coin. The man who

idence for including age as a distinguishing feature for ambitious amateurs, the indicator discriminated very poorly. Young amateurs were no more likely to establish careers in the House or Senate than older amateurs. Therefore, this factor was not used.

Each of these factors has several good properties for helping to distinguish among amateurs: (1) The characteristics of each category are unambiguous (the latter two are based on objective data, while celebrity status is determined by a few simple coding rules); (2) each factor is available well before the general election, and thus can be used in a predictive or forecasting model; and, most important, (3) each factor is derived from my theory of ambition and careers.

Can the theory explain election outcomes and predict who will run? The theory successfully identifies 60.4% of the amateurs who win a House seat (84 of 139).[36] Another way to examine the effectiveness of the theory is to examine the relative success of those the theory identifies as ambitious amateurs and those it does not. In contests against incumbents, 1.5% of amateur nominees not identified as ambitious win (29 of 1,971). Ambitious amateurs win 20.9% of their contests (29 of 139). In open-seat races the difference is less dramatic, but still significant: a fourth of nonambitious amateurs win open-seat races, but 48.2% of the ambitious amateurs win.[37] The following section attempts to predict when experienced challengers and amateurs run for Congress.

Political Experience in Congressional Elections

The primary aim of the test in this section is to predict when experienced candidates appear in House and Senate elections, using data from 1972 through 1988. Two types of explanatory variables are used: short-term

---

won would go to Congress, and the man who lost would take his place when he was done. Al Sabath won the toss. He came to Congress and stayed for 52 years. I've been on the city council all that time, and now that Al's dead, I figured it was my turn" (Thomas P. O'Neill, Jr., with William Novak, *Man of the House: The Life and Political Memoirs of Speaker Tip O'Neill* [New York: Random House, 1987], 139). The story got somewhat better with age; Sabath actually served for less than forty-six years.

36. This figure is derived from tables 5.1 and 5.2 in David T. Canon, "Actors, Athletes, and Astronauts: Political Amateurism in the United States Congress" (Ph.D. diss., University of Minnesota, 1987), 459–60. The rest of the figures in this paragraph and information from the years 1986–88 are from the data gathered by the author.

37. Interestingly, whether an experienced candidate defeated another experienced candidate in a primary also aids in predicting his or her success. Almost a fourth of the challengers emerging from these hotly contested primaries go on to defeat the incumbent, while only 13.3% of experienced candidates who are unopposed or who defeat an amateur in the primary do so.

(including district- and national-level), which vary from election to election, and structural/institutional, which change more slowly with electoral trends and the evolution of institutional rules. The latter have been largely ignored by previous research, despite the increasing awareness of the importance of institutions and the rules of the game.[38]

Most evident, and probably most important, at least in the statistical sense of "explaining variance," are the district-specific short-term variables. The presence or absence of an incumbent is so critical to challengers' strategic calculations that other considerations are less important in open-seat elections. That is, incumbency is so powerful that experienced challengers will usually run in open-seat races even when all the other relevant factors are not in their favor. For this reason, open-seat elections are treated separately.

National forces also influence whether a politician is willing to run for higher office. As economic conditions worsen and the popularity of the incumbent president declines, experienced candidates in the opposing party are more likely to leave their base office and run for Congress. Jacobson and Kernell add to this plausible claim by asserting that national forces are *primarily* felt through such strategic calculations by politicians and elites (with campaign contributors making similar calculations in allocating their financial resources).[39] Their theory is illustrated in figure 4.1. This theory is presented as an alternative to the typical modeling of the impact of economic conditions on congressional elections, where changes in personal income, inflation, and unemployment affect votes directly.

The evidence Jacobson and Kernell present does not directly test their theory. Instead of testing the link between national aggregate conditions and strategic politicians to see if higher-quality candidates run in times of perceived opportunity, they focus their research at the national level. Without a demonstrable link between aggregate national variables and quality of candidates, the alternative theory of midterm congressional elections is based on indirect evidence. While their theory is intuitively plausible and supported by the national-level data, the district-level link must be established to discover the factors that influence experienced candidates' decisions to run for higher office.[40]

---

38. James March and Johan P. Olsen, "The New Institutionalism: Organizational Factors in Political Life," *American Political Science Review* 78:3 (September 1984): 734–49.

39. Jacobson and Kernell, *Strategy and Choice,* 19–48.

40. See Alan I. Abramowitz, "National Issues, Strategic Politicians, and Voting Behavior in the 1980 and 1982 Congressional Elections," *American Journal of Political Science* 18:4 (November 1984) 710–21, and Richard Born, "Strategic Politicians and Unresponsive Voters," *American Political Science Review* 80:2 (June 1986): 599–612, for challenges

Fig. 4.1   The Jacobson and Kernell Theory

Dependent Variable

Despite my casual use of the term "experience," it is not at all obvious what range of political activity should fall within that definition. The most common specification is any elective office.[41] My dependent variable has four levels: elective office, any public experience (as legislative assistants, state party chairs, and appointed officials), ambitious amateurs (as specified in the previous section), and other amateurs. The categories are the same for the Senate, except that the highest category of experience includes only statewide elective office and House members.

Independent Variables

SHORT TERM—DISTRICT LEVEL

The *incumbent's vote*[42] in the previous elections is the best and most readily available indicator of potential vulnerability. Hinckley and Jacobson both present evidence that incumbents who had close contests in their previous elections face stronger challengers and are defeated with more regularity than their colleagues who enjoyed more comfortable margins.[43] Fenno notes the importance of "discouraging the opposition" through maintaining a strong election record.[44]

---

to the strategic-politicians hypothesis. William T. Bianco, in "Strategic Decisions on Candidacy in U.S. Congressional Districts" (*Legislative Studies Quarterly* 9:2 [May 1984]: 351–64) provides a preliminary test of the direct link between national conditions and candidate experience, and Gary C. Jacobson presents additional evidence at the aggregate level in "Strategic Politicians and the Dynamics of House Elections" (paper presented at the annual meeting of the American Political Science Association, Washington, D.C., 1–4 September 1988).

41. Jacobson, "Strategic Politicians and the Dynamics of House Elections, 1946–1986," 5; Bianco, "Strategic Decisions on Candidacy," 354; see Jonathan S. Krasno and Donald Philip Green, "Preempting Quality Challenges in House Election," *Journal of Politics*, 50:4 (November 1988): 920–36, for a more complex specification of challenger quality.

42. Italicized words are independent variables used in the model of political experience in congressional elections.

43. Hinckley, "House Reelections and Senate Defeats"; Gary C. Jacobson, "The Marginals Never Vanished: Incumbency and Competition in Elections to the U.S. House of Representatives," *American Journal of Political Science* 31:1 (February 1987): 126–41.

44. Richard F. Fenno Jr., *Home Style: House Members in Their Districts* (Boston: Little,

Freshman members are more likely to face formidable challengers. Members of Congress work the constituency with special care in their early or "expansionist" phase, after which they move into a "protectionist" phase. One member interviewed by Fenno said, "The first term is the hardest. If you win election a second time, you're in for quite a while."[45] Challengers hoping to unseat an incumbent are well advised to make their attempt early in the incumbent's career.

Age is an important variable in political careers.[46] I expect a curvilinear relationship between age and previous political experience of challengers for House and Senate elections. Experienced politicians are less likely to be either extremely young or extremely old when they decide to run for Congress. Amateurs, on the other hand, are more likely to be of any age—both young ambitious amateurs who run for the House and older retired insurance agents and lawyers are quite common.[47]

Finally, *scandals* involving incumbents will generally attract experienced challengers. While the number of scandals is relatively large (averaging ten per year over the past decade), timing may mitigate a scandal's impact on recruitment. If a minor scandal occurs early enough in the election cycle, it may be forgotten by the general election; late-breaking scandals may make a dent in the incumbent's vote, but unless a viable candidate who can exploit the issue is already running, the incumbent is likely to emerge unscathed.[48]

Brown, 1978), 13–14. The coefficients are the same (with opposite signs) when the incumbent's vote or the challenger's vote is used. Another variable may be considered an indicator of incumbent vulnerability—a strong primary challenge. This, it turns out, is not a good predictor of incumbent vulnerability in the general election because the strongest challenges to incumbents are in noncompetitive districts.

45. Ibid., 178.

46. Jeff Fishel, *Party and Opposition: Congressional Challengers in American Politics* (New York: David McKay, 1973), 36–38; Paul Brace, "Progressive Ambition in the House: A Probabilistic Approach," *Journal of Politics* 46:2 (May 1984), 559; Schlesinger, *Ambition and Politics,* 184–87.

47. I initially specified a variable for the incumbent's age to tap the "time for a change" notion, which could affect strategic thinking. The best-known example of the previous decade is Elizabeth Holtzman's (D-NY) defeat of Emmanuel Celler (D-NY). Celler held his seat for half a century, but by the end of his career, failing health and inattention to constituents' needs finally made him vulnerable. The variable was not significant. In most cases, a strong challenger will wait until the aging congressman retires, in order to avoid appearing overly ambitious.

48. Jacobson and Kernell, *Strategy and Choice,* 48.

SHORT TERM—NATIONAL LEVEL

Real disposable personal income is often used as a catchall variable for indicating changes in the national economy. Income levels are related to political variables such as presidential popularity, congressional election results, and the strategic calculations of congressional candidates. I will follow Tufte's practice of using percent change in state per capita real income.[49] The percent change in *state unemployment* for the year preceding the decision period is also included. The other national-level variable is a "shock" variable that alters the opportunity structure and strategic calculations for a short period of time. Events of this nature can affect both parties in a similar manner (as during World Wars I and II), or it can have an unequal effect on the parties (as in the early years of the Great Depression, or more recently with the *Watergate scandal*). When both parties are affected, the shock opens up opportunities for amateurs as traditional career paths are underused. Asymmetric shocks have a more complex impact. For example, in the wake of Watergate, the Republicans had a hard time recruiting quality candidates, but the Democrats had a surge of experienced challengers. At the same time, many Democratic amateurs capitalized on the GOP's problems.

STRUCTURAL/INSTITUTIONAL VARIABLES

Schlesinger's work presents many important findings that have not yet been recognized by scholars of congressional elections. Structural variables that can influence the types of candidates who run in congressional elections can be divided into two categories: those that relate to the opportunity structure and those that are institutionally derived. The distinction is based on the rule-governed nature of institutional variables (such as the type of state primary), which are determined by state law and thus are more readily subject to change. Opportunity-structure variables are derived from the aggregation of hundreds of elections over long periods of time. Change comes only incrementally, with the rare exception of major realignments, when career paths are abruptly altered (as demonstrated in chapter 3).

Schlesinger defines the "size" of the opportunity structure as the number of chances available to run for a given office in a specific period

---

49. Edward R. Tufte, "Determinants of the Outcomes of Midterm Congressional Elections," *American Political Science Review* 69:3 (September 1975): 812–26. State income and unemployment data are classified as national-level variables because they have a dominant national component.

(he uses twelve-year intervals). Size can affect the level of political experience in congressional elections in the following way. If a given district has a very low turnover rate, opportunities to run under the most favorable conditions (when the incumbent is not running) are obviously limited. When the incumbent eventually retires, many experienced politicians will be eager to run for the open seat. On the other hand, in a district with high turnover, open-seat elections may see occasional challenges by amateur candidates who may face less formidable opposition in the primary. Furthermore, current officeholders considering a run for an open House seat may value the seat less highly if incumbents are frequently turned out of office. Therefore, I expect an inverse relationship between the size of the opportunity structure and the political experience of congressional challengers in open-seat races. I define *turnover* in the opportunity structure as simply the number of times a seat has changed hands (so to speak) in the past ten years.

The *shape* of the structure of political careers may also have an impact on the experience of candidates in congressional elections. States are more likely to produce experienced candidates when stepping-stones to the House and Senate are clearly defined. In states where career paths are less highly structured, amateurs have greater opportunities to run and win.[50]

The *supply* of potentially experienced candidates for congressional races also serves as a predictor of the quality of the candidate pool. While it would be difficult to specify all the offices in each House district that potentially produce congressional candidates, the proportion of state legislative seats per House district within each party provides a good approximation of the supply of candidates. In districts in which there is a large supply of state legislators, the probability of having one or more experienced challengers is higher.[51] This variable is calculated by multiplying

50. It is not clear whether the shape of the structure has an effect on candidate experience directly (through the strategic calculus that potential candidates employ) or indirectly (by constraining opportunities). That is, candidates may not consciously consider the history of their district's career paths, yet a "rigid path" may preclude the inexperienced from considering running for office (e.g., in the machine-controlled districts of Chicago in past generations). An assumption underlying this variable is that career structures will be relatively homogeneous for all districts within a given state. This is clearly not a valid assumption in every case, but in general, the presence of state laws that govern some career decisions will tend to produce homogeneity within states.

51. There is a plausible counter-argument: the overlap of constituencies promotes movement from lower to higher office. Thus in states with a low supply, such as California, a state legislator may be *more* inclined to seek higher office because his or her district has a considerable shared constituency with the House seat. Brace finds that shared constituencies

the number of state house and senate seats per congressional district in a given year by the proportion of state legislative seats held by a given party. For example, the potential supply of House candidates was 1.49 in California in 1988 for Democrats and 1.13 for Republicans. In smaller states with large state legislatures, such as New Hampshire, the supply variable can be greater than 100.[52] In addition to a simple "supply" argument, this hypothesized relation reflects the relative desirability of the lower office. Holding other aspects of state,legislatures constant, the number of constituents in a district is an approximate indicator of the power or influence the lawmaker has. An assemblyman in New York who represents 120,000 people probably views his or her job as more important than does a legislator in New Hampshire who serves only 2,000. New York lawmakers are less likely, therefore, to want to leave their lower office for the House.[53]

The next set of variables are institutionally determined. This category includes the rules that govern the context of elections and the role of political parties (the competitive position of the party, the type of nominating system, and the party's active involvement in recruiting). The overwhelming consensus of the recent literature that elections can be best understood as individual or even isolated events concludes that parties do not matter. Yet the three areas outlined above may indicate that the epitaph was carved too soon.

---

between House and Senate seats predict whether a representative will seek a Senate seat ("Progressive Ambition in the House," 565). As David Rohde pointed out to me, Brace's argument makes sense at the individual level, but the "supply" argument is more compelling at the aggregate level—i.e., what is the impact of district overlap on a *given* state representative's likelihood of running for the House, compared with the likelihood of *any* state representative emerging as the challenger? The latter question is my concern; thus the supply variable is appropriate. This assertion is empirically supported in the analysis below.

52. This measure assumes a uniform distribution of legislative districts across the state, which is obviously not the case in all states. To cite an extreme example, the partisan distribution of state legislative seats is relatively even in Illinois, but there are few Republicans in the First Congressional District, to say nothing of a state legislator from the GOP. However, solving this problem would involve comparing thousands of state district and U.S. House district lines or making arbitrary assumptions about the partisan distribution of state legislative seats based on demographic patterns.

53. Fowler and McClure make this very argument in *Political Ambition,* chap. 4. However, state legislatures of the same size and partisan split have different patterns of career advancement. Peverill Squire shows that the legislature in New York is a careerist body, while California's is a "springboard" ("Career Opportunities and Membership Stability in Legislatures," *Legislative Studies Quarterly* 13:1 [February 1988]: 75). My supply variable ignores such differences, but my argument would become circular if modified to reflect career opportunities.

The competitive position of the party is the first consideration. Amateurs have more opportunities in weak minority parties within a district because the supply of experienced candidates is limited and those who do hold office will be reluctant to run without good prospects for success. By opposite reasoning, strong challengers are attracted to the majority party in open-seat and incumbent races. In the most secure one-party districts, incumbents frequently run unopposed, and occasionally open seats are uncontested as the majority party's "heir apparent" takes the seat.[54] The party's competitive position is measured here as its *normal vote* in the district.[55]

The *type of nominating system* may influence the type of candidate who runs. Nominating systems that are characterized by active party involvement are more likely to produce experienced candidates than those in which the party is relatively inactive. States with closed primaries and restrictive voting qualifications are more likely to meet these conditions.[56] On the other hand, states that encourage broad participation are likely to favor the amateur candidate.

The party's active role in the recruitment process is probably not as important as the factors outlined above. As V. O. Key notes, although

54. There were thirteen open-seat races from 1972 to 1988 in which a candidate did not have major-party opposition.

55. The original concept of "normal vote" was based on turnout and partisanship (Philip E. Converse, "The Concept of the Normal Vote," in *Elections and the Political Order*, ed. Angus Campbell, Philip Converse, Warren E. Miller, and Donald E. Stokes [New York: John Wiley and Sons, 1966], 9–39; see also Arthur H. Miller, "Normal Vote Analysis: Sensitivity to Change Over Time," *American Journal of Political Science* 23:2 [May 1979]: 406–25). Given the difficulty of collecting partisan identification data by congressional district and the problems associated with approximating partisanship from demographic variables, I use actual election results from past House, Senate, gubernatorial, and presidential elections. Jacobson also recognizes the problems of using partisan identification to measure party strength. He finds that challenger's vote works as well as party registration as a measure of party strength in his model explaining congressional vote (*Money in Congressional Elections*, 39–40). The election data, while not perfect indicators, provide a broad measure of a party's vote-getting potential and probably more closely reflect candidates' actual calculations of their party's strength. This operationalization also follows Jon R. Bond, Cary Covington, and Richard Fleisher, "Explaining Challenger Quality in Congressional Elections," *Journal of Politics* 47:2 (May 1985): 510–29.

56. On the impact of closed primaries, see Edward Keynes, Richard J. Tobin, and Robert Danziger, "Institutional Effects on Elite Recruitment: The Case of State Nominating Systems," *American Politics Quarterly* 7:3 (July 1979): 283–302, and Richard J. Tobin and Edward Keynes, "Institutional Differences in the Recruitment Process: A Four State Study," *American Journal of Political Science* 19:4 (November 1975): 667–81. On restrictive voting rules, see Malcolm E. Jewell and David M. Olson, *American State Political Parties and Elections* (Homewood, Ill.: Dorsey Press, 1982), 126–32.

parties nominate candidates for office, "to assert that party leadership develops candidates is more an attribution of a duty noted in the textbooks than a description of real activity."[57] There is always an adequate supply of "self-starter" experienced candidates for races in which there is a reasonable chance of winning. Furthermore, the influence of party organization in recruitment is very difficult to measure. The recruitment literature usually attacks the problem by directly asking candidates, "Was the party important in your decision to run for office?" or "Were you contacted by your local party leaders?" It is not clear to me that these types of questions will elicit the true importance of parties in the decision to run.[58]

A more reliable approach is to rely on institutionalized practices and actual ability to achieve party goals. One such practice is *party endorsements* of preferred candidates, which vary from states that have no pre-primary endorsements to those that have party convention endorsements as a prerequisite to primaries. My expectation is that parties tend to endorse more experienced candidates. A second variable is Mayhew's measure of *candidate activity* in primary elections.[59] Though Mayhew does not emphasize this conclusion, his measures of candidate activity reflect the ability of strong party organizations to restrict competition (partly through endorsement practices) in primary elections. I expect that candidate activity (the number of candidates in primary elections) will be negatively related to candidate experience.[60]

57. Quoted in Fowler, "Cycle of Defeat," 132; see Paul S. Herrnson, *Party Campaigning in the 1980s* (Cambridge, Mass.: Harvard University Press, 1988), for an alternative view.

58. The problem is exacerbated if the survey is taken in the primary election. Interviews with unsuccessful candidates may give an inaccurate picture of the influence of party in recruitment. As Key and others have pointed out, one function of the party in recruitment is to limit the opposition to the chosen candidate. Thus, if the researcher interviews candidates who have been discouraged by the party, the positive influence of the party would be understated.

59. David R. Mayhew, *Placing Parties in American Politics* (Princeton, N.J.: Princeton University Press, 1986), 335–44.

60. Mayhew gathered his data from some nine thousand House, Senate, and state legislative primaries in the late 1960s and early 1970s. The nature of the political process and the strength of party organizations may have changed by the latter part of the period I am studying. Two considerations lessen this concern: (1) The other institutional variables that are measured every two years are fairly stable, and (2) Mayhew's variables are *relative* measures of candidate activity; thus a general decrease in the role of parties would not significantly affect his measures (see Mayhew, *Placing Parties in American Politics*, 337–44).

Redistricting is the final institutional variable that influences whether congressional candidates will have had previous political experience. Based on the descriptions in *Congressional Quarterly Weekly Reports*, I determined whether an incumbent's chances for reelection were increased, decreased, or unaffected by redistricting. This measure indicates primarily whether the incumbent's district has a significantly different partisan composition than before redistricting. Altered districts that contain a larger proportion of the challenger's partisans are expected to attract more experienced candidates.[61]

The same set of variables cannot be used for Senate races, for obvious reasons. Barring civil war or imperialistic land-grabbing by neighboring states, redistricting is not a relevant consideration. Turnover also will not be used; while some states, such as Iowa, are famous for one-term senators, it is not likely that the turnover rate will be related to the previous political experience of senatorial candidates because Senate seats so infrequently become available. The supply variable is not used in Senate races because there is no single path to the Senate that is comparable to the role played by state legislatures for the House. The normal-vote variable is modified for Senate elections to reflect state rather than district lines.

Some aspects of the decision to run obviously cannot be quantified. Family or personal considerations may often prevent an otherwise qualified candidate from seeking higher office. Or, conversely, issue or group concerns, ideological predispositions, or desire to help the party may lead otherwise strategic politicians to run for office despite unfavorable district-level conditions (economic or otherwise). Despite these limitations, the model captures the most important variables that affect the decision to run; furthermore, I assume such nonstrategic behavior is randomly distributed.

---

61. One possibly important variable has been excluded from the model—ideological differences between incumbents and their districts. Incumbents who are "out of touch" with their districts may be more likely to face experienced challengers. However, given the methodological problems associated with determining an ideological baseline for each district, and given the evidence that most campaigns are candidate-centered, nonideological affairs, I chose to ignore this variable. (See Gerald C. Wright, Jr., and Michael B. Berkman, "Candidates and Policy in United States Senate Elections," *American Political Science Review* 80:2 [June 1986]. 567–88, for an alternative view.) Presidential popularity was included in some initial runs, but the crudeness of the measure limited its usefulness (there are no district-level measures of popularity). By the exclusion of presidential popularity, the remaining estimates are biased by about 5% and the standard errors are virtually unchanged.

Timing the Decision to Run

A key assumption of the strategic-politicians model is that the state of the economy *at the time of the decision to run for office* is more important than the influence of that same variable in the fall. This argument is compelling, but is difficult to put into practice because candidates finalize their campaign plans as early as two years or as late as six months before the general election.[62] In aggregate models, such district-level variation must be ignored; Jacobson and Kernell find that economic data from March, April, and May are better predictors of fall congressional votes than data from the preceding or following quarters.[63] More recently, Jacobson has argued that second-quarter data are the most reliable because this is when most *final* decisions to run must be made.[64] While this is a plausible argument for most districts, many states have already held primary elections by June; therefore it may be more theoretically justifiable to use first-quarter data in aggregate models.[65]

The candidates' complex decision-making processes are not adequately captured by either first- or second-quarter data. The ideal way to test the impact of national economic variables on the behavior of strategic politicians in congressional elections is to examine *projections* of fall economic conditions at the time each individual choice is made to run for Congress. (Republicans contemplating a run for the House in 1988 were not concerned about the last-quarter GNP or real-income figures for 1987. To the extent that economic conditions matter, challengers were trying to guess whether the bottom would fall out of the economy or whether the recovery could be sustained until November.) Unfortunately, the data to conduct this ideal test are not available. Announcements of decisions to run are not made available in any systematic manner, and projections of economic variables are not made at the district or even state level. However, my district-level model has the luxury of estimating the timing of the actual decision to run more accurately than aggregate models that must be confined to a single quarter. I use state-level economic data from the three-month period prior to each state's filing deadline.

---

62. Maisel, *From Obscurity to Oblivion*, 19–22. Also see Clyde Wilcox, "The Timing of Strategic Decisions: Candidacy Decisions in 1982 and 1984," *Legislative Studies Quarterly* 12:4 (November 1987): 565–72.

63. Jacobson and Kernell, *Strategy and Choice*, 68.

64. Jacobson, "Strategic Politicians and the Dynamics of House Elections," 7.

65. In 1984, eleven states held primaries in May or earlier, another twelve had their primaries in June, and another seven states with later primaries had state nominating conventions in June or before.

The Model

My model of political experience in congressional elections can be summarized as shown in figure 4.2. The model is tested with the probit technique due to the ordinal nature of the dependent variable. The equations and specifications of the variables, which all follow from the discussion above, are included in appendix B. The first test was for races from 1972 to 1988 in which a challenger faced an incumbent ($n=2,936$). For open-seat elections the model is slightly different: the incumbent's previous vote margin is replaced with a dummy variable for the party of the previous incumbent (in redistricted districts in 1982 and 1972, estimated vote totals along new district lines are used to specify the variable).[66] An additional structural variable, turnover in the district, is included; freshman status and scandals are dropped from the equation because they involve incumbents.

In Senate elections I only estimate an equation for races involving challenges to incumbents. There were only forty-one open-seat Senate races from 1972 to 1988, which is not enough cases to estimate the model, given the number of independent variables. The results for the Senate equation are not expected to be very strong, for several reasons. First, the maximum likelihood estimates require much larger sample sizes than OLS regressions because of the asymptotic nature of their properties. Second, the nature of Senate elections is less conducive to this analysis because *some* experienced politician is likely to run for a Senate seat even if there is little chance of winning, and the amateurs who run in Senate elections are more likely to be celebrity amateurs who run viable campaigns. Thus, two errors in prediction are more likely in Senate races: amateurs will often run when an experienced candidate is predicted, and experienced politicians will often run in hopeless races.

Results

HOUSE—INCUMBENT RACES

The results of the test of incumbent races confirm most of the expectations established by the theory (see table 4.2).[67] Interpreting results is

---

66. The party dummy variable is used rather than the previous vote margin because the strength of the retired incumbent is not relevant for candidates' decisions to run. The important consideration is the latent strength of the party in the district, which is captured by the normal vote variable and the party dummy.

67. Before discussing the results, two considerations must be mentioned. First, the radically changed nature of congressional elections over the last decade (campaign finance and the emergence of state legislatures as a clear stepping-stone) caution against pooling the

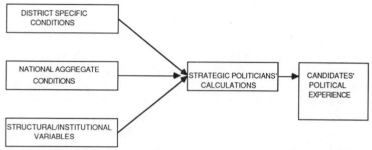

Fig. 4.2   A Model of Candidate Experience in Congressional Elections

more complex for probit analysis than for OLS regression because the impact of any given independent variable on the dependent variable depends on both the value of the independent variable and the values of all the other variables in the model. Furthermore, change in the dependent variable cannot be estimated linearly (as in regression), but must be calculated from the cumulative standard normal probability distribution. (A more extended discussion of how to interpret probit results is presented in appendix B.)

Twenty of the twenty-two variables are in the expected direction, and seventeen are statistically significant (one other almost reaches the .05 level). At the district level, the previous challenger's vote, whether the incumbent was involved in a scandal, and whether the incumbent was serving in his or her first term all significantly affect the experience of the challenger. The incumbent was 11.7% more likely to face an experienced challenger if the previous challenger received 49% of the vote than if he

---

1972–88 elections. However, dividing the data into two periods, 1972–78 and 1980–88, produced very similar results. (See Canon, "Contesting Primaries in Congressional Elections," 10–12, for an additional discussion of this point). Second, violations of the Gauss-Markov assumptions and their implication for probit analysis merit attention. Aldrich and Nelson indicate that little work has been done in this area and that even when effects can be demonstrated, at least in the case of serial correlation, corrections have "proven intractable in the logit and probit cases" (John H. Aldrich and Forrest D. Nelson, *Linear Probability, Logit, and Probit Models* [Beverly Hills: Sage Publications, 1984], 81). Pooled cross-sectional time-series data present a potential nightmare of problems. Such models can be cross-sectionally correlated and heteroskedastic and time-wise autoregressive. Though conclusive tests cannot be conducted, first-order serial correlation does not appear to be a problem; the potential for heteroskedasticity was minimized by using *change* in many variables, rather than absolute levels, and multicollinearity is not a problem as only two of the simple correlations among independent variables are above .25. For a more extended discussion, see Canon, "Actors, Athletes, and Astronauts" (Ph.D. diss.), 286–87.

Table 4.2   Challengers in Incumbent Races (House, 1972–88)

Variable	Estimate	Expected Direction	Significant at	Change in Probability
Constant	−2.57		<.0001	
District-Level Variables				
Previous challenger's vote	0.020	Yes	<.0001	2.22%
Scandal	0.35	Yes	<.0001	13.21
Challenger's age	0.0012	Yes	.17	(1.02)
Challenger's age squared	−0.0001	Yes	.30	
Freshman status	0.21	Yes	.0002	7.76
National-Level Variables				
Watergate—Rep.	0.47	Yes	<.0001	18.16
Watergate—Dem.	−0.28	Yes	<.0001	−8.96
Real income/in	0.043	Yes	.07	(.54)
Real income/out	−0.015	Yes	<.0001	−2.15
Unempl/in	−0.12	Yes	<.0001	−3.97
Unempl/out	0.076	Yes	.001	2.72
Structural/Institutional Variables				
Challenger's normal vote	0.024	Yes	<.0001	3.57
Rep. shape	0.081	Yes	.035	.34
Dem. shape	0.12	Yes	.014	.54
Supply	0.0089	Yes	<.0001	.24
Endorse	−0.027	Yes	.029	−.92
Number primary candidates	−0.22	Yes	<.0001	−.67
Open primary	0.15	No	.017	5.56
Participation/open	−0.082	Yes	.15	(−2.76)
Participation/closed	−0.17	No	.006	−5.67
Redistricting/hurt	1.01	Yes	<.0001	38.84
Redistricting/help	−0.070	Yes	.33	(−2.41)

NOTE: Changes in probability for variables that are not statistically significant are in parentheses.

n = 2,936

MU (1) = 0; MU (2) = .156; MU (3) = .754.

Estimated R^2 = .25.

Distribution of dependent variable: (1) = 1,970; (2) = 138; (3) = 426; (4) = 402.

or she received the average, 32.1%. A scandal in the previous two years had a similar impact on the incumbent's chances of facing an experienced challenger, and freshmen were almost 8% more likely to face an experienced challenger. The expectation that experienced challengers were less likely to be very old or very young was true at one extreme (83% of challengers over sixty-six years of age were amateurs, compared to two-thirds of those under sixty-six, but there was no general relationship between age and experience. The national variables perform very well. The Watergate dummies are strong predictors of candidate experience. The 18.2% change in probability when a Republican is running is large enough to change the predicted value of the dependent variable by one or even two levels. All four of the economic variables are significant, with unemployment having the largest impact. A one-point increase in unemployment increases the chance of an experienced challenger from the party out of power by 2.7%. The opposite holds for the party in power.

The structural variables also perform very well. Redistricting was the most significant variable in the model. An incumbent hurt by redistricting is virtually guaranteed to face an experienced challenger (the probability increases by 38.8%, though an incumbent who benefited from the re-drawn district lines was only marginally more likely to have an amateur challenger (and the coefficient was not statistically significant). The only other variables that do not reach significance, or are not in the expected direction, are those that pertain to voter participation. Counter to my expectations, open primaries and broader participation do not aid amateur candidates. However, political parties *do* exert influence on the levels of experience through their endorsement practices and their ability to restrict the field of candidates, while the rigidity of the opportunity structure and the supply of candidates also prove to be significant predictors, though their impact is quite small.

HOUSE—OPEN SEAT RACES

The results presented in table 4.3 show that patterns of contesting open-seat races are more predictable than indicated by previous research. While Bianco finds that the normal vote of a district was the only significant predictor of candidate experience in open-seat races (only half of his variables have signs in the right direction),[68] this model has fourteen of the eighteen variables with the signs in the right direction, and eight that reach significance (five at the .001 level and three at .10).

The most interesting aspect of the open-seat results is the tremendous difference in the significance of the three types of variables. As was true in earlier studies, the national-level variables—real income, unemployment, and the Watergate dummies—all fail to reach significance, and their coefficients are very small. On the other hand, both of the district-

68. Bianco, "Strategic Decisions on Candidacy," 359–62.

Table 4.3 Challengers in Open-Seat Races (House, 1972–88)

Variable	Estimate	Expected Direction	Significant at	Change in Probability
Constant	−2.28		<.0001	
District-Level Variables				
Open party	0.36	Yes	<.0001	2.82%
Challenger's age	0.10	Yes	<.0001	
Challenger's age squared	−0.0011	Yes	<.0001	−.67
National-Level Variables				
Watergate—Rep.	−0.14	Yes	0.22	(−3.59)
Watergate—Dem.	−0.0017	No	0.44	(−.68)
Real income/in	−0.0087	No	0.27	(−.27)
Real income/out	−0.0063	Yes	0.26	(−.26)
Unempl/in	−0.0023	Yes	0.10	(−.18)
Unempl/out	−0.0005	No	0.37	(−.07)
Structural/Institutional Variables				
Challenger's normal vote	0.015	Yes	<.0001	2.82
Rep. shape	0.11	Yes	.06	(.31)
Dem. shape	−0.039	No	.31	(.21)
Turnover	−0.029	Yes	.31	(.38)
Supply	0.0073	Yes	.0016	.15
Endorse	−0.018	Yes	.24	(.42)
Number primary candidates	−0.094	Yes	.096	(−.16)
Redistricting/hurt	−0.16	Yes	.20	(−3.92)
Redistricting/help	1.16	Yes	<.0001	15.2

NOTE: Changes in probability for variables that are not statistically significant are in parentheses.

n = 771

MU (1) = 0; MU (2) = .531; MU (3) = 1.27.

Estimated R^2 = .21.

Distribution of dependent variable: (1) = 119; (2) = 113; (3) = 198; (4) = 321.

level variables and three of the eight structural/institutional variables are significant and in the right direction. Being of the same party as the previous incumbent also increases the probability of being experienced by almost 3%. The challenger's age is important in open-seat races: very young and very old candidates are less likely to be experienced. The proportion of candidates with elective experience grows from 26.5% in the 25–30 age group, to 39.0% (31–37), to 43.8% (38–44), and peaks at 52.4% in the 45–51 age group. It then falls to 40.0%, 28.4%, and 5.8% in the next three groups. When controlling for all other variables in the model, the probability of having previous experience falls by about 1% for every seven years above or below the global maximum of 45.8 years.

Perhaps even more important is the discovery of the significance of the structural/institutional variables. This whole set of variables has never been used in the study of congressional elections. That they are significant in open-seat races as well as in incumbent contests indicates their theoretical importance. The normal-vote and redistricting variables are most important. A five-point change in the normal vote leads to a 3% increase in the likelihood of an experienced challenger. If a party was hurt by redistricting there is 4% less chance that its eventual nominee will have political experience (though this variable does not quite reach significance). On the other hand, if a party was helped by redistricting it is 15% more likely to field an experienced candidate. The shape of the opportunity structure (for Republicans), the supply of candidates, and the party's ability to restrict the field of candidates are also significant, though their impact on the dependent variable is small.[69] Turnover in a district proved not to be a significant predictor of experience, which is not surprising given the stability of House incumbency (87.8% of the open-seat districts had changed hands only once or not at all in the previous ten years).

SENATE RACES

In the Senate races, fifteen of the eighteen variables are in the expected direction, but only five of them reach statistical significance (see table 4.4). The previous challenger's vote, the normal vote, freshman status, and whether the incumbent was involved in a scandal were all significant predictors of experience. Scandal produces a change in probability of 13%, among the largest for any variable in the House or Senate models. A 4% change in each of the vote variables increases the probability of an experienced challenger by about 2%. Of the structural/institutional variables, only the shape of the Democratic career structure had a significant

69. Two other tests were also conducted. One-party districts were analyzed separately because all the action is in the primaries rather than in the general election. Economic and party-related variables should operate differently in this context, but almost none of the variables were significant. The lack of significant results may be due in part to the small number of cases (only 152 districts had intra-party challenges in one-party districts). Separating the data into presidential and midterm elections yields several interesting results. Scandals are significant only in midterm elections, and presidential popularity is significant in the presidential years, but not in the midterm years, which is consistent with expectations concerning "presidential coattails." The other variables have coefficients that are very similar to those presented in table 4.2.

Table 4.4   Challengers in Incumbent Races (Senate, 1972–88)

Variable	Estimate	Expected Direction	Significant at	Change in Probability
Constant	−2.23			
District-Level Variables				
Previous challenger's vote	0.022	Yes	0.0036 .	1.99%
Scandal	.88	Yes	0.043	12.9
Challenger's age	0.095	Yes	0.11	
Challenger's age squared	−0.00088	Yes	0.091	(−.62)
Freshman status	0.32	Yes	0.054	5.22
National-Level Variables				
Watergate—Rep.	−0.25	Yes	0.24	(−6.46)
Watergate—Dem.	0.16	Yes	0.33	(3.55)
Real income/in	0.0094	Yes	0.33	(.23)
Real income/out	−0.021	Yes	0.31	(−.50)
Unempl/in	−0.050	Yes	0.32	(−1.22)
Unempl/out	0.087	Yes	0.18	(1.98)
Structural/Institutional Variables				
Challenger's normal vote	0.024	Yes	0.013	(2.25)
Rep. shape	0.032	Yes	.37	(.21)
Dem. shape	0.22	Yes	.040	(1.29)
Endorse	0.041	No	.24	(.95)
Number primary candidates	0.099	No	.43	(.69)
Open primary	−0.20	Yes	.13	(−5.06)
Participation/open	0.11	No	.31	(2.37)
Participation/closed	0.02	Yes	.46	.54

NOTE: Changes in probability for variables that are not statistically significant are in parentheses.
n = 227
MU (1) = 0; MU (2) = .320; MU (3) = 1.46.
Estimated R^2 = .19.
Distribution of dependent variable: (1) = 43; (2) = 20; (3) = 89; (4) = 75.

impact. Open primaries appear to be more likely to produce inexperienced candidates, though the variable just failed to reach statistical significance. The age of experienced challengers reaches a global maximum at 54.2 years (challengers are slightly less likely to have experience above or below this age; the variable is significant at the .10 level). Overall, the model works moderately well in Senate races. The estimated R^2 is only .19 and the model correctly predicts less than half of the cases. Some of the relationships may have been expected to be stronger, given that measurement error is less evident in the Senate model (the economic variables are measured at the state level).

In general, the results confirm many of the expectations generated by my theory of ambition and the strategic-politicians model.[70] The structural variables are a significant contribution to our understanding of the factors that frame the context of the decision to run for office. While these findings do not contradict the characterization of congressional elections as entrepreneurial contests between individual politicians, they do emphasize the importance of the *context* of choice and the rules of the game. Not all candidates are similarly situated, and the varying contexts and rules are crucial in determining what types of candidates will run for the House and for the Senate.

Experienced Challengers and Election Outcomes

Ultimately, the significance of whether an amateur or an experienced candidate runs in a congressional election hinges on the outcome of the race. Common sense dictates that experienced candidates should be more successful. Survey research indicates that voters value political experience in candidates for public office. Of thirty desirable qualities for political candidates ranked in various polls, ranging from youth and good health to courage and intelligence, political experience was the only one consistently mentioned as the "most important characteristic."[71]

Journalists, in their coverage of political campaigns, also focus on the candidates' experience. In their excellent study of the print media's coverage of the 1978 congressional elections, Clarke and Evans find that incumbents receive roughly twelve times as much coverage of their political attributes as challengers.[72] This difference cannot be explained by the process of reporting; the effort expended in covering the races was similar for both sides. Clarke and Evans say:

70. I attempted a more direct test of the strategic-politicians hypothesis by coding the dependent variable to reflect candidates who had *current* elective experience. Those politicians would behave more strategically than others because they usually have to give up their current office to run for higher office (state senators or others at the midpoint of a four-year term are the exception). The estimated coefficients for the independent variables were almost identical given the various specifications of the dependent variable, somewhat contrary to expectations.

71. David A. Leuthold, *Electioneering in a Democracy* (New York: John Wiley and Sons, 1968), 24–25.

72. Peter Clarke and Susan Evans, *Covering Campaigns: Journalism in Congressional Elections* (Stanford, Cal.: Stanford University Press, 1983), 61.

Reporters work hard, but fail to find much to write about on the political background of challengers. Why? The answer is probably simple, if depressing: challengers usually do not have the raw material—past experience in office, legislative skills, constituent services. House members, on the other hand, have an almost endless reservoir to tap.[73]

Though they do not address this question in their study, their evidence indicates that challengers who *do* have substantial experience would be less disadvantaged in media coverage because reporters would have something to cover. Thus, experienced challengers should be expected to do better than their amateur counterparts partly because voters value their experience and reporters give them more media attention.

Aggregate-level results provide some evidence for the link between experience and votes. On the average, experienced challengers in the years 1972–78 received 7% more of the two-party vote than inexperienced candidates.[74] Name recognition is the important intervening variable between the micro- and macro-level findings: politically experienced candidates should be stronger because they enjoy an existing vote base that leads to higher name recognition. Green and Krasno conclude that a highly experienced challenger receives 10% more of the vote than a complete amateur, even after controlling for the candidates' relative ability to raise campaign money.[75] Despite this evidence and the commonsense notion that experienced candidates are stronger than inexperienced challengers, parts of the picture remain unclear. Born presents a strong challenge to the strategic-politicians theory by finding little evidence that the presence of experienced politicians helps explain election outcomes at either the aggregate or the individual level.[76] The 1978 Center for Political Studies survey showed an unprecedented weakness in name recognition for congressional challengers, despite a higher proportion of candidates in the sample having had previous political experience (21.3%) than those who were not in the sample (18.8%), because of their relative inability to raise money.[77]

73. Ibid., 61—62.

74. Jacobson and Kernell, *Strategy and Choice*, 31.

75. Donald P. Green and Jonathan S. Krasno, "Salvation for the Spendthrift Incumbent: Reestimating the Effects of Campaign Spending in House Elections," *American Journal of Political Science* 32:4 (November 1988): 900. This finding contradicts Jacobson's earlier assertion that previous experience has only indirect effects on candidate recall through campaign expenditures (*Money in Congressional Elections*, 147–52).

76. Born, "Strategic Politicians and Unresponsive Voters."

77. In this study I have put aside considerations of campaign spending—the other half of the equation in the Jacobson/Kernell model—because I am concerned with determining the

For these reasons it is necessary to examine more closely the link between previous experience and election outcomes. The question I attempt
to answer here is whether experienced candidates fare better in elections,
independent of the effects of their strategic calculations. In other words,
they may do better because of their self-selection into races in which they
should be expected to receive a higher percentage of the vote. Is it reasonable to expect that if more experienced challengers ran, that in itself
would create more close elections and, ultimately, more incumbent
defeats?

Simple vote totals and controls for other influences on the vote indicate
that previous political experience has an independent impact on congressional elections. The vote totals without controlling for factors that would
increase the challenger's vote replicate the data presented by Jacobson.[78]
Challengers with elective experience from 1974 to 1984 received almost
9% more of the vote (41.0% compared to 32.3%; these totals exclude the
1980 election because of a coding problem due to redistricting). When
controlling for normal vote, scandal, and redistricting, the difference between inexperienced and experienced candidates diminishes, but is still
significant. As expected, both amateurs and experienced candidates improve their vote margins when district conditions are in their favor. Amateurs in these races fare relatively better, thus closing the gap, but challengers with previous elective office still fare 5.7% better than amateurs.

The same result holds when open-seat cases are examined. With no
controls, the difference between experienced and inexperienced candidates is 8.4%. With the controls, this difference shrinks to 5.9%. With
the strongest candidates running in open-seat races, it is heartening that
the differences persist even when experienced candidates are compared to
the most serious (and probably best funded) of the amateur candidates.[79]
These results confirm the wisdom of the Republican National Committee's strategy of increasing their power at the state legislative level to
build a strong pool of experienced candidates that someday may end the
Republicans' seemingly permanent minority status in the House.

---

independent importance of political experience in the electoral arena. Including money
makes the task more complicated because of the reciprocal effects between experience and
money (Jacobson, *Money in Congressional Elections,* 49–50 and chap. 5; Green and
Krasno, "Salvation for the Spendthrift Incumbent").

78. Jacobson, *Politics of Congressional Elections,* 1st ed., 39.

79. These results come from tables 4.16 and 4.17 in Canon, "Actors, Athletes, and Astronauts" (Ph.D. diss.), 457–58. If the typology of amateurism is applied to outcomes, the
results are as expected. Ambitious amateurs and politicians with nonelective experience
receive comparable vote totals, while other amateurs (policy and hopeless) receive less and
elected politicians receive more.

Conclusion

It is clear that amateurs face very different opportunities in congressional elections than do experienced candidates. When experienced candidates choose to run, amateurs generally are pushed from the electoral process. The model of the decision to run for office confirms that experienced politicians are sensitive to district and national conditions when they choose to run. The combination of strategic behavior by experienced politicians and the pushing-out rule forces amateurs into less desirable races. Yet amateurs are not elected only in unexpected upsets of incumbents. Almost a fourth of open-seat House elections (but only 5% of open-seat Senate races) are won by amateurs.

The challenge to a theory of ambition and political careers is to help predict these exceptions. I made a step in that direction in this chapter by distinguishing ambitious amateurs from other amateurs on the basis of their behavior in previous elections, their risk-taking in the primary, and their celebrity status. The test of the theory confirms its basic utility (60% of the amateur general-election winners were correctly predicted), but also indicates room for additional improvement. The first revision would be to specify the baseline as uncontested races rather than as races in which amateurs run. The second improvement would involve enhancing the theory's ability to predict when amateurs will run if the likelihood of success is high.

Future work should also more closely examine the link between political realignments and changing career structures. The multivariate model presented here is insufficient for discovering the basis of career-path changes that occur in realignments, because these changes are rooted in the complex interaction between strategic behavior and changing issue cleavages. More detailed examination of policy amateurs and their successful campaigns during periods of electoral upheaval may prove fruitful. Unconstrained by the baggage of previous policy positions and unhindered by the strategic considerations of perpetuating a political career, amateurs may be better positioned to ride into office on the crest of partisan waves.

Five

Amateurs in Congress

In chapter 1 I mentioned the media's fascination with celebrity candidates. Fred Grandy (of TV's "Love Boat"), the Kennedys (Kathleen Townsend and Joe), Tom McMillen (of the NBA Washington Bullets), and Ben Jones (of TV's "Dukes of Hazzard") received top billing in the 1986 and 1988 congressional elections. At the local level, Clint Eastwood's election as mayor of Carmel, California, generated much attention, including an inspired series in Garry Trudeau's comic strip, "Doonesbury." At the other end of the political career ladder, Ronald Reagan's acting career provided the basis for many insights and anecdotes during his eight years as governor of California.[1]

Occasionally the fascination with celebrities takes on a more analytic quality as observers wonder about the link between previous careers and behavior. Michael Barone noted that baseball's "Vinegar Bend" Mizell (R-NC), decathlon champ Bob Mathias (R-CA), and NFL quarterback Jack Kemp (R-NY), all elected between 1966 and 1970, were Richard Nixon's "team players," implying a connection between their sports-based loyalties and their political behavior.[2] A decade later, Barone wondered about the political future of former talk-show host Robert K. Dornan (R-CA) after his reelection to the House in 1984: "The interesting question is whether this politician who made his earlier political and media career literally sounding off is now prepared to be a constructive legislator, or will he again be more of a zealot or even zany."[3]

1. Garry Wills, *Reagan's America: Innocents at Home* (Garden City, N.Y.: Doubleday, 1987).

2. Michael Barone, Grant Ujifusa, and Douglas Matthews, *The Almanac of American Politics, 1974* (New York: E. P. Dutton, 1973), 750.

3. Michael Barone and Grant Ujifusa, *The Almanac of American Politics, 1986* (Washington, D.C.: Barone and Co., 1985), 190. The following incident indicates the latter was more likely. "His first months back in office were not reassuring. At a conservative conference Dornan called New York Democrat Thomas Downey a 'draft-dodging wimp'; Dornan was apparently still angry that Downey had spoken against his appointment to an arms control position in the administration in 1983. When Downey approached him on the

To cite one of many other examples, Jeremiah Denton (R-AL), an ama-teur, had to convince his colleagues that he was "not a nut" after charging that a peace group founded by Betty Bumpers, wife of Arkansas senator Dale Bumpers, was guided by Communists. More outrageous to many senators was Denton's amendment to a criminal-code revision in the Ninety-seventh Congress to ensure immunity from prosecution for raping a spouse. In proposing the amendment he said, slapping his hand on the committee table, "Damn it, when you get married, you kind of expect you're going to get a little sex."[4]

Common wisdom holds that politicians who have been seasoned at lower levels of office are less likely to be so extreme in their behavior. For example, Augustus Hawkins, a Democrat, served for twenty-eight years in the California State Assembly, including a few terms as speaker, before being elected to the House. "Such experience does not usually produce verbal militance," Barone notes, "and Hawkins is known as one of the quieter members of the Congressional Black Caucus."[5]

Observations of the relative extremism of some amateurs are occasion-ally translated into normative statements about the importance of pre-vious political experience. Earlier I cited Robert Dahl's admonition that politicians require training as much as carpenters or doctors do. Charles Jacob noted that inexperience could be a problem in the House, and George Will lays some of the blame for the recent "crisis" in the Senate on the shoulders of amateurs.[6]

---

floor of the House, Dornan grabbed the New Yorker by the necktie; if it wasn't a fist-fight, much less a duel of old, it was still the closest thing to a congressional tussle Washington has seen in a few years."

4. Alan Ehrenhalt, *Politics in America: Members of Congress in Washington and at Home, 1984* (Washington, D.C.: Congressional Quarterly Press, 1983), 12.

5. Barone, Ujifusa, and Matthews, *Almanac of American Politics, 1974*, 102.

6. Charles E. Jacob, "The Congressional Elections," in *The Election of 1984: Reports and Interpretations,* ed. Marlene M. Pomper (Chatham, N.J.: Chatham House Publishers, 1985), 120–21; Brinkley, "This Week with David Brinkley," transcript of show #155, 14 October 1984 (guests: Richard Wirthlin, James Johnson, Sen. Paul Laxalt; interviewers: David Brinkley, Sam Donaldson, George Will), 13. The U.S. Congress is almost always "in crisis" according to some scholar or journalist, but in recent years these complaints have been more frequent than at any time since the widespread discontent that led to the reforms of the mid 1970s. Thomas Eagleton (D-MO), who retired at the end of the Ninety-ninth Congress, said the Senate was in a "state of incipient anarchy" and that the rules of un-limited debate have led to "unbridled chaos." Warren Rudman (R-NH) chimed in, calling the situation "anarchy period—you can leave off the incipient" (*Washington Post,* 9 De-cember 1985, A15). The confrontation between Republicans and Democrats early in 1988 over campaign finance reform, in which Majority Leader Robert Byrd issued warrants of arrest for Republican senators who were trying to avoid quorum calls, is more evidence of the increasing frustration.

Is amateurism really a problem? Most amateurs obviously are not zealots or zany, but are the concerns of Dahl, Jacob, and others well founded? In this chapter, I will determine whether there are differences between amateurs and politicians who are elected to Congress with some previous political experience, and whether distinctions among amateurs based on typology of amateurism can explain differences in congressional behavior.

Member Goals and Political Behavior

In the previous two chapters, the distinctive role of the amateur was self-evident. A discussion of political career structures must consider the point at which an individual begins his or her career. Differences between the strategic positions of amateurs and experienced candidates in electoral politics are also clear: a bad decision may end a political career for the latter, while the former may suffer little cost or may even benefit from a losing effort.

That differences extend to institutional behavior is less obvious. Indeed, the dominant theoretical perspective in studying legislative behavior in the last decade and a half—that of purposive behavior—assumes that *all* members of Congress are dominated by the desire for reelection. Why are amateurs distinctive? I have argued that the goals held by those who have chosen politics as their vocation—experienced politicians and ambitious amateurs—are likely to differ from the goals of those who have not.

The goals held by politicians have been central to congressional research since Mayhew's analysis of the links among political careers, institutional structures, and policy outcomes through the "electoral connection." Mayhew describes Congress as an institution ideally suited to meet congressmen's electoral needs. The combination of growing personal staffs and constituency service, forgiving leadership, and specialization in committees allows members to transform their individual pieces of "turf" into permanent real estate in their single-minded pursuit of the reelectoral goal.[7]

Fenno's study of committees in Congress expanded the range of individuals' goals beyond reelection to include power within the body and making good public policy. Fenno suggests that all members of Congress probably hold a mix of all three goals and that goals evolve throughout the progression of a legislative career.[8] Dodd develops this point, arguing

7. David R. Mayhew, *Congress: The Electoral Connection* (New Haven: Yale University Press, 1974), 81–180.

that goals are reflected in predictable "stages of mastery."[9] "To become successful," Dodd says, "a legislator must exercise mastery of four types of resources: those associated with reelection, policy development, institutional influence, and organizational control."[10] The attainment of these stages is determined by the nature of the organizational resources at the member's disposal.

These studies provide a solid basis for understanding legislative behavior. Committee preferences, attempts to gain leadership positions, effort expended on constituency service, and positions on roll call votes are all seen as goal-directed.[11] Yet scant attention has been given to explaining *why* members hold different mixes of goals. My theory of political ambition and careers provides some clues. I assume that experienced politicians' and ambitious amateurs' goals progress in the patterned hierarchy described by Dodd, while policy amateurs' and hopeless amateurs' goals do not. Hopeless amateurs spend their entire careers attempting to transform their decidedly marginal districts into safe seats; thus they will be consumed by constituency goals.[12] Policy amateurs will pursue their policy goals upon entering the House, without "mastering the stage" of electoral security. These goals should have an observable impact on behavior; I assume that the manner in which a member is elected reveals a great deal about the way he or she will behave in office. I will test the propositions that inexperienced members will have different careers with-

8. The three goals are outlined in Richard F. Fenno, Jr., *Congressmen in Committees* (Boston: Little, Brown, 1973), 1, and the progression of goals is discussed in Richard F. Fenno, Jr., *Home Style: House Members in Their Districts* (Boston: Little, Brown, 1978), chap. 6.

9. Lawrence C. Dodd, "Congress and the Quest for Power," in *Congress Reconsidered,* ed. Lawrence C. Dodd and Bruce I. Oppenheimer (Washington, D.C.: Congressional Quarterly Press, 1977), 269–307; Lawrence C. Dodd, "The Cycles of Legislative Change: Building a Dynamic Theory," in *Political Science: The Science of Politics,* ed. Herbert F. Weisberg (New York: Agathon Press, 1986), 82–104.

10. Dodd, "Cycles of Legislative Change," 87.

11. The most recent work in the purposive tradition adds complexity and flexibility to assumptions concerning member goals (Richard L. Hall, "Participation and Purpose in Committee Decision Making," *American Political Science Review* 81:1 [March 1987]: 105–27; Steven S. Smith's work-in-progress on policy leadership). In an adaptation of Kingdon's analysis of voting decisions (John W. Kingdon, *Congressmen's Voting Decisions* [New York: Harper and Row, 1981]), Hall argues that members hold different goals depending on the question at hand.

12. I prefer the term "constituency goals" to "reelection goals." As Steven S. Smith and Christopher J. Deering point out, "many members mention a richer set of constituency-oriented motivations than the reelection label suggests" (*Committees in Congress* [Washington, D.C.: Congressional Quarterly Press, 1984], 85).

in the body, that policy amateurs will be more ideologically extreme, and that ambitious amateurs will have higher levels of participation in legislative activity than policy and hopeless amateurs. I will also discuss the two competing theories outlined in chapter 2—socialization theory and recruitment theory—as alternative frameworks for understanding behavior.

The Legislative Career in the House and Senate

Early in the 1960s, congressional scholars discovered the "congressional career" as a key variable in explaining institutional structures and change. The first change noted in political careers was the transition from politics as an avocation to the congressional careers of the twentieth century, which are as stable as the professions of law, medicine, and business. This shift is indicated by a transition from limited tenure, high turnover, and less structured career paths to longer but less flexible political careers.[13]

Just as the topic of legislative careers was beginning to receive more attention, important aspects of careers changed. As marginal districts vanished, scholars attempted to sort out the causes and consequences of the incumbency advantage. Voluntary retirements from the House in the 1970s indicated another significant change in congressional careers.[14]

---

13. Nelson W. Polsby, "Institutionalization of the U.S. House of Representatives," *American Political Science Review* 62:1 (March 1968); 144–69, and H. Douglas Price, "Congress and the Evolution of Legislative 'Professionalism,' " in *Congress in Change: Evolution and Reform* (New York: Praeger Publishers, 1975), 2–23. "Less flexible" refers to the fact, noted in chapter 1, that career structures are more unidirectional and less permeable than they were in the nineteenth century. The practices of rotation (Samuel Kernell, "Toward Understanding Nineteenth Century Congressional Careers: Ambition, Competition, and Rotation," *American Journal of Political Science* 21:4 [November 1977]: 669–93) and moving in both directions in the career structure (the most dramatic example of being John Quincy Adams's sixteen years in the House after his tenure as president) do not exist today.

14. Several of the central articles on vanishing marginals are David R. Mayhew, "Congressional Elections: The Case of the Vanishing Marginals," *Polity* 6:3 (Fall 1974): 295–317; Edward R. Tufte, "The Relationship Between Seats and Votes in Two-Party Systems," *American Political Science Review* 67:3 (September 1973): 540–54; John Ferejohn, "On the Decline of Competition in Congressional Elections," *American Political Science Review* 71:1 (March 1977): 166–76; Morris P. Fiorina, "The Case of the Vanishing Marginals: The Bureaucracy Did It," *American Political Science Review* 71:1 (March 1977): 177–81; and Gary C. Jacobson, "The Marginals Never Vanished: Incumbency and Competition in Elections to the U.S. House of Representatives," *American Journal of Political Science* 31:1 (February 1987): 126–41. In the latter, Jacobson indicates that between 1952 and 1982, incumbency safety did not really increase; thus marginal districts, properly defined, never really vanished. The 1984–88 elections, in which 97.5% of incumbents were re-

The massive reforms of the 1970s prompted others to explain how this could happen in an institution that had seemed so stable.[15] Attention also turned to changing careers within the institution: Smith and Deering examined the changing role of committees and Barbara Sinclair and I each looked at leadership.[16] Some see the legislative career as central in the process of institutional change.[17]

None of these scholars has examined the underlying patterns of the trends in political careers. The political career is discussed in undifferentiated terms: all members face the same set of institutional structures and demands. This work does not provide any reason to assume that a subset of members behaves differently as a group.[18] I will examine differences between amateurs and experienced politicians and among amateurs by looking at three aspects of the legislative career: tenure, legislative leadership positions, and committee assignments.

elected, may force yet another revision of this analysis. See Monica Brauer and John R. Hibbing, "Which Incumbents Lose in House Elections: A Response to Jacobson's 'The Marginals Never Vanished,' " *American Journal of Political Science* 33:1 (February 1989): 262–71, for an early reassessment. On voluntary retirement, see Stephen E. Frantzich, "Opting Out: Retirement from the House of Representatives, 1966–1974," *American Politics Quarterly* 6 (1978): 251–76; and John R. Hibbing, "Voluntary Retirement from the U.S. House: Who Quits?" *American Journal of Political Science* 26:3 (August 1982): 467– 83.

15. Norman J. Ornstein, "Causes and Consequences of Congressional Change: Subcommittee Reforms in the House of Representatives, 1970–73," in *Congress in Change: Evolution and Reform,* ed. Norman J. Ornstein (New York: Praeger Publishers, 1975), 88– 114; Lawrence C. Dodd and Bruce I. Oppenheimer, "The House in Transition: Change and Consolidation," in *Congress Reconsidered,* 2d ed., ed. Lawrence C. Dodd and Bruce I. Oppenheimer (Washington, D.C.: Congressional Quarterly Press, 1981), 31–61; James L. Sundquist, *The Decline and Resurgence of Congress* (Washington, D.C.: The Brookings Institution, 1981). More recently, Dodd and Oppenheimer were concerned that congressional scholars did not foresee the new centralization in Congress, indicating yet again the difficulty posed by analyzing a moving target (Lawrence C. Dodd and Bruce I. Oppenheimer, "The New Congress: Fluidity and Oscillation," in *Congress Reconsidered,* 4th ed., ed. Lawrence C. Dodd and Bruce I. Oppenheimer [Washington, D.C.: Congressional Quarterly Press, 1989], 443–49).

16. Smith and Deering, *Committees in Congress;* David T. Canon, "The Institutionalization of Leadership in the United States Congress," *Legislative Studies Quarterly* 14:3 (August 1989): 415–43; Barbara Sinclair, *Majority Leadership in the U.S. House* (Baltimore: Johns Hopkins University Press, 1983).

17. Dodd, "Congress and the Quest for Power" and "Cycles of Legislative Change"; Joseph Cooper and William West, "The Congressional Career in the 1970s," in *Congress Reconsidered,* 2d ed., 83–106; Burdett A. Loomis, "Congressional Careers and Party Leadership in the Contemporary House of Representatives," *American Journal of Political Science* 28:1 (February 1984): 180–202.

18. The exception is Loomis's piece on leadership ("Congressional Careers and Party Leadership").

Tenure in Congress

Most members of Congress come to Washington with the expectation of staying as long as the voters permit. The dominance of the reelectoral goal cannot be denied. (Occasionally an amateur such as Mick Staton [D-WV], described earlier, does not want to make a career in the House, but this is clearly the exception.) Yet several points lead to the expectation that amateurs may have shorter careers than experienced politicians: (1) A disproportionate number of amateurs are elected in landslide elections in which a larger number of candidates from their party are swept into office. In many cases there is a "corrective election" two years later as the partisan tide recedes; 1966 and 1982 are prime examples of this tendency.[19] (2) Amateurs may have a higher incidence of voluntary retirement. (3) An amateur may not easily make the transition to life as a congressman, which may translate into ineffectiveness and voter dissatisfaction. However, to make conclusive statements about the relationship between amateurism and tenure, one must control for the competitiveness of the district, the trend toward longer careers, and the age of the congressman when elected.[20] I will present the data on tenure for all amateurs and experienced candidates from 1930 to 1984 for the House and from 1913 to 1984 for the Senate. The typology of amateurism will be used for House members elected from 1972 to 1984.

TENURE IN THE HOUSE

Amateurs do have shorter careers in the House. They serve an average of 7.99 years, while experienced members serve 8.70 years on average (the difference is significant at the .02 level).[21]

19. The 1974 Watergate class was an exception. Forty-eight of the forty-nine Democrats who defeated Republican incumbents in 1974 were reelected in 1976.

20. Age may be considered an explanation for differences between amateurs' and experienced members' tenures (arguing that an amateur's age upon election is partly a product of the place of amateurs in the career structure and of their strategic calculations), or it may be considered an external factor that must be controlled. I will discuss it as a control.

21. These figures include members who are currently serving. If those members are excluded, the difference between amateurs and experienced House members is not significant. In the Ninety-ninth Congress, experienced members had served an average of 10.54 years, while amateurs had been in office only 8.71 years on average. (It is interesting to note that these figures are approximately two years and one year higher, respectively, than the means of members who served between 1930 and 1984, even though the averages will increase as the current officeholders finish their careers.) The inclusion of the Ninety-ninth Congress with members who were already defeated or had retired is based on the assumption that the number of amateurs elected in the recent decade is not greater than in the previous periods

Which of the factors mentioned above account for this difference? First, the corrective elections that follow landslides produce large differences in the tenures of members of opposing parties. Amateurs are disproportionately affected by this pattern. Amateurs who are swept into office in landslide elections are also swept back out more quickly in subsequent elections than either their counterparts in the other party or experienced candidates of the same party. In 1946, for example, when Republicans made a net gain of fifty-six House seats, twenty-seven amateur Republicans and ten amateur Democrats were elected to the House. The careers of the Democratic amateurs averaged 17.7 years, while the twenty-seven Republicans were defeated (or retired) in an average of 4.0 years! In 1948, the Democrats charged back, gaining the most seats of any post–World War II congressional election (seventy-five). Twenty-eight amateurs were elected in 1948—twenty-five Democrats and only three Republicans. As expected, the Democrats were not as able to hold on to their seats through the 1950s, averaging 7.3 years in office compared with 19.3 years for the Republicans. Experienced politicians followed the same pattern in 1946, but they are more insulated from the effects of corrective elections than amateurs (experienced politicians' average length of service was 7.0 years for the fifty-seven Republicans and 12.1 years for the thirty-two Democrats). The figures for 1958, 1966, and 1974 follow the pattern of shorter tenure for the landslide winners, with amateurs disproportionately feeling the corrective effect, although the differences are not as dramatic as those in 1946 and 1948. Many hopeless amateurs are affected by this pattern.[22]

The expectation that amateurs may voluntarily retire more frequently than experienced politicians is based on the assumption that the latter may be more committed to a political career, through what Black calls "investment transferability."[23] The higher the rise in the structure, the

---

(which is empirically verified: approximately 23% of the House members in the Ninety-ninth Congress were amateurs, which is nearly identical to the 1930–84 average). In the Senate, the assumption of the proportional election of amateurs in the recent decade is not valid; therefore members currently serving are treated separately.

22. One interesting exception to this rule is that in realigning elections, as opposed to isolated elections with large partisan tides, the correction factor is not as prevalent because formerly marginal districts move permanently into the majority party's control. Furthermore, there are no significant differences between the average tenures of amateurs and experienced candidates in realigning elections (the figures are an identical 7.2 years for both amateur and experienced Democrats, 8.6 years for amateur Republicans, and 8.1 years for experienced Republicans in the 1930–36 elections).

23. Gordon Black, "A Theory of Political Ambition, Career Choices and the Role of Structural Incentives," *American Political Science Review* 66:1 (March 1972): 155–59.

greater the sunk cost, and thus the greater the desire to stay or try for higher office. Amateurs do not have as extensive an investment, so they may find it easier to change careers once again and leave politics; hence the link to shorter tenure in office.[24] There is some evidence for this hypothesis. Fewer amateur House members retire voluntarily (20.1%, compared with 24.0% of all experienced House members). However, marginally more House members who had political experience prior to their service in the House are elected to the Senate (5.1%, compared with 4.1% of the amateurs), indicating that those who have invested in a political career are more likely to continue in politics.[25]

Amateurs' ineffectiveness is difficult to isolate as a cause of defeat, but anecdotal evidence is plentiful. One of the more celebrated recent examples was John LeBoutillier's defeat after only one term in New York's Sixth District in 1982. Ehrenhalt reports, "LeBoutillier's abrasive outspokenness offended congressional colleagues in both parties. Among his more pungent comments were his descriptions of Sen. Charles Percy (R-IL) as a 'wimp' and Speaker Thomas P. O'Neill Jr., as 'big, fat and out of control.' "[26] Robert Mrazek used LeBoutillier's personality as a campaign issue, claiming that his "obnoxious behavior rendered him ineffective." Bella Abzug (D-NY) may have been in a class of her own in the outspokenness department. Barone describes her reputation in the House:

> Once in Congress, Abzug jarred the sensibilities of aging congressmen even more than [William F.] Ryan ten years earlier. When once requested by Doorkeeper Fishbait Miller to remove her hat, Bella reportedly told him to perform an impossible act. Some, including the writers of Nader's Congress Project, said that her support of any measure would cost it 20 or 30 votes.[27]

24. Deceased Congressmen's widows, who are mostly amateurs, were expected to have the weakest attachment to a career in politics. However, their careers are not statistically distinguishable from those of the body as a whole. Some, such as Lindy Boggs (D-LA, Hale Boggs's widow), have established safe seats and appear to be headed for lengthy and productive careers in the House.

25. These figures include only House members who completed their careers in the Ninety-eighth Congress or earlier. Other limited evidence for the "sunk costs" hypothesis is revealed in the previous political careers of ladder climbers. House members who are subsequently elected to the Senate hold 1.47 prior public offices on average, compared with 1.34 for those who finish their careers in the House (difference is significant at the .09 level), but their pre-House careers are, on average, about one year shorter, indicating their progressive ambition.

26. Ehrenhalt, *Politics in America, 1984,* 1017.

27. Barone, Ujifusa, and Matthews, *Almanac of American Politics, 1974,* 696–97. However, Abzug did not suffer electoral consequences because she came from a safe seat.

A crude test based on the proportion of amateurs defeated after one term in non–corrective-election years indicates that the ineffectiveness of amateurs is not a general explanation for their shorter tenure.

The competitiveness of the district, changes in congressional careers, and the age of the candidate are competing explanatory factors that must be considered. If amateurs are disproportionately elected in competitive districts, their shorter careers may be a function of the high natural turnover in their districts, rather than of anything intrinsic to the nature of amateurism.[28] The normal vote (as defined in chapter 4) in each district from 1972 to 1984 shows that amateurs are not elected in more competitive districts. In races in which an incumbent was defeated, candidates with previous elective experience ran in districts only slightly more favorably disposed to their party (a normal vote of 46.6%, compared with 44% for those without elective experience). In open-seat races, ambitious amateurs are elected from the *least* competitive districts. None of the differences among the various categories is statistically significant.

Since the nineteenth century, the length of the congressional career has increased dramatically. If amateurs were elected at disproportionate levels when careers were shorter, then perhaps the present negative relationship between amateurism and tenure is due to this secular trend toward longer careers. This is not the case, for two reasons. First, the correlation between tenure and year of election in the period of this study is .02. Second, as previously noted, the rate at which amateurs are elected to the House follows a cyclical rather than secular trend.[29]

The relationship between previous experience and tenure becomes stronger when the candidate's age is controlled. Overall, the mean age of amateurs upon election is 44.0 years; of experienced members, 46.6 years. Of the 220 House members elected between 1930 and 1984 who were older than sixty, only 15.9% were amateurs. This is significantly less than the 24.2% of all members who are amateurs. A multiple regression, with tenure in the House as the dependent variable and previous experience, age, and a year elected (to capture any secular change in House service), shows the significance of the relative age of experienced

28. One could argue that running in more competitive races is a characteristic of amateurs forced upon them by the pushing-out rule. Indeed, hopeless amateurs are those who are unexpectedly elected from such districts. But if amateurs *generally* must run in more competitive races, then differences in tenure may be entirely attributable to this point.

29. Nonetheless, to test for a possible relationship, paired comparisons between amateurs and experienced members were made for each year from 1930 to 1984. Both the signs and magnitudes of the differences are fairly randomly distributed. For example, the amateur class of 1934 had the third longest tenure of any class (11.62 years), while the 1932 class had the second shortest (5.54 years).

House members. Previous political experience adds .86 years to one's expected stay in the House, compared with only .71 years in the simple bivariate relationship ($t=2.32$). Age is in the expected direction; a candidate elected at age sixty can expect to serve three and a half years less than a thirty-year-old beginning a career in the House ($t=7.8$).

To this point I have made no distinctions among amateurs because the data were not available for the entire period. My theory would predict that ambitious amateurs would have careers not significantly different from those of experienced members, whereas policy amateurs' and hopeless amateurs' careers would be shorter. These expectations are met. For members who served between 1972 and 1984, the average tenure of hopeless amateurs is 3.93 years; policy amateurs lasted 3.79 years, while ambitious amateurs had the longest tenure at 5.62 years.[30] Experienced candidates served an average of 5.35 years. The hypothesized differences are all significant at the .05 level. The hopeless amateurs' shorter tenure is not surprising given the nature of the districts in which they are elected, but policy amateurs' careers are unexpectedly short. The theoretical literature on the incentives for policy ambiguity in political campaigns is given a strong endorsement by these results.[31] Policy amateurs are penalized for their blunt approach to politics.

TENURE OF THE SENATE

The careers of amateur and experienced senators are different from those in the House. The average tenure for amateurs who no longer serve in the Senate is 11.96 years; those with some public experience actually have slightly shorter careers—11.10 years. Senators still serving in the Ninety-ninth Congress have longer tenure than those who have completed their careers (amateurs average 14.25 years, experienced senators, 14.63 years; neither difference is significant at the .10 level). Why is there no relationship between tenure and experience in the Senate?

Several of the factors that were significant in the House will be less so in the Senate. First, corrective elections that return many seats to the party previously defeated in a landslide election do not have as great an

30. The distribution of amateurs elected between 1972 and 1984 is as follows: nineteen hopeless, twenty-one policy, fifty-two ambitious, twenty-two ambitious/policy, six hopeless/policy, and seven widows of former congressmen. See David T. Canon, "Actors, Athletes, and Astronauts: Political Amateurism in the United States Congress" (Ph.D. diss., University of Minnesota, 1987), tables 5.1 and 5.2 and pp. 459–60.

31. Kenneth A. Shepsle, "The Strategy of Ambiguity," *American Political Science Review* 66:2, (June 1972): 555–68; Benjamin J. Page, "The Theory of Political Ambiguity," *American Political Science Review* 70:3 (September 1976): 742–52.

impact on the Senate, given the six-year time lag.[32] Second, the argument concerning "investment transferability" and voluntary retirement does not hold for the Senate, which seems to generate its own ambition independent of the strategic considerations imposed by an advancing political career—both for lengthy careers in the body and for attempts at the presidency.[33] Amateurs are no different from their experienced counterparts in the cultivation of political careers within or beyond the Senate. John Tower (R-TX), Howard Baker (R-TN), and Russell Long (D-LA) enjoyed lengthy careers within the Senate, and John Glenn (D-OH), Bill Bradley (D-NJ), and Baker are evidence that amateurs are not immune to White House fever.

The impact of the age of members will be similar to its effect in the House. Those who enter with previous experience have often had lengthy careers in lower office, or have left politics and reentered later in their careers (Terry Sanford, the sixty-nine-year-old freshman and former governor of North Carolina, is the most recent example). Older experienced freshmen will depress the average tenure of experienced senators. The average age of all senators with major elective office is 50.1 years, compared with 48.1 years for amateurs.

A multiple regression confirms the bivariate analysis: tenure is not significantly related to previous political experience. Of the same three variables that were included in the House analysis (previous experience, age, and year elected), only age is significant ($t=6.02$). A senator elected at age sixty can expect to serve five years less than a member who is elected at age forty.

The relationship between previous experience and tenure becomes significant if appointed senators are included in the analysis. Eighty-six of the 150 senators appointed between 1913 and 1984 served one year or less. Fifty-three percent of the appointees had no major elective experience, compared with 24% of those who were elected to office. Thus, if

---

32. Despite the lag, corrective elections operate to some extent; witness the 1986 election, in which seven of the sixteen seats picked up by the Republicans in the 1980 Senate sweep reverted to Democratic control. As was true in the House, amateurs may be disproportionately affected by these receding partisan tides.

33. See Roger H. Davidson and Walter J. Oleszek, *Congress and Its Members*, 2d ed. (Washington, D.C.: Congressional Quarterly Press, 1985), 37–40, for a discussion of careers in the Senate. See Robert L. Peabody, Norman J. Ornstein, and David W. Rohde, "The United States Senate as a Presidential Incubator: Many Are Called but Few Are Chosen," *Political Science Quarterly* 91:2 (Summer 1976): 237–58, and Paul R. Abramson, John H. Aldrich, and David W. Rohde, "Progressive Ambition among United States Senators: 1972–1988," *Journal of Politics* 49:1 (February 1987): 3–35, on presidential aspirations.

appointees are included, the mean tenure of amateurs falls to 6.81 years, compared with 9.25 years for senators with some public experience. In the multivariate analysis, having previous experience adds 2.5 years to expected tenure in the Senate ($t=3.49$), and a twenty-year age difference reduces tenure by 4.8 years ($t=6.69$).

Committee Assignments in the House

The varying goals held by the three types of amateurs and by members of Congress with previous experience are expected to produce differences in committee service. Personal goals are translated into assignment preferences, which in turn have a significant impact on committee membership, legislation, and individual careers.[34] Before the typology of amateurism and committee assignments can be discussed, the mechanics of the assignment process must be understood.

Lobbying for desired committee assignments is one of the first tasks undertaken by freshman members of Congress. Party leaders, members of the Steering and Policy committees (or of the Committee on Committees for Republicans), relevant interest groups, key members of the desired committee, and members of the state delegation are contacted for information and endorsements.[35] Predispositions and newly acquired information are combined to formulate members' requests or revealed preferences. The members' true preferences reflect the value of the committee to each member; revealed preferences also take into account the likelihood of receiving a given assignment. Thus, prestige committees would be ranked highly in an account of true preferences, yet are rarely requested by freshmen because more senior members dominate these committees.

The next step involves the actual assignments. Cohen says, "The process of assigning House and Senate members to congressional committees is one of the most mysterious—and one of the least discussed—aspects of the legislative process."[36] The process is equally perplexing to some members. They may be pleasantly surprised, as was Wyche Fowler

34. Irwin N. Gertzog, "The Routinization of Committee Assignments in the U.S. House of Representatives," *American Journal of Political Science* 20:4 (November 1976): 693–712; Richard E. Cohen, "The Mysterious Ways Congress Makes Committee Assignments," *National Journal* 11 (3 February 1979): 183–88; Smith and Deering, *Committees in Congress,* chap. 4.

35. John F. Bibby, *Congress off the Record: The Candid Analyses of Seven Members* (Washington, D.C.: American Enterprise Institute, Studies in Political and Social Processes, no. 383, 1983), 4–9.

36. Cohen, "Mysterious Ways Congress Makes Committee Assignments," 183.

(D-GA), who received a spot on the prestigious Ways and Means Committee in his second term. (When asked how he had managed that coup, he said, "Beats the hell out of me.") Or they may be deeply frustrated, as was James Oberstar (D-MN), a third-term, hardworking party loyalist who was not given a Ways and Means seat despite having a majority of the Steering Committee on an early ballot.[37] Shepsle provides a comprehensive analysis of assignments in the pre-reform period (when assignments were made by the Ways and Means Committee for Democrats), and Smith and Ray examine the post-reform period.[38] Both studies conclude that competition, rather than personal characteristics, is central in determining which members receive their first requests: is there an available seat on the desired committee, and how sought-after is that seat? Intra- and interzone competition are also important as members of the Committee on Committees attempts to "serve their constituents" (that is, members of their zones).

The finding that structural factors rather than individual-level concerns are central in determining assignments does not seem to square with recent observations that freshman members are becoming more successful in receiving desired assignments.[39] Gertzog argues that the process has become routinized, with 91% of members receiving a desired assignment by their second term.[40] If competitive factors were determinative, there would not be such satisfaction with eventual assignments. The contradiction appears only when too much focus is placed on the assignment process rather than on the sources and accommodation of preferences. Revealed preferences for the main legislative committees, as indicated through written requests and active lobbying, are accommodated as much as possible by Committee on Committees members (preferences for minor committees are handled through a process of co-optation). This accommodationist practice works through two channels, the first reactive and the second more formative: party leaders, who can adjust the size of

37. Ibid., 183, 185. Assignments are made in a sequential process whereby the top vote-getter receives an assignment and the slots are filled one at a time until all are filled. Thus, in the extreme case, if five slots are to be filled (as there were in this case) a member could finish second on every ballot, defeating four eventual nominees in successive rounds, but never receive a nomination.

38. Kenneth A. Shepsle, *The Giant Jigsaw Puzzle: Democratic Committee Assignments in the Modern House* (Chicago: University of Chicago Press, 1978); Steven S. Smith and Bruce A. Ray, "The Impact of Congressional Reform: House Democratic Committee Assignments," *Congress and the Presidency* 10:2 (Autumn 1983): 219–39.

39. Smith and Ray, "Impact of Congressional Reform," 227–28; Shepsle, *Giant Jigsaw Puzzle*, 193.

40. Gertzog, "Routinization of Committee Assignments."

committees to incorporate freshman requests, and zone representatives, who encourage a wide distribution of requests to meet the available supply in a given Congress.

The centrality of member preferences could be viewed more directly in a nonrecursive model that would reflect the intensity of preferences. Intensity would be indicated by member predispositions (member and district characteristics) and the supply and demand variables (state, interzone, and intrazone), and would have direct effects on requests and both direct and indirect effects on assignments. The two most complete models of the assignment process treat all first requests as equal along the dimension of underlying motivations or predispositions.[41] Differences in intensity of preferences may reveal a more central role for individual-level variables.

Conclusive tests of this model await further research. In the limited test I present here, I assume that assignments reflect preferences and that preferences reflect goals that are determined from the electoral context. The first assumption is obviously second-best—it is preferable to use request information or actual Steering Committee tallies—but given the routinization of the process, it is still a realistic assumption for all but the minor committees. Virtually nobody receives a prestige assignment who does not request and actively pursue the nomination, and Gertzog and Shepsle both conclude that major legislative-committee requests are generally honored.[42] The second assumption follows from my theory, which sees distinctions among amateurs that can be drawn on the basis of their behavior in the electoral arena. Policy amateurs are more likely to seek policy-committee assignments that will further their specific policy goals, while hopeless amateurs will seek constituency committees to shore up their shaky electoral base. Ambitious amateurs and experienced politicians will serve on a mix of committees, but will have greater representation on the prestige committees.

The other two theories I have discussed through this study offer more general predictions: both recruitment theory and socialization theory predict that experienced freshmen will receive better assignments than amateurs, but for different reasons (specifically, that experienced mem-

---

41. Shepsle, *Giant Jigsaw Puzzle;* Smith and Ray, "Impact of Congressional Reform." Clearly, requests do not all reveal equal intensity of preferences. It is difficult to discover intensity, but predictions can be made from district characteristics. Shepsle's model of freshman requests indicates that "best case requests" have probabilities as high as .99. It is reasonable to assume that members who virtually *must* request these committees have stronger preferences and will be more successful in gaining these assignments.

42. Gertzog, "Routinization of Committee Assignments," and Shepsle, *Giant Jigsaw Puzzle.*

bers will receive more prestige committee assignments and amateurs more "undesired" assignments; see table 5.1 for the categories of committees). Recruitment theory holds that the assignment process will favor those who have prior legislative and state-government service because they will be viewed as more politically seasoned and more likely to possess the skills required of successful House members. Socialization theory holds that members who know their way around a legislature will be better able to do what it takes to gain a favorable assignment. The following is an example of a member who benefited from "knowing the ropes":

> I wanted a seat on the Agriculture Committee. My experience in the state legislature made me realize that you just don't get things automatically. You have to go after them. I had the support of our members on the Committee on Committees and I also sought out other influential members of that committee.[43]

Recruitment theorists see experienced members as passive recipients of favorable treatment rather than promoters of their own careers; the perceptions of those making assignment decisions are central. Nicholas Masters in his seminal study of congressional committee assignments, considers the importance of previous experience (such as legal experience on the Judiciary Committee or military experience in the armed forces) and concludes:

> But all agreed that holding elective office, particularly a state legislative office, outweighed any other type of professional experience as a qualification for any committee assignment. Holding elective office is regarded as a profession by members of the committees and they feel that the rewards of the system should go to professionals.[44]

More recent anecdotal evidence demonstrates that this bias may still be evident. Bibby recounts the experience of a freshman congressman who was lobbying Steering Committee members for a seat on the Appropriations Committee:[45]

43. Shepsle, *Giant Jigsaw Puzzle,* 42.
44. Nicholas A. Masters, "Committee Assignments in the House of Representatives," *American Political Science Review* 55:2 (June 1961): 356.
45. Loomis refers to Clem McSpadden's assignment to the Rules Committee as a freshman in 1972 as additional evidence that experienced members receive preferential treatment; McSpadden had served for twenty years in the state senate ("Congressional Careers and Party Leadership," 193).

Table 5.1   Types of Committees in the U.S. House

Prestige Committees	Constituency Committees
Appropriations	Agriculture
Budget	Armed Services
Rules	(Education and Labor)
Ways and Means	Interior
	Merchant Marine
Policy Committees	Public Works
	Science and Technology
Banking	Small Business
Commerce	Veterans' Affairs
(Education and Labor)	
Foreign Affairs	
Government Operations	
Judiciary	

Undesired Committees
District of Columbia
House Administration
Post Office and Civil Service
Standards of Official Conduct

SOURCE: Smith and Deering, *Committees in Congress*, 90.

. . . several of them would start off with, "So what? What else
is new? You want to be on Appropriations." I would tell them
that I had been involved in politics for a while and had served
as Speaker [in the state legislature] for six years and that I had
to make some tough decisions. Clearly, that was helpful in the
process.[46]

Terry Seip's observations about the Congress of the mid nineteenth
century indicate that the bias for previous experience may be long-
standing:

Although previous officeholding experience was not an
essential prerequisite either to election or success in Congress,
those who had it frequently seemed to wield more influence
that did political newcomers. Experienced politicians, such as
John H. Reagan and James W. Throckmorton of Texas,
received much better committee assignments, they were more
active, and they had more impact during their first term in the
Forty-fourth House than did, for example, their fellow   .

46. Bibby, *Congress off the Record*, 4–5.

freshmen, Charles Nash of Louisiana and Jeremiah Williams of Alabama, neither of whom had ever held public office. There were obviously other factors involved, such as personality and political context, but it is no less apparent that an individual's quickness of adaptation to the House or Senate, his activity and influence, and even his constituents' expectations were to some degree correlated with his level of prior political experience.[47]

I will examine freshman committee assignments from 1973 to 1985 to test the various theories' predictions. This test is only exploratory: these data cannot confirm differences between experienced and inexperienced members and among amateurs, but they can disconfirm them or indicate patterns that may justify additional research.

There is weak evidence for the expectation of socialization and recruitment theory (that experienced candidates receive higher-quality assignments than amateurs) and strong confirmation of my theory. Specifically, 14.9% of amateurs are placed on "less desired" committees, compared with 12.4% of members with previous experience, while 5.8% of amateurs and 8.4% of experienced members win prestige committee assignments. "Super-freshmen," former congressmen who return to the House, fare significantly better—more than a fourth (four of fifteen) received a prestige assignment, while only one was stuck on a less desired committee.

There is stronger evidence for the typology of amateurism. Policy amateurs are the most likely to receive policy-committee assignments (70%, compared with 53.2% for all other members), hopeless amateurs disproportionately serve on constituency committees (88.9% versus 69.8%), and experienced politicians and ambitious amateurs completely dominate initial assignments to prestige committees (8.1% of ambitious amateurs, 7.7% of experienced politicians, and only 2.1% of other amateurs). Hopeless amateurs are more likely to receive assignments to the least desired committees (22.2%, compared with 13.0% for others), contributing additional evidence for rejection of the Clapp/Masters hypothesis.[48]

In recent years, initial assignments have increasingly become permanent assignments as the routinization of the assignment process produces

47. Terry L. Seip, *The South Returns to Congress* (Baton Rouge: Louisiana State University Press, 1983), 73.
48. The Clapp/Masters hypothesis argues that members from marginal districts are more likely to receive favorable committee assignments from a sympathetic leadership. Heinz Eulau reviews this dispute in his essay "Legislative Committee Assignments" (*Legislative Studies Quarterly* 9:4 [November 1984]: 604–611).

a greater percentage of satisfied freshmen. Yet transfers should be examined to see whether patterns established in the initial assignment process persist. The obvious change in committee membership is the movement to the prestige committees. Whereas only 7.8% of all freshmen from 1973 to 1985 were able to receive an assignment to Ways and Means, Appropriations, Rules, or Budget, more than a third of all members past their second term serve on these committees.[49] As a result, a smaller proportion of senior members serve on policy and constituency committees. The ladder-climbing in the committee structure does not completely erase differences that are evident among junior members. Most notably, policy amateurs are still more likely to serve on policy committees (47.4%, compared with 37.9% of other members) and far less likely to serve on the prestige committees (15.8% versus 37.8%). These patterns must be confirmed by a multivariate analysis that controls supply and demand factors and district-level variables, but there is some indication that previous political experience and goals, as revealed in the electoral process, help explain the shape of member careers in the institution.[50]

Legislative Leadership Positions

Who in Congress aspires to leadership positions and what influences their ability to gain those positions? Most scholars point to the characteristics of the individual; the prospective leader must be a political moderate, a compromiser, and a coalition builder. Of the three major studies of leadership in Congress in the last two decades,[51] Peabody's most thoroughly examines the question of who becomes a party leader.

49. In recent Congresses the percentage has ranged from 37.7% in the Ninety-eighth Congress to 33.5% in the Ninety-seventh Congress.

50. Senate committee assignments will not be discussed, for two reasons. First, committees have not been as important in meeting either policy or power goals held by senators. Second, committee assignments take on less meaning in the Senate because members generally hold at least three assignments—sometimes as many as six.

51. Randall B. Ripley, in *Party Leaders in the House of Representatives* (Washington, D.C.: The Brookings Institution, 1967), provides a broad overview of leadership selection, functions, styles, and institutions in the House. Robert L. Peabody, in *Leadership in Congress: Stability, Succession and Change* (Boston: Little Brown, 1976), examines leadership succession and change in the House and the Senate. Sinclair, in *Majority Party Leadership in the U.S. House*, focuses on coalition building in the House. See also Garrison Nelson, "Change and Continuity in the Recruitment of U.S. House Leaders, 1789–1975," in *Congress in Change: Evolution and Reform,* ed. Norman J. Ornstein (New York: Praeger Publishers, 1975), 155–83, on the backgrounds of House leaders, and "Partisan Patterns of House Leadership Change" (*American Political Science Review* 71:3 [September 1977]: 918–39), on patterns of change; Barbara Hinkley, "Congressional Leadership Selection and Support" (*Journal of Politics* 32:2 [May 1970]: 268–87), on the leadership ladder; and

He concludes that "the most pervasive and continuing influence upon leadership selection for party office has been exerted by the personality and skill of the candidates" for leadership positions.[52] This observation lends support to recruitment theory's argument that the "political personality" rises to the top of the political career structure. Seasoned politicians who have made politics their vocation from the start are more likely to possess the characteristics outlined above. Political mavericks can survive in the House or Senate, but without exception cannot climb the leadership ladder.[53]

Recruitment theory would capture the most essential component of leadership selection if the process were completely passive, but a member's qualities are only half of the equation. As Loomis points out, "As with most steps up the political ladder, advancing into the legislative leadership includes elements of self-starting from below as well as being tapped from above."[54] Peabody's accounts of bruising battles for leadership positions make it clear that aspiring leaders cannot idly sit by and expect their colleagues to rally behind them.[55]

The proper political personality is a necessary but not a sufficient condition for leadership selection. Many who have the requisite backgrounds and characteristics to become leaders choose not to do so. Holding a leadership position generally requires neglecting personal legislative and policy concerns: many would rather make their mark in the House through committee work and policy expertise. Furthermore, the first rung on the ladder, party whipping, is not an attractive job to most. One House aide noted, "It is a myth that anybody can whip. There are very, very few people who can work the House, and fewer who like it."[56]

How then does one explain the varying degrees of desire to achieve

---

Aage R. Clausen and Clyde Wilcox, "Policy Partisanship In Legislative Recruitment and Behavior" (*Legislative Studies Quarterly* 12:2 [May 1987]: 243–63), on the ideological position of leadership in voting.

52. Peabody, *Leadership in Congress,* 498.

53. This argument does not see previous experience as a *qualification* for leadership. It is not conceivable that most members will even recall that a candidate for a top leadership position had a distinguished record in a state legislature twenty years earlier. However, if previous experience is viewed as a qualification by party leaders who make appointments for lower leadership positions, the relationship between previous experience and leadership may be more direct (because of the automatic escalator). There is some evidence for this claim: 80.6% of the appointed at-large whips (twenty-five of thirty-one) had previous political experience in the Ninety-ninth Congress, while only 68.2% of the elected regional whips (fifteen of twenty-two) were experienced.

54. Loomis, "Congressional Careers and Party Leadership," 191.

55. Peabody, *Leadership in Congress.*

56. Jacqueline Calmes and Robert Gurwitt, "Profiles in Power: Leaders Without Portfolio," *Congressional Quarterly Weekly Report* 45 (3 January 1987): 17.

leadership positions and success in doing so among members who are similarly situated and have comparable backgrounds and personalities? The varied goals that members hold can explain these differences. Experienced members and ambitious amateurs who have established careers in the House or Senate may choose to pursue the goal of power within the institution. Policy amateurs and hopeless amateurs are not likely to hold this goal; they will be driven by policy concerns and constituency concerns, respectively.

LEADERSHIP IN THE HOUSE

The backgrounds of top party leaders in Congress from 1900 to 1986 give limited support to both the theory of amateurism and recruitment theory, and soundly reject socialization theory, which argues that previous experience is unrelated to the likelihood of serving in the leadership. Every Speaker in the twentieth century except Carl Albert has had some previous political experience.[57] Every one since Joseph Cannon, except Carl Albert and Henry Rainey (who served as Speaker for less than two years in 1933–34), has served in his state legislature (four as leaders). If the process were strictly random, the odds of at least one amateur among fifteen Speakers is .08. The probability of having eleven or more of thirteen who have served in state legislatures is less than .003, and the probability that four Speakers had been party leaders in their state legislature is less than .0001.[58] Members with previous political experience clearly are more successful in gaining the speakership

In testing the two theories,[59] I will move beyond the core leadership to include the extended circle comprising members of the whip system (chief deputy whip, deputy whips, at-large whips, and regional whips), the caucus chair and secretary, and members of the Rules Committee. The broader circle of leadership must be examined to explain who gains

57. Albert was one of the many veterans who were elected to Congress after World War II. He enlisted as a private in 1941, was discharged with a Bronze Star as a lieutenant colonel in February, 1946, and was elected to the House that November.

58. That is, $P(X < 1)$ where $n = 15$ and $p = .25$ is .080; $P(X > 11)$ where $n = 13$ and $p = .40$ is .003, and $P(X > 4)$ where $n = 15$ and $p = .025$ is $< .0001$. The proportions of members with previous experience elected to the next two levels of leadership are not significantly different than would be expected by chance. Eleven of the fourteen majority leaders in the twentieth century, six of the eight minority leaders (who did not also serve as majority leader), fifteen of the eighteen Democratic whips, and only seven of the twelve Republican whips, have had previous experience.

59. Given that socialization theory can be rejected with the simple bivariate analysis, the theoretical focus in the rest of the discussion will be on recruitment theory and my theory.

top leadership positions. The whip system has become the training ground and incubator for aspiring leaders. Prominent Democrats who were weaned in the whip system include Jim Wright (TX), Tony Coelho (CA), Norman Mineta (CA), Bill Alexander (AR), Dan Rostenkowski (IL), and Charles Rangel (NY).[60]

According to recruitment theory, the distribution of these positions should be heavily skewed in favor of those with previous political experience. My theory, on the other hand, predicts that only policy and hopeless amateurs will not hold leadership positions. The evidence supports the latter prediction. Almost a third of House members elected between 1972 and 1984 with previous political experience were in the leadership, while this is true of *none* of the policy or hopeless amateur Democrats. Forty percent (ten of twenty-five) of the ambitious amateurs are in this category, the largest proportion of any group. Additional evidence for rejecting the prediction of recruitment theory that only experienced candidates are advantaged in the leadership quest is that, of the fifty-eight Democratic leaders elected since 1972, forty-seven (81.0%) had previous political experience, which is indistinguishable from the overall proportion of 80.7% of Democrats with previous experience. Republicans tend to follow the pattern predicted by recruitment theory, with 76.1% of all members elected since 1972 having previous experience and 88.8% (twenty-four of twenty-seven) of the leadership positions being held by this subgroup.[61]

Within the expanded leadership system, only a small percentage of

60. The explosion in the size of the Democratic whip system may undermine its value as a stepping-stone to higher positions (Lawrence C. Dodd and Terry Sullivan, "Majority Party Leadership and Partisan Vote Gathering: The House Democratic Whip System," in *Understanding Congressional Leadership*, ed. Frank H. Mackaman [Washington, D.C.: Congressional Quarterly Press, 1981], 227–60; Loomis, "Congressional Careers and Party Leadership"). The number of at-large whips doubled from the Ninety-sixth to the Ninety-eighth Congress, and then doubled again in the next four years; the number of deputy whips has tripled in that period. Six years ago, deputy whips had a reasonable chance of moving into the number four leadership position of chief deputy whip. Now they must compete with nine others. Changes in the Republican whip system have been more gradual: a new whip region in 1975, an increase in the number of whips in each region from three to four and two new deputy whips in 1981, two class whips in 1985, and three new deputy whips in 1987. The whip system is not as extensively used by Republicans as a stepping-stone to higher leadership positions (see Canon, "Institutionalization of Leadership").

61. The numbers are too small to say much with certainty about Republican amateurs. Two of the three Republican amateurs who hold leadership positions are ambitious amateurs. The third, Duncan Hunter (CA), was elected as a hopeless amateur, but his district was made safe by redistricting in 1982, allowing him to pursue other goals. His vote total increased from 53% in 1980 to 69% in 1982.

those serving in the leadership win top positions. Of the 122 Democrats and 70 Republicans who served in the leadership between 1973 and 1986, fewer than a dozen held the positions of whip, floor leader, or Speaker. However, not all leaders attempt to climb the ladder. Three distinct career types can be identified: dabblers, whippers, and ladder climbers.[62] Dabblers are those who serve in the whip organization for one or two terms and then leave. More than half of the Democratic dabblers remain in office after leaving the whip system (57.5%); the others retire or are defeated (27.5%) or seek higher office (15%).

Whippers are the relative few who continue as at-large or regional whips year after year (the coding rule was three terms or more). Some— such as Pennsylvania's John P. Murtha ("The 'P' is for Power," his billboards proclaim) and Alabama's Tom Bevill—enjoy the cajoling and persuading, while others perform the whipping function out of a sense of duty or loyalty to the party. These members do not aspire to move beyond this limited but valuable role, and often they are heavily involved in committee work and other legislative concerns. Only five of the forty-three whippers (11.6%) left the leadership voluntarily, and only two were defeated.

Ladder climbers aspire to the speakership. Generally they move from regional whip to at-large whip to deputy whip and wait their turns to compete for the top positions (occasionally the intermediate level is skipped).[63] Jim Wright, for example, moved from regional whip to deputy whip, then jumped to majority leader (when John McFall did not move from whip to majority leader because of a scandal), and then to Speaker. In fourteen years, Bill Alexander had patiently worked his way from regional whip to deputy whip to chief deputy whip; he then lost a bid for the number three leadership position to Tony Coelho. Members are included in this group if they have served at least three terms in the whip system and have climbed at least one level. Of the twelve in this category, seven can be considered "super ladder climbers" by virtue of having progressed at least to the level of deputy whip. Five others who were elected before 1972 are in this category (Bill Alexander, Dan Rostenkowski, Charles Rangel, Jim Wright, and Tom Foley).[64]

62. In this analysis, the leadership does not include Rules Committee members, who tend to remain on the committee rather than use it as a stepping-stone. This discussion will apply only to the majority party, as the Republican party whip system has not become nearly so routinized and bureaucratized.

63. The move from regional whip to at-large whip is clearly a step up the leadership ladder. In the past decade, ten made the move in this direction and only one went from at-large whip to regional whip.

64. These data are updated to include the 100th Congress in Canon, "The Institutionalization of Leadership in the U.S. Congress."

The discovery of these distinct career paths is important in its own right, especially considering that today's successful ladder climbers are the top leaders of the future (due to the routinization of leadership succession), but of greater interest for this work are the striking differences in the political backgrounds of the three groups. All twelve of the ladder climbers had previous political experience, compared with approximately three-fourths of the other two types (nineteen of the twenty-five dabblers and fourteen of the nineteen whippers). The probability of this happening by chance is less than .0001. Hopeless and policy amateurs are found only among the dabblers, while ambitious amateurs (and the mixed ambitious/policy amateurs) are most commonly whippers. This is consistent with the expectation that the power goal is usually held by experienced politicians and ambitious amateurs.

A conclusive test of the importance of amateurs' previous experience and goals in explaining leadership selection must consider alternative explanations. For example, policy and hopeless amateurs elected in large numbers in 1980 may not have gained leadership positions because they did not have the necessary seniority. I will specify a probit model for all members elected since 1972 who were serving in the Ninety-ninth Congress that controls the seniority, opportunity (as indicated by an opening in a member's region and by the extent of representation in the member's region among at-large whips), party loyalty, and ideology, which should be reflected in a curvilinear relationship between a member's deviation from his or her party's mean conservative coalition score and his or her likelihood of gaining a leadership position (i.e., the extremes are not selected).[65] I hypothesize that my typology of amateurism and political experience can serve as a predictor of leadership selection.

Table 5.2 shows estimates for a probit model that reflects my typology of amateurism for one for recruitment theory, which does not make distinctions among amateurs. The dependent variable indicates whether or not the member served in the leadership. I tried a more complex four-level dependent variable that made distinctions among different levels in the leadership, but the results were similar to those presented here. In the first model, which tests my theory of amateurism (that ambitious amateurs are likely to serve in the leadership, while hopeless and policy amateurs are not), six of the nine explanatory variables are significant (at the .10 level) and in the right direction. Democratic seniority, the ideological extremes of Democratic members, Republican party support, and whether the member had previous experience or was an ambitious amateur are all sig-

65. This is an improvement over the general practice of reporting means and medians. Reporting that both the leadership and the general membership has a mean conservative coalition score of 35 ignores the dispersion around the mean.

Table 5.2 Leadership in the House, 99th Congress: Testing the Typology of Amateurism

Variable	Amateurism Typology			Recruitment Theory		
	Maximum likelihood estimate	Expected direction	Significant at	Maximum likelihood estimate	Expected direction	Significant at
Constant	-2.67	—	.0001	-3.46	—	.0001
EXPER	1.05	Yes	.005	.14	—	—
EXPER2	—	—	—	.00029	Yes	.091
DPARTY	.00028	Yes	.273	.011	Yes	.264
RPARTY	.011	Yes	.020	-.00026	Yes	.021
DCC^2	-.00025	Yes	.042	.00007	Yes	.035
RCC^2	.00006	No	.244	.24	No	.194
OPPATLG	.31	Yes	.091	.40	Yes	.143
OPPREG	.41	Yes	.082	.066	Yes	.088
DYROFF	.074	Yes	.007	.049	Yes	.013
RYROFF	.046	Yes	.126		Yes	.112

Estimated R^2 = .261
N = 343

Estimated R^2 = .207
N = 343

Distribution of the dependent variable:
(0) = 258 (1) = 85

LEADER = B1 + B2(EXPER) + B3(RPARTY) + B4(DPARTY) + B5(RCC^2) + B6(DCC^2) + B7(OPPATLG) +
B8(OPPREG) + B9(DYROFF) + B10(RYROFF) + e

Definitions of the variables:

LEADER   one if the member has served in the leadership, zero otherwise;

EXPER   one if the member has previous political experience or is an ambitious amateur; zero if the member is a policy
          amateur, "hopeless" amateur, or widow;

EXPER2   zero if the member is an amateur, one if the member has some previous nonelective public experience, two if the
          member has previous elective experience;

RPARTY   Republican members' party support score, corrected for absences:
          RPARTY = Support/(Support + Opposition);

DPARTY   Democratic members' party support score, corrected for absences:
          DPARTY = Support/(Support + Opposition);

RCC^2 difference between a Republican member's conservative coalition score and the party's mean conservative
          coalition score squared, corrected for absences;

DCC^2 difference between a Democratic member's conservative coalition score and the party's mean conservative
          coalition score squared, corrected for absences;

OPPATLG   one if there is an opening for an at-large whip in the member's region, zero otherwise;[a]

OPPREG   one if there is an opening for a regional whip in the member's region, zero otherwise;

DYROFF   number of years in office for Democratic members;

RYROFF   number of years in office for Republican members.

[a]Regional balance is not strictly followed in appointing at-large whips. That is, if an at-large whip retires, that member's state
does not have an absolute claim to that position. Yet the argument is that an ambitious amateur has a *better* chance of gaining an
appointive whip position if there is an opening than if there is not.

nificant at the .05 level, and the opportunity variables (both for regional and at-large whips) reach the .10 level of significance.[66] The most important finding here is that the experience variable in the amateurism model holds up even in the presence of competing explanations and outperforms the variable in the recruitment-theory model that does not make distinctions among amateurs (the size of the coefficient falls from 1.05 to .14 and is no longer significant, though the rest of the recruitment-theory model is fairly robust). Having previous political experience or being an ambitious amateur increases the probability of serving in the leadership by 20.4%. The two other most significant variables, seniority and ideology, have less impact: a Democrat who serves four years longer than the party average is 12.6% more likely to serve in the leadership, while a Democrat whose conservative coalition score is ten points above or below the party average is 8.7% less likely to be on the leadership team.[67]

While it certainly is not surprising that goals can be linked to behavior, it is significant that goals inferred from behavior in the electoral arena are so strongly linked to tenure in the House, committee assignments, and success in gaining leadership positions.

LEADERSHIP IN THE SENATE

Leadership in the Senate does not resemble the hierarchical organization of the other body. Most noticeable is the size of the apparatus; there are thirteen Senate Democrats in the extended leadership circle, compared with seventy-four in the House, while Republicans manage with only four in the Senate (minority leader, whip, conference chair, and conference secretary), as opposed to thirty-three in the House. Clearly, the smaller Senate requires fewer leaders, but the House system is proportionally larger.[68]

66. Multicollinearity is a problem with the conservative-coalition and party-support variables (they are correlated at .97 and .18 for the Republicans and Democrats, respectively). The strong linear relationship between the two variables for Republicans inflates the standard errors and makes significance tests unreliable. Excluding one of the variables is not feasible because specification error biases the remaining variables. Multicollinearity is less of a problem for Democrats because of the inclusion of southern Democrats. A separate control for southern Democrats did not dramatically change the results.

67. These results should be viewed with some caution because they include only 343 members who served in the Ninety-ninth Congress and were elected after 1972. Including all members should serve to strengthen these results.

68. Almost a fourth of all House members hold leadership positions, compared with 17% in the Senate. One would expect the opposite, due to economies of scale.

A more important difference is the lesser role that leadership positions play in pursuing the power goal in the Senate. Peabody begins his chapter on Senate leadership, ". . . why do so few Senators gravitate toward elected party leadership, while the vast majority choose to make their mark on public policy primarily through legislative specialization?"[69] Intuitively this tendency would not be expected in the Senate, where, unlike in the House, policy goals and leadership goals are not zero-sum. Party leaders generally continue to hold four or five subcommittee chairmanships or ranking minority positions. Some leaders, such as Lyndon Johnson, Robert Taft, and Alben Barkley, had substantial impact on the substance of a broad range of legislation while holding their party's top position.[70]

The history of individualism in the Senate, which has reached new proportions in the 1980s, accounts for much of the preference senators have for policy expertise over leadership; the former allows for more individual initiative and rewards, while the latter is a collective enterprise. Peabody concludes that idiosyncratic factors also play a role: "For most of these Senate influentials, personal style, geography, ideology, and not a little luck move them toward or away from positions of formal leadership."[71] Determining the composition of the leadership may not be so unpredictable: differing structures and different levels of institutionalization affect career paths within the body and the types of members who seek leadership positions.

Leadership in the Senate has become very different for the two parties. The Democratic leadership is more institutionalized and, by virtue of its majority status in all but six of the last thirty-four years, more powerful. The institutionalization of Democratic leadership is manifested in several ways. Polsby argues that an institutionalized organization will be well bounded, relatively complex, universalistic rather than particularistic in its use of criteria, and automatic rather than discretionary in its conduct of business.[72] Several of these descriptions hold for Democratic leadership but not for Republican: succession at top levels is relatively automatic,[73]

69. Peabody, *Leadership in Congress,* 321.

70. Ibid., 321–22.

71. Ibid., 323.

72. Polsby, "Institutionalization of the House," 145.

73. Routinized succession in the Democratic leadership was established for the whip-to-minority-leader step until the 101st Congress, when Alan Cranston (CA) decided not to run for the top spot. Nonetheless, the two top contenders for majority leader in the 101st Congress, Daniel Inouye (HA) and George Mitchell, were respectively third and fourth in the leadership hierarchy in the 100th Congress. At lower levels there is some indication of an

the tasks of the organization are well organized and defined through the regional whip system, and membership is more stable. Survivability, the ultimate test of organizational institutionalization, most clearly illustrates the differences between the two parties. While the Democratic whip system became better defined in the 1980s, the Republican system was disbanded in the Ninety-seventh Congress.

Two indicators of institutionalization require more discussion: the internal complexity and stability of the system and its boundaries. Internal complexity refers to a division of labor and separation of function between levels of the organization. In the highly institutionalized House whip system, this is most easily demonstrated by the regional whips' role of head-counting and the at-large whips' function of persuasion. In the Senate, neither party's whip organization is really that well defined, but the Democrats' newly formed regional whip system comes closer. The Democratic whip system is comprised of a head whip, a chief deputy whip, and four regional deputy whips with an assistant deputy whip under each.

The Republicans abolished their whip system partly because the division of labor broke down. According to a top leadership aide, the whip system was discontinued for several reasons. First, the system was underutilized, partly because nobody knew what they were supposed to do. "Functions were fairly ill defined," an aide said. "There was not a clear sense of getting anything done, so the assistant whips did not feel they were having an impact. More basically, there just was not that much for them to do."[74] Second, the system was disbanded in 1981, when the Republicans took control of the Senate. One would think that this would create more need for a whip system, but an aide explained that the main service provided by the whip system was floor coverage, and the presiding officer of the Senate, now a Republican, could play that role. The other two important functions of the whip system, whip counts and the dissemination of information, are done through other channels. (Howard Green, the party secretary, handles whip counts, and the policy committee serves as the primary source of agenda and policy information.) Thus,

---

escalator; for example, Inouye moved to the number three position, chairman of the conference, after serving several terms as an assistant whip, Robert Byrd (WV) moved from conference secretary to whip, and in 1989, Alan Dixon (IL) was elected chief deputy whip after having served in the whip system since 1981.

74. In 1987 and 1988 I conducted interviews with twelve top-level staffers and former staffers in the House and Senate leadership. Ten interviews were conducted in person and two over the phone; they ranged in length from twenty-five to fifty-five minutes. Unattributed quotes in this chapter are from these interviews.

the Republican system had no internal complexity; indeed, it had no clearly defined function.[75]

Well-bounded organizations are characterized by clearly identified members, selective membership, and stability in tenure. The last two are less evident in the Republican leadership system. As mentioned above, almost 40% of the Republican membership held assistant whip positions in the Ninety-sixth Congress; apparently anybody who wanted the title could have it. Generally, less than 20% of Democratic membership is in the whip system; the current figure is one in six. As expected, the less bounded system also has greater turnover. In its last year, the Republican whip system had a 50% turnover rate, whereas the Democratic membership remained completely unchanged from the Ninety-seventh Congress through the Ninety-ninth, except for the loss of Walter Huddleston (KY) to electoral defeat in 1984. Such stability is not observed even in the highly institutionalized Democratic whip system in the House.[76] The average tenure of Republican whips in the last year of their system was 1.87 years; for Democrats in the Ninety-ninth Congress it was 7.8 years.[77]

These differences should have an impact on the type of member who seeks a leadership position in each of the two parties. In general, the expectation is that an institutionalized leadership system offers more opportunity to advance the power goal. One aide said:

> The lack of clearly delineated lines to higher office undermined the attractiveness of the assistant whip position [in the Republican system]. In the most highly developed whip system, that of the Democrats in the House, there is an expectation that you get a bit of a leg up in moving up the leadership system. This is clearly an incentive that didn't exist in our whip system, and this influences the type of member who is looking to serve in that position.

75. The whip system was briefly reinstituted early in 1987 after the Republicans were back in the minority. A leadership aide said that every senator who volunteered (nine in all) became a regional whip. Their duty again was primarily floor coverage, but the system did not work because the whips were never there when Simpson needed them. The aide said, "When I would call the senators' offices to get them onto the floor for their four-hour shift, their administrative assistant would often say, 'Oh, I didn't know he was a regional whip.' They didn't take the job too seriously."

76. There was a shake-up in the 100th Congress, with five new whips appointed and only three carrying over from the Ninety-ninth Congress.

77. This dramatic difference can be explained by the policy in the Republican system of assigning all freshman senators to the whip system.

Institutionalized structures that use lower-level leadership positions as stepping-stones to top leadership positions attract ambitious senators who see some payoff in party service. Permeable structures are less likely to be populated by this type. The election of a majority leader (such as Howard Baker or Robert Dole) who is elected without having served time in the leadership undermines the incentive to sacrifice policy goals for a position that has no power and little prestige. To test these claims I will examine the type of senator in each party's leadership.

Much is revealed by the caliber of senators who serve in the leadership systems. In recent years, Democratic assistant whips have included Paul Sarbanes (MD), Don Riegle (MI), Chris Dodd (CT), John Glenn (OH), Patrick Leahy (VT), and David Pryor (AR). In the 100th Congress, three promising freshmen were appointed to the whip system—former House members Wyche Fowler (GA) and Tim Wirth (CO) and former Transportation Secretary and House member Brock Adams (WA). These senators do not represent the top echelon of the Democratic party in the Senate, but they are among the Senate's leaders or rising stars. Compare this group to Republican whip members before the system was disbanded in 1981: Rudy Boschwitz (MN), Harrison Schmitt (NM), John Warner (VA), Malcom Wallop (WY), Jesse Helms (NC), Larry Pressler (SD), Gordon Humphrey (NH), and S. I. Hayakawa (CA). With all due respect, this is not a tremendously impressive list of senators.[78]

A more systematic analysis of the types of members who serve in leadership positions reveals that Democrats are much more likely to have previous legislative experience, whereas the Republican membership is dominated by freshmen and amateurs. Democratic House members who come to the Senate are likely to carry with them a view of a whip system that furthers power goals. In fact, three of the top four Democratic leaders in the Ninety-ninth Congress served *both* in the state legislature and in the House, while eight of the eleven assistant whips (including the chief deputy whip) had previous legislative experience (three in both the House and state legislature, two in only the House, and three in only the state legislature). Of the Senate whips, only John Glenn (OH) had no previous elective experience. These levels of prior experience have a 5% probability of occurring by chance. On the other hand, five of the sixteen Republican assistant whips in the Ninety-sixth Congress had no previous public experience and eight had no legislative experience. Clearly, the structure of the leadership system has an impact on its membership.

78. Some prominent Republicans have served in the whip system, such as Richard Lugar (IN), Peter Domenici (NM), and William Cohen (ME), but in general the characterization is fair.

Behavior in the House and Senate

Comparing the behavior of one congressman to another is difficult at best. Objective data, such as number of bills sponsored or introduced and success rates, can mask more than they explain. This is best illustrated by the typical campaign ploy of pointing out a member's rate of participation in roll call votes as an indicator of effectiveness. Effectiveness is often more closely related to cloakroom lobbying, or to diligent committee work. Reputational measures or in-depth interviewing attempt to tap differences in members' power, influence, and effectiveness.[79] A broad theory of legislative behavior would address all aspects of behavior, but this is clearly beyond the aspirations of my study. The theoretical concerns I address touch on the ideas of influence, but my focus is on behavior as goal-directed activity. Specifically, I will examine the relationship between previous political experience, goals, and behavior by examining roll call voting and amending behavior.

Roll Call Voting

In this section I will entertain two simple hypotheses: (1) Policy amateurs will be more ideologically extreme than their colleagues, and (2) Policy amateurs will be less likely to moderate their views with increasing seniority. These hypotheses follow from the argument that members who hold strong policy goals will be less likely to compromise their positions. In the Senate analysis, as in previous sections, the number of observations is not large enough to allow distinctions among amateurs. Thus, in the Senate I will test only the proposition of recruitment theory that amateurs are more ideologically extreme and the hypothesis of socialization theory that they moderate their views with increasing seniority.

VOTING IN THE HOUSE

Conservative coalition support and opposition scores are used to measure House members' ideological positions. This measure obviously reflects constituency, personal, and other factors that must be controlled. In addition, the summary measure is not an ideal indicator of members'

---

79. The reputational approach is used by John R. Hibbing and Sue Thomas, "The Modern United States Senate: What is Accorded Respect?" (paper presented at the annual meeting of the American Political Science Association, Washington, D.C., 1–4 September 1988); interviewing is used by Lawrence C. Evans, "Influence in Senate Committees" (Ph.D. diss., University of Rochester, 1987).

positions on specific policies. This analysis can thus be seen only as a preliminary test that may justify additional research.

Conservative coalition scores were gathered for the 1983–86 sessions of Congress (redistricting limits the usefulness of analysis across decades, so only the more recent period is used). According to the scheme employed by *Congressional Quarterly,* both support and opposition scores are calculated as proportions of all votes in a given set. As such, both scores are lowered by a member's failure to vote, whether the failure is due to illness, strategic considerations, or plain lack of interest. To correct for the effects of abstention, adjusted support scores were calculated for each member by dividing the support score by the sum of the support and opposition scores. The result produces a measure that represents the support of a given member on those roll calls in which the member voted.

The simple bivariate relationship between previous experience and adjusted conservative coalition scores shows that there are only small differences between amateur and experienced House members. Amateurs tend to be somewhat more ideologically extreme—Democratic amateurs' conservative coalition scores are 3.6 to 3.8 points lower than those of their experienced counterparts, while Republican amateurs' are about one point more conservative—but the differences are not significant.

When the typology of amateurism is introduced, significant differences *among* amateurs become evident. Ambitious amateurs tend toward the party mean, while policy and hopeless amateurs are more extreme. Though the number of cases is small, ambitious amateurs who are northern Democrats have scores that are exactly twice as large as those of policy amateurs (28.7 and 14.3—the average for all northern Democrats was 25.3), while southern Democratic policy amateurs are about eighteen points less conservative than ambitious amateurs from the South. Republicans follow similar patterns (differences are statistically significant because the *n*s are larger), with ambitious amateurs resembling their experienced counterparts and policy and hopeless amateurs being more ideologically extreme.[80] Thus, apparent similarities between amateurs and experienced members in the aggregate mask significant differences among types of amateurs.

The next obvious question is whether these differences can be attributed to the goals that members hold (as revealed by their behavior in the electoral arena and their policy positions), or whether constituency factors and other considerations are central. That is, maybe policy ama-

---

80. Hopeless amateurs were not expected to be more ideologically extreme because of their tenuous electoral position.

teurs appear to be ideologically extreme because they are from districts that are more extreme. The regression presented in table 5.3 indicates that Democratic policy amateurs have scores that are, on average, 12.4 points lower than those of ambitious amateurs and experienced politicians, while differences between these two groups for Republicans average 11.6 points when controlling for party, seniority, and district ideology. A simpler specification that does not make distinctions among amateurs (a simple dichotomous variable) verifies the bivariate analysis—the typology of amateurism demonstrates differences among members, while recruitment theory does not.[81]

The second hypothesis from socialization theory is that freshman members, especially amateurs, will moderate their initially extreme ideological positions once they gain experience in the House—i.e., in the parlance of statistics, they will regress toward the mean. The expectation of my theory is that policy amateurs will *not* regress toward the mean, but will maintain their initial positions. There is little evidence for either hypothesis. Based on time-series data from the years 1983–86, there is no general trend toward the mean for freshman members, and policy amateurs are only slightly less likely to regress to the mean (13.8% of all policy amateurs who were one standard deviation above the mean moved at least five points toward the mean, whereas 15% of all members did so).[82]

VOTING IN THE SENATE

In the Senate analysis the population size was increased by extending the analysis back to 1959, the first year in which *Congressional Quarterly* calculated conservative coalition scores. I included scores from the first session of each Congress (the odd-numbered years from 1969 to 1983). Amateur Democrats are 7.6 points more liberal than their experienced freshman counterparts, and Republican amateurs are 11.3 points

81. Seniority is added as a control because there is some evidence that members temper their ideological positions with time in office (Alan L. Clem, "Do Representatives Increase in Conservatism as They Increase in Seniority?" *Journal of Politics* 39:1 [February 1977]: 193–200). There is a small but significant relationship between seniority and conservative coalition scores for Democrats, but not for Republicans. These results for the entire model follow similar patterns for 1983, 1985, and 1986. The Republican experience variable is significant in all four regressions and the Democratic variable is significant in two of the four. The other independent variables remain largely the same, as does the general fit of the model.

82. These numbers reflect the mean proportions of shifts in a member's conservative coalition scores in the periods 1983–84, 1984–85, and 1985–86.

Table 5.3   Conservative Coalition Scores and Previous Political Experience
in the U.S. House, 1984: Controlling for Alternative Explanations

Independent Variables	Estimate	Expected Direction	Significant at
Constant	69.18	—	.0001
DEMEXPER	−6.20	Yes	.064
REPEXPER	5.81	Yes	.026
PRES72	−.98	Yes	.0001
PARTY	20.59	Yes	.0001
DEMYROFF	.58	Yes	.008
REPYROFF	−.03	No	.417

$R^2 = .742$
Adjusted $R^2 = .738$
N = 400

Dependent variable and conservative coalition scores adjusted for attendance.

DEMEXPER	one if the member is politically experienced or is an ambitious amateur, two if a hopeless amateur, three if a policy amateur, for Democrats;
REPEXPER	one if the member is politically experienced or is an ambitious amateur, two if a hopeless amateur, three if a policy amateur, for Republicans;
PRES72	Democratic presidential vote in 1972 for the congressional district;
PARTY	zero for northern Democrats, one for southern Democrats, two for Republicans;
DEMYROFF	number of years in the House for Democrats;
REPYROFF	number of years in the House for Republicans.

NOTE: The number of cases is not equal to 435 because amateurs elected before 1972 are excluded from the analysis.

more conservative (differences significant at the .05 level). Both groups are more extreme than nonfreshman senators (see table 5.4). The data presented in table 5.5 show that the socialization hypothesis (that initial differences will disappear) can be rejected. Among Democrats, the difference in the mean scores of experienced and inexperienced new members is 10.7 points in Year One. This discrepancy narrows to 4.7 points in Year Three, but then increases to 7.9 points in Year Five. The pattern among Republicans provides clearer evidence for rejecting the hypothesis. The difference between the two groups steadily grows from 5.2 points in Year One to 10.8 points and 19.9 points in successive years. A multivariate analysis shows that these differences persist and remain significant when period effects and seniority are controlled.[83]

83. When southern Democrats are excluded from the analysis, differences between amateurs and experienced members among northern Democrats are significant only in the most recent period.

Table 5.4   Conservative Coalition Scores and Previous
Political Experience in the U.S. Senate, 1959–83

	Democrats	Republicans
Incumbents	44.2	72.0
	(448)	(243)
New members,	25.2	85.6
no experience	(46)	(39)
New members,	32.8	74.3
experience	(200)	(136)

NOTE: The cell entries represent the mean, adjusted conservative coalition score of each group. Number of cases in
each category are in parentheses.

Table 5.5   Socialization in the Senate: Changes in Conservative
Coalition Scores, 1959–83

	Year 1		Year 3		Year 5	
	Dems	Reps	Dems	Reps	Dems	Reps
Incumbents	44.2	72.0	44.2	72.0	44.2	72.0
	(448)	(243)	(448)	(243)	(448)	(243)
New member,	22.0	84.3	26.7	84.4	26.5	89.1
no experience	(14)	(16)	(17)	(13)	(15)	(10)
New member,	32.7	79.1	31.4	73.6	34.4	69.2
experience	(66)	(51)	(68)	(43)	(66)	(42)

NOTE: The cell entries represent the mean adjusted conservative coalition score of each
group. Number of cases in each category are in parentheses.

This analysis indicates the merit of further research that would examine the link between the typology of amateurism and roll call voting. The
next step is to examine voting records in specific issue areas. The expectation is that differences among amateurs should be more pronounced
when areas of policy interest are identified and analyzed. Better controls
for the influence of members' constituencies should also be included in
future models.

Legislative Activity in the House

An understanding of how members choose to spend their time is of
central importance in understanding the operations of Congress. In the
1950s and 1960s, policy expertise and the norms of specialization, and
legislative work were held in high regard. Consequently, committees

were at the center of policy-making. In the 1970s, new members shifted the locus of activity on several fronts. Motivated by a desire to establish their careers more quickly, they demanded a greater role in the legislative process through the "subcommittee bill of rights," challenged the seniority system, expanded the role of the Democratic Caucus, and increased participation on the floor. They also shored up their electoral base by expanding home offices and devoting more time and resources to constituency needs.

There is a great deal of variation within these general patterns of how members spend their time, yet scholars have not explained *why* members choose different mixes of activities. The three theoretical frameworks discussed in this study offer explanations. Proponents of recruitment theory see personality as dictating the mix of activities; socialization theory places previous experiences in the forefront; my theory sees member goals (as indicated by previous experiences) as central.

Recruitment theory defines two extremes in the mix of legislative activity: "show horses," the publicity seekers who avoid detailed legislative work, and "work horses," who pride themselves on policy expertise.[84] James Payne discovers substantial evidence for the validity of the distinction. After rejecting the alternative explanations of time pressures, reelectoral needs, and socialization, he asserts that previous political experience accounts for the differences. He discovers that only 10% of the show horses had at least four years of previous legislative experience, while 53% of the work horses and 70% of the "clear work horses" had such a background. He concludes, "Any explanation of the show horse/work horse pattern which relied upon forces working on a member once he entered Congress—constituency pressure or legislative norms, for example—would be insufficient to account for the relationship."[85]

Frantzich's study of bill sponsorship in the Ninety-fourth Congress provides evidence for socialization theory. He discovers that forty-four of the forty-six members who were in the "low activity" category of sponsorship had previous legislative experience. He concludes:

84. The two scholars who first made this distinction were Donald R. Matthews ("The Folkways of the United States Senate: Conformity to Group Norms and Legislative Effectiveness," *American Political Science Review* 53:4 [December 1959]: 1064–89) and Charles L. Clapp (*The Congressman: His Work as He Sees It* [Washington, D.C., The Brookings Institution, 1963]). Phil Gramm (R-TX) is often given as an example of a "show horse." One aide said, "Don't get between Phil Gramm and a TV camera; you might get hurt." Al Gore (D-TN) is another "show horse" who exploits a timely issue and then quickly moves on to the next.

85. James L. Payne, "Show Horses and Work Horses in the United States House of Representatives," *Polity* 12 (Spring 1980): 456.

The decision of whether to introduce legislation probably stems partially from one's evaluation as to whether the effort will reap rewards or not. Members' perceptions of futility seem to be learned early and changed little. House members having long experience dealing in the frustrating world of political compromise learn to temper their appetites for legislative success much more than political neophytes. . . . House members entering the chamber with no previous political experience consistently introduce more legislation than do their peers with wide previous experience in other offices.[86]

I will not provide a comprehensive analysis of how members spend their time, but rather present data on a key aspect of legislative behavior: the number of amendments offered on the floor. Amending behavior is an excellent measure of legislative activity. First, the substantive importance of amending activity grew dramatically in the 1970s.[87] Second, amending activity is probably a more valid indicator of policy preferences and intensity than bill sponsorship or speech-making.[88] I will examine contested amendments offered in the Ninety-third, Ninety-fourth, and Ninety-sixth Congresses.[89]

Amendments obviously are not always substantive, or even good indicators of serious activity. Members known for their obstructionist tactics, such as Craig Hosmer (R-CA), H. R. Gross (R-IA), Bella Abzug (D-NY), and Robert Bauman (R-MD), were among the most frequent offerers of amendments in the 1970s. Hosmer, who holds the 1970s record of forty-seven offered amendments, came up with some unusual proposals, such as suggesting that the Air Force drop the "Vietnamese equivalent of voodoo dolls" on the Viet Cong to frighten them into surrendering.[90]

86. Stephen E. Frantzich, "Who Makes Our Laws? The Legislative Effectiveness of Members of the U.S. Congress," *Legislative Studies Quarterly* 4:3 (August 1979): 418–19. This conclusion illustrates the theoretical difficulties of the socialization perspective (I should make it clear that Frantzich does not subscribe to this theory). One could argue just as easily (and, to my mind, more persuasively) that previous legislative experience would make the introduction of legislation *more* likely because of familiarity with the process.

87. Steven S. Smith, "Decision Making on the House Floor" (paper presented at the annual meeting of the American Political Science Association, Washington, D.C., 28–31 August 1986); 31. Smith elaborates this argument in a recent book, *Call to Order: Floor Politics in the House and Senate* (Washington, D.C.: The Brookings Institution, 1989).

88. Charles L. Clapp, *The Congressman: His Work as He Sees It* (Washington, D.C.: The Brookings Institution, 1963); Frantzich, "Who Makes Our Laws?" 413.

89. I am very grateful to Steven S. Smith (and to his small army of research assistants at the Brookings Institution) for providing the amending data. An amendment is coded as contested if the split on a teller or recorded vote was 60 to 40 or closer.

90. Barone, Ujifusa, and Matthews, *Almanac of American Politics, 1974*, 125.

Limiting the analysis to contested amendments excludes the flakiest ones.

What expectations are generated by the three theories for levels of amending behavior in the House? Payne and Frantzich paint a picture of members with previous legislative experience as work horses who shun publicity and allocate their time to more useful activity than flooding the floor with legislation. However, the theoretical expectations could cut both ways. With socialization theory, "futility" and "know the ropes" arguments are at odds, while members with the proper "political personality" may or may not be inclined to floor activity.

Though the direction of behavior cannot be predicted by these theories, stability or change can. Recruitment theory sees established patterns persisting over time. Socialization theory, on the other hand, predicts that if the "know the ropes" argument holds, amateurs should be expected to offer fewer amendments in their freshman term, but then converge toward the mean in successive terms. If experience breeds skepticism of the value of floor activity (the "futility" argument), amateurs should, on average, submit more amendments initially and then move toward the mean of experienced members as they recognize the error of their ways.

My theory of amateurism predicts that hopeless amateurs will tend to offer fewer amendments, since a preponderance of their time will be spent on constituency activities. This assertion is consistent with Frantzich's finding that electorally insecure members submit fewer pieces of legislation than members in safe districts and are far less successful in getting bills passed.[91] Policy amateurs are expected to be more active on the floor as they pursue their policy agenda. No distinct patterns of behavior are expected for ambitious amateurs or experienced members.

Overall, amateurs proposed more amendments than those with previous legislative experience or other public experience, though this number steadily decreased from the Ninety-third to the Ninety-sixty Congress while the number increased for members with legislative experience. In the Ninety-sixth Congress, the means for these two groups are statistically indistinguishable. As expected, hopeless amateurs were significantly below the mean (1.3 amendments per capita, compared with a House mean of 3.1 for the three Congresses).

Means are not the best indicators of central tendencies because the population is heavily skewed. More than a fourth of all members did not offer any amendments at all, and another 35% offered only one or two amendments. Yet 5% to 6% offered more than ten amendments, with ex-

---

91. Frantzich, "Who Makes Our Laws?" 416, 422.

tremes ranging from twenty-five to forty-seven in the various Congresses. Thus a two-population median test is used to determine whether there are significant differences between groups. The differences are significant for the Ninety-third Congress, but then disappear in succeeding Congresses.[92] The numbers of policy and hopeless amateurs are not large enough to generate statistically significant chi-squares in most of the median tests, but the results are in the expected direction. In the Ninety-third Congress, all three hopeless amateurs are below the median, and all four policy amateurs are above.[93] In the Ninety-fourth, five of the six hopeless amateurs are below the median (the one above offered three amendments), while seven of the twelve policy amateurs are above. In the Ninety-sixth, six of the eight hopeless amateurs are below, while fourteen of the sixteen policy amateurs are above (chi-square of 5.96, significant at the .01 level, when compared with the population as a whole).

As expected, senior members are more likely than junior members to submit amendments. There is strong evidence that once members become more comfortable with the legislative process, they become more active. Smith finds, "Each freshman class from the 91st to the 93rd increased its amending activity when they became sophomores. Each succeeding freshman class during the reform period also exhibited more activity than the preceding freshman class."[94] What about the socialization process for amateurs and those with previous legislative experience? First, neither the "futility" nor the "learn the ropes" argument holds for the Ninety-third and Ninety-fourth Congresses. Members with previous legislative experience start out at *lower* levels (1.2 amendments per capita) and then increase (to 2.1) in their sophomore years. Amateurs start at a *higher* level (2.9; the difference is significant at the .04 level) and stay there in their second year. These are the only two Congresses for which I have data for successive years, but several other observations from the Ninety-sixth Congress are worthy of mention. First, differences among members who are past their first term are not significant. Second, there is a complete reversal in differences between amateurs and those with previous legislative experience; the latter move from the least active to the most active among freshmen in the House.[95]

Amending behavior yields a mixed bag of results. Policy amateurs of-

92. See tables 5.18, 5.19, and 5.20 in Canon, "Actors, Athletes, and Astronauts" (Ph.d. diss.), 476–78.

93. This includes ambitious/policy amateurs and hopeless/policy amateurs.

94. Smith, "Decision Making on the House Floor," 25.

95. All amateurs are included together here because the *n*s are not sufficiently large to separate the policy and hopeless amateurs.

fer more amendments and hopeless amateurs fewer, as predicted by my theory. Socialization theory's prediction of the relationship between previous experience and amending activity was rejected, though a tendency is evident for various groups to regress toward the mean. The movement of members with previous legislative experience to more active floor roles is difficult to explain. In a period of change in which the floor is becoming a more respected and utilized method for expressing views, experienced members are perhaps more able and quicker to adapt to the radically changed environment.

Conclusion

The simple dichotomy between amateurism and political experience generally cannot explain behavioral differences or divergent career patterns among members of Congress. With the exception of differences in tenure between amateurs and experienced members, and the dominance of top legislative leadership positions by experienced members, the two groups are indistinguishable. Thus there is scant evidence for the claims of recruitment theory that see persistent differences based on previous experiences. Socialization theory was also rejected in the various tests, as differences among members did not disappear.

   The central assertion of my theory of amateurism—that amateurs cannot be viewed as a single group, but must be distinguished by the goals they hold—is strongly confirmed. Policy and hopeless amateurs have patterns of behavior and careers within the body that are distinct from those of ambitious amateurs and experienced politicians. Policy amateurs' careers are significantly shorter and more focused. That is, they are more likely to gain policy-committee assignments, are more likely to be active on the floor, are more ideologically extreme in their voting, and do not pursue power goals through legislative leadership positions. Hopeless amateurs also have shorter careers, are more likely to serve on constituency committees, are less likely to be active on the floor, and generally do not gain leadership positions. (They are also more ideologically extreme, which is not consistent with the theory.) Ambitious amateurs, on the other hand, resemble experienced politicians in every regard. Their career patterns are similar, they are more ideologically moderate, and they pursue a variety of goals. These patterns generally are more descriptive of the House than of the Senate. Nonetheless, behavioral differences between amateurs and experienced senators on roll call voting and in the leadership system merit additional attention.

Six

Conclusions and Consequences

The U.S. House and Senate are not exclusively the domain of the politically experienced. More than one-fourth of House members and 10% of senators in recent years do not have previous public experience. This study has examined the theoretical and practical implications of amateurism in the U.S. Congress. Existing theories do not illuminate the topic because they either ignore amateurs or treat them as a single group. Ambition theory is guilty of the former, as it encompasses the behavior of current officeholders only, while recruitment and socialization theory fail on the second count. A complete theory of ambition must recognize amateurs' distinct place in the political system, and also must realize that amateurs are not all the same. My theory of ambition and careers is based on these two themes.

All amateurs begin at the same place in the career structure, but they respond differently to opportunities, which has implications for their behavior in Congress. In electoral politics, policy amateurs compensate for limited name recognition by emphasizing issues, while hopeless amateurs capitalize on national tides and scandals to win upset races. Experienced politicians and ambitious amateurs generally attempt to avoid issue-based campaigns and are rarely in a position to defeat an incumbent unexpectedly. Once in office, policy amateurs and hopeless amateurs are motivated by policy concerns and constituency concerns, respectively, while ambitious amateurs generally share the same mix of constituency, policy, and power goals held by experienced members. This chapter does not dwell on the details of these differences as presented in the previous chapters; rather, it summarizes the theoretical contributions and outlines the broader implications of having a significant number of amateurs at high levels in the political system.

Theoretical Developments

Career structures for the House and Senate change rapidly and dramatically in response to national partisan conditions (see chapter 3). Previous work in ambition theory has assumed that career structures are relatively stable because, at the *aggregate* level, career paths change very slowly. But when differences between parties are examined, significant patterns appear, both for experienced and amateur politicians. In periods of increased political opportunity (such as the early 1930s for Democrats and 1980 for Republicans), proportionally more amateurs are elected to office. Career politicians respond to changing opportunities by accelerating their decisions to run for higher office, by reentering politics after being out of public life for more than five years, and by using alternative career paths more frequently, thus indicating that career paths change in several dimensions.

The unusually large number of amateurs elected in periods of high electoral opportunity presents a special problem for current ambition theory. I suggest that office-seeking behavior must be examined in two distinct periods: when career structures are changing and when they are stable. When career structures change, the type of candidate who is elected can be explained by the national partisan balance, by the relationship of the "new breed" of politician of the changing issue agenda, and by the shifting demand for and supply of experienced candidates. In "normal" periods, district-level forces will be dominant, though national economic conditions will also come into play.

Chapter 4 makes two theoretical contributions. First, I redirect an analysis of the decision to run to the political amateur, examining the implicit hypothesis of previous work that amateurs are swept aside whenever experienced candidates choose to run. Although the hypothesis is largely confirmed, something of a paradox is presented by the reality that many amateurs *are* elected to Congress, and most must defeat an experienced candidate along the way. The trick for ambition theory is to identify the ambitious amateurs who laterally enter the career structure. I suggest three factors to distinguish between ambitious amateurs and "sacrificial lambs": celebrity status, previous attempts at a congressional seat, and victories over experienced candidates in the primary election. These factors successfully identify 60% of the amateurs who win general-election campaigns. Second, I present an integrated theory of ambition that combines individual-level factors, national-level concerns, and structural variables and that makes distinctions among amateurs. The multivariate probit test of this model performs better than a version that makes a simple distinction between experienced and inexperienced candidates.

Chapter 5 provides evidence of a link between institutional and office-seeking behavior. Campaigns are more than empty rhetoric and position-taking. For some candidates, campaigns provide valuable clues about the policy goals they hold or the ambition that drives them; for others, the election results indicate constraints that will govern the member's every move. One of the central contributions of this book is the discovery that among policy, ambitious, and hopeless amateurs, differences that begin with their election continue through their tenure in office. It is not useful to characterize all political amateurs as neophytes or gadflies.

This analysis could be extended to members of Congress who have previous political experience in order to test my assumption that most will evolve through predictable stages from dominant concern with reelection to interest in institutional positions of power. My argument has been that the unique place of amateurs in the political system facilitates their policy advocacy and provides them with disproportionate rewards of strong national tides.

Amateurs in the Political System

In discussing this book with friends, the first question I am confronted with is, Are amateurs good or bad for Congress? At the risk of sounding like an equivocating social scientist, I answer this question by saying, It depends. An amateur can be seen as an invigorating breath of fresh air or a thorn in the side of the leadership, a committed believer or a ranting ideologue. In general, it is clear that amateurs play an important role in many aspects of the democratic process, especially in areas of political change. Although some of these points are speculative and require additional research, amateurs have a hand in (1) providing democratic accountability in congressional elections, (2) resisting socialization pressures in the House and Senate, (3) party building, (4) policy change, and (5) institutional change.

Democratic Accountability

House incumbents have enviable job security. Their 98.5% reelection rates in 1986 and 1988 indicate the increasing ease with which they are returned to office. Without the gutsy campaigns of many amateurs (challenges that few experienced candidates are willing to accept), incumbents would be even more entrenched. Hopeless amateurs are especially important in this process. The accountability they impose through their upset victories helps provide the electoral check that is so central to the democratic process. Policy amateurs who win also play this role, but even those who are not elected raise public awareness and provide a well-defined electoral choice on issues such as opposition to the Vietnam War, advocacy of a cleaner environment, opposition to the defense buildup, concern about school busing, or a fervent belief in the free market and cutting the size of government. Amateurs are often uniquely situated to play this role because they do not have the investment in a political career that demands caution and ambiguity rather than risk-taking and policy advocacy.

Legislative Norms and Governability

I have presented anecdotal evidence from the careers of S. I. Hayakawa, Gordon Humphrey, Jeremiah Denton, Bella Abzug, Robert Dornan, Vin Weber, John LeBoutillier, Newt Gingrich, and John Hiler indicating that some amateurs may be less sensitive to legislative norms. But others, such as John Glenn, Bill Bradley, and Frank Lautenberg, have gone to great lengths to establish their credibility and learn the workings of the institution.[1] The implications for congressional leadership are also unclear. While Tip O'Neill expressed frustration with the "bedwetters" in the 1974 Watergate class, the Republican leadership benefited greatly from the unswerving loyalty of the 1980 class of amateur "Reagan robots." Asher discovered that prior legislative experience is not a significant indicator of most attitudes on norms, but his sample size was probably not large enough to allow conclusive statements about behavioral differences.[2] Systematic inquiry into this question is beyond the scope of this study.

Fenno sees adherence to legislative norms as a central ingredient of legislative effectiveness. In an orientation seminar sponsored by the APSA and conducted by eight experienced congressmen, freshman members were repeatedly told that their colleagues would be "sizing them up" and passing judgment.[3] Members who followed the norms of legislative work, specialization, courtesy, and institutional loyalty had the best chances of being judged favorably. "And with the favorable judgment," Fenno notes, "comes the most enduring basis for influence in the

1. James Miller described how Lautenberg hired Mary Jane Checchi, a seasoned Hill staffer, to teach him how to survive in the Senate. Checchi complained of the difficulty of remolding a "businessman's mind," but eventually was pleased with the progress Lautenberg made (James Miller, *Running in Place inside the Senate* [New York: Simon and Schuster, 1986], 139–40).

2. Herbert B. Asher, "Learning of Legislative Norms," *American Political Science Review* 67:3 (September 1973): 510–11.

3. Richard F. Fenno, Jr., "The Freshman Congressman: His View of the House," in *Congressional Behavior*, ed. Nelson W. Polsby (New York: Random House, 1971), 134.

House—that is, the 'confidence,' 'respect,' and 'trust' of one's fellow Members."[4]

Previous legislative experience may influence effectiveness in more obvious ways. Members are convinced that having served in a state legislature helps ease the transition to the House and makes them better lawmakers. The following are excerpts of new members' impressions from a study for *State Legislatures:*

> U.S. Rep. Lynn Martin (R-IL) had perhaps the most trenchant response. "I would hate to be here without that experience," she said. If everything a member of Congress needs to know equals 100, Martin said, then with state legislative experience "you at least start at 10, and that 10 makes you think that maybe you will survive."
>
> Rep. Barney Frank (D-MA) believes that "legislating is an activity which is essentially similar on the state and national levels." That view is shared by Rep. Charles Hatcher (D-GA), who said that "the experience of knowing how the legislative process works was a tremendous asset." . . . For Rep. Larry Craig (R-ID), knowledge of how the legislative process operates enabled him to avoid what he sensed as "a high level of frustration among some of my freshman colleagues."
> According to the Idaho congressman, much of this frustration stems from the "inability to transform campaign rhetoric and obligations into legislative reality." Rather than trying immediately to knock over windmills, Craig explained, "those of us who have experience as legislators have found that the only way you affect the windmill is to find the door, gain access and then affect the mechanisms of the windmill."[5]

Partisan Realignments and Party Building

The observation that amateurs play an important role in partisan realignments (see chapter 3) calls for a shift in the focus of realignment theory. The immediately interesting consequence of electoral change

---

4. Ibid. Attitudes towards norms in Congress have greatly changed since Fenno's and Asher's writings, but evidence indicates that "general benefit" norms still survive, while "limited benefit" norms have eroded (David W. Rohde, "Political Change and Legislative Norms in the U.S. Senate: 1957–1974," in *Studies of Congress,* ed. Glenn R. Parker [Washington, D.C.: Congressional Quarterly Press, 1985], 147–88).

5. Andrea Kailo, "From the Statehouse to Congress: Five Stories," *State Legislatures* 8:4 (April 1982): 21.

may not be its impact on the partisan composition of Congress or on the emergence of new issues on the legislative agenda. Instead, it may be more useful to examine the calculations of political actors concerned with how best to advance their political careers in an uncertain, changing environment. Their interpretations of developing events, and their decisions about how to react to them, become integral parts of the realignment process (or of the blunting of a potential realignment, as the case may be). I address some of these questions in a paper with David Sousa and demonstrate the importance of individuals' career decisions for partisan realignments. The merger of ambition theory and the "governing side" of realignment theory with a focus on policy and career goals opens up a whole new research agenda.[6] I will briefly discuss two of the important topics here: party building and policy change.

One requirement for a strong regional or national party is a good supply of experienced candidates. The adage "you can't beat somebody with nobody" is especially true in an era of weakened party ties and candidate-centered campaigns. Such an environment would seem to limit amateurs' usefulness to parties. However, amateurs play a critical role in party building during partisan realignments. In "big bang" realignments, as in the 1930s for the Democrats, the party is forced to rely on amateurs because of the imbalance between the supply of and the demand for experienced candidates. After several elections, the career paths return to their normal patterns. Similarly, in "secular" realignments, as in the South in the past two decades, the GOP has been forced to rely heavily on political amateurs because there are virtually no experienced Republican state and local politicians in some districts.[7] I will discuss the southern case in more detail.

6. David T. Canon and David J. Sousa, "Realigning Elections and Political Career Structures in the U.S. Congress" (paper presented at the annual meeting of the American Political Science Association, Chicago, 3–6 September 1987). See David W. Brady, "Congressional Party Realignment and Transformation of Public Policy in Three Realignment Eras," *American Political Science Review* 79:1 (March 1985): 28–49, and "Critical Elections, Congressional Parties, and Clusters of Policy Changes," *British Journal of Political Science* 8:1 (January 1978): 79–99; Barbara Sinclair, *Congressional Realignment: 1925–1978* (Austin: University of Texas Press, 1982); and Jerome M. Clubb, William H. Flanigan, and Nancy H. Zingale, *Partisan Realignments: Voters, Parties, and Government in American History* (Beverly Hills: Sage Publications, 1980) for discussions of the governing side of realignments. To summarize this literature in one sentence, it is concerned with demonstrating the consequences of electoral upheaval rather than with describing the components of change.

7. David S. Broder, "Republicans Gain Strength in Region's Political Cauldron," *Washington Post,* 18 May 1986, A1, A12.

Before the Republican emergence, amateur candidates were likely to be prominent local businesspeople or willing party leaders who ran in order to promote their nonpolitical careers or simply to provide a Republican line on the ballot. V. O. Key was skeptical that these candidates would ever build a competitive party; he described amateurs in the southern Republican party at mid century in the following manner:

> They are not politicians and are not desirous of office. They are sound, reputable people—and undoubtedly they are. They are honest, and, again, undoubtedly they are. The people, however, who build political parties are politicians. They are keenly desirous of public office, an honorable ambition, perhaps the most honorable of all ambitions. Only through the clash of such ambitions can the ideals of democracy be approached.[8]

Barry Goldwater's success in the South in 1964 changed the political landscape. As the Republican party-in-the-electorate grew, and as nominally Democratic voters began to vote for Republican presidential and congressional candidates, a few amateurs were elected to the House and to lower offices (of the nine newly elected Republican southerners in 1964, seven were amateurs). These developments profoundly affected the calculations of politically ambitious officeholders and "pre-politicals" contemplating political careers. The Republican party suddenly became a viable vehicle for political success and was able to attract dozens of ambitious Democratic politicians seeking to advance their careers under a new party label. As the Republicans have attracted experienced Democratic politicians and nurtured a pool of home-grown political talent, the party's prospects have slowly brightened.

Amateurs will continue to play an important role in the Republican party's efforts to gain majority status in the South. In districts in which Republicans have not been elected to lower office and where the party has not been successful in recruiting party switchers, amateurs will fill the congressional ticket. Furthermore, these amateurs no longer are likely to fit Key's descriptions. The new generation of Republican amateurs in the South is both "keenly desirous of office" and highly motivated ideologically—for example, Connie Mack (FL), Jack Fields (TX), Joe L. Barton (TX), and Newt Gingrich (GA). These young ambitious amateurs have been instrumental in the Republicans' gains in the South.

8. V. O. Key, Jr., *Southern Politics* (New York: Alfred A. Knopf), 296–97.

Partisan Realignments and Policy Change

The infusion of amateurs into Congress during realignments may also have an important impact on policy change. Brady and others argue that the new majorities elected in realigning periods (especially in the 1930s) are swept into office on the basis of their party's perceived position on highly salient national issues; new members are sensitive to the electoral importance of these issues and follow the emerging policy agenda.[9] Policy amateurs, who are disproportionately elected during these partisan sweeps, have the convictions of converts. They bring with them an ideological fervor that is untempered by previous experiences and frustrations in public office. This was especially evident in the "Reagan Revolution" in 1981 as twelve policy amateurs were elected to the House (as well as nine other Republican amateurs). Janet Hook described the 1980 "Reaganauts" as "young, inexperienced, and ideological." She said they were "more concerned with the national issues that brought them to office than the local issues that would keep them there; some of these freshmen even opposed federal programs that were mother's milk to their own districts."[10] As mentioned above, the amateurs in the 1980 class who survived, such as John Hiler (IN), Jack Fields (TX), Bill McCollum (FL), and Vin Weber (MN), have been more attentive to their districts while maintaining their ideological zeal.

Another dimension of the amateur's role in periods of electoral change may have implications for political parties. Not only were the new amateurs sensitive to the national issues that were driving electoral change, but many of them lacked the ties to traditional party organizations in their home states and districts. This claim is based on two observations. First, in the upheaval of the 1930s, Democrats were being elected to Congress from districts and states in which the party was moribund. Second, some amateurs used the salience of national issues to defeat more experienced, locally oriented "organization men" in primaries.

The same phenomenon can be observed today, on a smaller scale, in the Republican party. In 1980, many amateurs were elected and then re-elected by identifying themselves as members of the Reagan team. They also brought with them a new brand of politics. Many of the amateur Republicans criticize the "old guard" who are willing to compromise with the Democrats. Increasingly frustrated with their party's seemingly per-

---

9. Brady, "Congressional Party Realignment."
10. Janet Hook, "House's 1980 'Reagan Robots'' Face Crossroads," *Congressional Quarterly Weekly Report* 46 (13 August 1988): 2262–63.

manent minority status in the House, these "Young Turks" advocate confrontation. By establishing themselves as a new type of politician (i.e., anti-Washington or even anti-politician), they make a virtue of their inexperience. The recent election of Newt Gingrich (R-GA) to replace Richard Cheney (R-WY) as Minority Whip in the House is a prime example of the new power of the more confrontational, less experienced generation. At this point, evidence for the "old guard/new guard" tension created by the election of large numbers of amateurs is mostly anectodal, but the pattern seems clear.

Institutional Change

The changing composition of Congress can contribute to institutional change. Polsby states the central question: "Do periods of congressional reform coincide with, or succeed periods of electoral instability so that they take place because there are an abnormal number of unsocialized members?"[11] A testable proposition is that amateurs comprise a large proportion of these unsocialized members. Peter Swenson's study of the revolt against Speaker Cannon in the early twentieth century demonstrates that reform-minded amateurs were largely responsible for the reforms.[12] The reforms weakened the powers of the Speaker and to some extent diminished the value of the career based on party loyalty and a low profile.

The period of reforms in the 1970s was prompted by similar concerns—individual members stifled by a strict seniority system and excessive control by powerful committee chairmen—but the backgrounds of the reformers were different than during the Cannon revolt. The members who led the reform effort were largely a very politically experienced group who had already tasted political success at the state level and were now frustrated with the slow path to power in the House. Julia Butler Hansen, whose reform plan was adopted in 1974, had served as a Democrat in the Oregon state house for twenty-one years, the last eight as speaker. Phil Burton (D-CA) and Frank Thompson (D-NJ), the other two most active members of the Hansen committee, also had extensive state legislative experience, Thompson as minority leader. A systematic study of this reform period could establish whether experienced

11. Nelson W. Polsby, "Studying Congress through Time: A Comment on Joseph Cooper and David Brady, 'Toward a Diachronic Analysis of Congress,' " *American Political Science Review* 75:4 (December 1981): 1010.

12. Peter Swenson, "The Influence of Recruitment on the Structure of Power in the U.S. House, 1870–1940," *Legislative Studies Quarterly* 7:1 (February 1982): 7–36.

politicians were instrumental in the reform effort and whether there is a relationship between previous experience and support for reforms.

The differences between the two periods can be explained by the roles of the individual and political parties in Congress. The candidate-centered nature of current politics has obvious implications for the operations of Congress. If members cannot count on the party to help them retain office, they are responsible for their own careers. Thus they are less likely to be sympathetic to the party-centered norms of the body that restrict their careers. Machine politicians of the late nineteenth and early twentieth centuries could rely on their party affiliation to perpetuate a political career. Today, everyone must carve out an individual niche, amateur and experienced politician alike. Experienced members are more likely to change existing institutional structures to suit their needs, but keep the *nature* of those structures the same. Thus, they maintain the idea of some structured system of delegation of authority and decentralization through the committee system, but serve their own interests by dividing the territory into more domains. In the modern period, amateurs may be more willing to tolerate existing institutional arrangements and operate as mavericks outside the system.

I will not conclude with a call for careerism, apprenticeships, and an end to amateurism in Congress. The pejorative connotation of the term "amateur" certainly has some validity. Tip O'Neill complains about the "bedwetters," Bella Abzug tells Fishbait Miller to perform an impossible act, and John LeBoutillier rails against the "big, fat and out of control Speaker." But in general, amateurs can have a beneficial impact on the political system as agents of political change, as instruments of party building, and as the last defense against irrevocable tenure for House members.

Appendix A
Coding Prior Political Experience

The coding process was organized around two principles: the functional characteristic of the office and the level of government at which the office exists. The five functional categories of office were executive, legislative, legal, administrative, and party. Each was broken down according to the various offices at the local, state, and federal levels and whether the office was elective or appointive. The distinction between the two was generally easy to determine. In some cases, such as many of the legal positions, the office can be elected or appointed. When it is not clear from the member's biography how he or she gained the office, the case was coded in the more inclusive category, public office. Thus, the percentage of House members coded as having prior elective experience may be understated to a very small degree (probably less than 1%). Here is the exhaustive list of offices coded:

FEDERAL	STATE	LOCAL
	Executive	
Vice president	Governor	Mayor
	Lt. governor	Supervisor
	Secretary of state	City manager
	Auditor	Auditor
	Treasurer	Treasurer
	Attorney general	Clerk
	Other statewide	Other local
	Legislative	
Senate	Senate	City council
House	House	Board of supervisors
	School board	Other local
		legislative body

Legal

Judge	Judge	Judge
Federal attorney	District attorney	City/county attorney
		Sheriff
		Justice of the peace

Administrative/Bureaucratic

Cabinet	State commissioner	Coroner
Assistant secretary	or secretary of a	Assessor
Diplomat	state agency	Surveyor
Ambassador	Governor's staff	Other local
House or Senate staff		

Party

Chair	Chair	Not coded
Member of national	Member of state	
party organization	party organization	

Membership on other miscellaneous national government commissions and various ad hoc state commissions were coded.

Appendix B

Probit Analysis of Political Experience in Congressional Elections: Model and Interpretation

Equation 1: Incumbent races (House)

Chall = B1 + B2(VoteChl) + B3(Scand) + B4(Age) + B5(AgeSq)
+ B6(Freshman) + B7(Rep74) + B8(Dem74) +
B9(RealInc*In) + B10(RealInc*Out) + B11(Unemp*In) +
B12(Unemp*Out) + B13(NormVt) + B14(RShape) +
B15(DShape) + B16(Supply) + B17(Ncand) +
B18(Endorse) + B19(PrimOp) + B20(ParticOp) +
B21(ParticCl) + B22(RDHelp) + B23(RDHurt) + U

Where:

B1–B23 = maximum likelihood estimators for each independent variable;

Chall = one if challenger has no previous experience, two if the challenger is an ambitious amateur (as defined in pp. 87–92), three if the challenger has previous appointive experience, and four if the challenger has previous elective experience;

Out = one if challenger is from the party out of power, zero otherwise;

In = one if the challenger is from the party in power, zero otherwise;

VoteChl = the percentage of the vote received by the challenger in the last election;

Scand = one if the incumbent was involved in a scandal at any time since the most recent election and before the primary, zero otherwise;

Age = the age of the challenger at the time of decision;

AgeSq = the challenger's age squared;

Freshman = one if the incumbent has served two years or less, one otherwise;

Rep74 = one if the incumbent is a Republican in 1974, zero otherwise;

Dem74 = one if the incumbent is a Democrat in 1974, zero otherwise;

RealInc = the percentage change in real per capita state income (at annual rates) in the six months before the candidate decision period;

Unemp = the change in state's unemployment rate in the year preceding the decision period;

NormVt = the average percentage of the district vote received by the incumbent party's candidates for the Senate, governorships, and presidency in the past six years (when a district has been altered through redistricting I use *Congressional Quarterly's* estimates of the previous party vote within the new district);

RShape = the number of offices held by Republican incumbents in the House in the previous two decades in each state;

DShape = the number of offices held by Democratic incumbents in the House in the previous two decades in each state;

Supply = the number of state house and senate seats per congressional district multiplied times the proportion of state legislative seats held by the challenges party;

Ncand = the number of candidates in a variety of congressional and state elections in each state;

Endorse = a scale of party involvement and effectiveness in endorsing candidates, ranging from one (effective party control at nominating conventions) to six (no endorsements);

PrimOp = one if the state's primary is open, zero otherwise;

ParticOp = one if the state's voter registration laws are not restrictive, based on the residency requirements, the closing date for registration, and whether or not voters may register through the mail; zero otherwise;

ParticCl = one if the state's voter registration laws are restrictive; zero otherwise;

RDHelp = one if the incumbent was helped by redistricting in 1972 or 1982, zero otherwise;

RDHurt = one if the incumbent was hurt by redistricting in 1972 or 1982, zero otherwise;

U = stochastic error term.

Equation 2: Open-seat races (House)

Chall = B1 + B2(OpenPar) + B3(Age) + B4(AgeSa) +
B5(Dem74) + B6(Rep74) + B7(Inc*In) + B8(Inc*Out) +
B9(Unemp*In) + B10(Unemp*Out) + B11(NormVt) +
B12(DShape) + B13(RShape2) + B14(Supply) +
B15(Endorse) + B16(Ncand) + B17(Turnover) +
B18(RDHurt) + B19(RDHelp) + U

All the variables are the same as those specified in equation 1 except:

OpenPar	= one if the former incumbent was from the challenger's party; zero otherwise;[1]
Rep74/Dem74	= one if a challenger from the respective party that ran in the 1974 election, zero otherwise;
Turnover	= the number of times a seat has turned over in the past ten years;
RDHurt/RDHelp	= one if the challenger's party was hurt (helped) by redistricting, one otherwise (the expected signs will obviously be the opposite of those specified for RDHurt and RDHelp in equation 1).

Equation 3: Incumbent races (Senate)

Chall = B1 + B2(VoteChl) + B3(Scand) + B4(Age) + B5(AgeSq)
+ B6(Freshman) + B7(Rep74) + B8(Dem74) +
B9(RealInc*In) + B10(RealInc*Out) + B11(Unemp*In) +
B12(Unemp*Out) + B13(NormVt) + B14(RShape) +
B15(DShape) + B16(Endorse) + B17(Ncand) +
B19(PrimOp) + B20(ParticOp) + B21(ParticCl) + U

All the variables are the same as those specified in equation 1 with the following exceptions. First, the "shape of the opportunity structure" variables (RShape and DShape) are computed from a forty-year period rather than a twenty-year period. Second, the highest level of experience in the dependent variable only includes U.S. representatives and those who hold statewide elective office.

1. In 1972 and 1982 *CQ*'s estimate of the 1970 and 1980 results for congressional races given the new district lines are used. Often an incumbent will retire because of unfavorable redistricting; thus being of the same party as the previous incumbent is not necessarily an advantage to a challenger. If the estimated vote for the challenger's party in 1972 and 1982 is greater than 50, OpenPar equals one.

Interpreting the Results

Interpreting probit is more complex than interpreting OLS regression because the impact of any given independent variable on the dependent variable depends both on the value of the independent variable and the values of all the other variables in the model. To determine the relative influence of the independent variables one can hold all the independent variables constant (usually at their mean level, or at 0 for dummy variables) except the one of interest, which is varied by some increment from its mean level. Alternatively, one can specify different levels of probability that the dependent variable takes on a value of one and then find the values for each coefficient that make the sum of the coefficients equal the Z-value that corresponds to each specified probability. I use the former method. The last column in each table shows the change in probability along the standard normal distribution that a challenger will be politically experienced given a 10% change from the mean value of each independent variable. For dummy variables, the column indicates the change in probability when the independent variable goes from zero to one.[2] Also listed in each table is the maximum likelihood estimate, the expected direction, and the corresponding level of significance for each independent variable. Insignificant changes in probability are presented in parentheses. The independent variables are grouped in the tables by the three types of variables: district-level, national-level, and structural-institutional. An estimated R^2 is presented as a measure of the goodness of fit.

Two features are not self-explanatory. The *MUs*, or "cut points" of the standard Z-scores, are reported at the bottom of the tables.[3] If the values of the independent variables yield a Z-score less than zero, the predicted value for the candidate is one (an amateur). In incumbent races, if the Z-

2. The 10% figure and 0–1 distinction for dummy variables are obviously not comparable, but theoretically it does not make sense to talk about 10% of a scandal or redistricting; either the incumbents were involved in a scandal or hurt by redistricting or they were not. The economic variables are also treated in a different fashion. The means for unemployment and real income change are close to zero for the entire period; thus a 10% change in the mean level would not give a realistic estimate of the impact of these variables. Thus, the change in the probability figure for these variables indicates a 1% change in the level of unemployment or income. Similarly, changes in the party endorsement variable are computed in one-level increments, rather than a 10% change. The change in probability for the age variables in the open-seat and Senate races are calculated as a 10% change from their global maximums (45.8 years and 54.2 years, respectively). In House incumbent races, the 10% change is calculated from the mean age of 43.2 years rather than the less meaningful global maximum of 73.8 years.

3. See Richard D. McKelvey and William Zavoina, "A Statistical Model for the Analysis of Ordinal Level Dependent Variables," *Journal of Mathematical Sociology* 4 (1975): 103–20, for a technical discussion.

score is from 0 to .156, the predicted value is two (an ambitious amateur), from .156 to .754 it is three (public experience), and above .764 the candidate is predicted to have had elective experience. The change in probability figure permits the reader to create scenarios in which the resultant Z-score applied to the *MU* cut points produces predictions of different types of candidates. The baseline Z-score (produced when all the independent variables are held at their mean levels) is −.515. Any Z-score below zero yields a prediction of an amateur candidate. To move to the next level (an ambitious amateur) the combination of independent variables would have to produce a Z-score of at least .156; thus the probability would have to be increased by 25.9% (this number is the area under the standard normal curve between a Z of −.515 and .156). A scandal-ridden Republican running in 1974 would fit this bill (these two variables increase the likelihood of an experienced candidate by 31.4%. Other combinations of variables can give the same result.

The McKelvey and Zavoina N-Chotomous Multivariate Probit program that is used to estimate my equations also provides an estimate of the percentage of cases "correctly predicted." My equations do not fare well with this summary measure because of the skewed nature of the dependent variable (there are only 138 "ambitious amateurs" and 1,970 regular amateurs). With a dichotomous dependent variable, the model predicts about 80% of the cases correctly; with the four levels this falls to about 68% in incumbent races and 46% in open-seat races. However, there are problems inherent in the measure that limit its usefulness. The measure does not distinguish between observations that "just barely miss" (that is, if the sum of the $B_i X_i$s is just over "cut point" MU) from those that are clearly errors in prediction.[4]

4. John H. Aldrich and Forrest O. Nelson, *Linear Probability, Logit, and Probit Models* (Beverly Hills: Sage Publications), 1984.

Index